To my wife Bert, the very real love of my life, I dedicate this book about my second great devotion. Without her patience, help, and understanding I might not have undertaken this work.

Books written, coauthored, or edited by Kenneth Bressett:

Alaska's Coinage Through the Years (with Maurice Gould and Kaye and Nancy Dethridge)

Basics of Coin Grading for U.S. Coins

Bible Lore and the Eternal Flame

Buying and Selling United States Coins

Coin Collecting (Boy Scouts of America Merit Badge Series)

Coin Collecting: An Introduction to the World of Numismatics

Collectible American Coins

Collecting U.S. Coins

The Fantastic 1804 Dollar (with Eric P. Newman)

A Guide Book of English Coins

A Guide Book of United States Coins (editor since 1974)

A Guide Book of Modern United States Currency (editor)

A Guide Book of United States Currency

Handbook of Ancient Greek and Roman Coins (editor)

The Handbook of United States Coins (editor since 1974)

Hawaiian Coins, Tokens, and Paper Money (with Maurice Gould)

Let's Collect Coins!

Milestone Coins: A Pageant of the World's Most Significant and Popular Money

Money of the Bible

Official American Numismatic Association Grading Standards for United States Coins

Official Whitman Statehood Quarters Collector's Handbook

A Penny Saved: R.S. Yeoman and His Remarkable Red Book

United States Coin Price Trends

COLLECTOR SERIES™

COIN COLLECTING

AN INTRODUCTION TO THE WORLD OF NUMISMATICS

FOURTH EDITION

KENNETH BRESSETT

FOREWORD BY MICHAEL GAROFALO

Whitman™
SINCE 1934

COLLECTOR SERIES™

Coin Collecting:
An Introduction to the World of Numismatics

Whitman™
SINCE 1934

4001 Helton Dr., Florence, AL 35630
whitman.com

ISBN: 978-07948-51255 / ZT1806-0525 / Ebook ISBN: 978-07948-39109

Printed in China

Correspondence concerning this book may be directed to Whitman, Attn: *Coin Collecting*, at the address above.

Disclaimer: Expert opinion should be sought in any significant numismatic purchase. This book is presented as a guide only. No warranty or representation of any kind is made.

Caveat: The value estimates given are subject to variation and differences of opinion. Before making decisions to buy or sell, consult the latest information. Past performance of the rare-coin market is not necessarily an indication of future performance.

1909 VDB
PCGS MS64RD
2425.64/40268803
1908 NO MOTTO $20
MS 63
3287550-011
NGC

Contents

Foreword

I grew up in the 1960s. Many boys, and a few girls, found coin collecting to be a fun hobby, a way to make friends, and a great way to earn a scouting merit badge. Sixty years ago, the coins were made of silver; silver dollars could be purchased for face value at a bank, and if you looked through enough coins you might find an occasional coin from the 19th century, such as a worn V nickel or a Barber dime, in your change. You might even find an Indian Head cent, as a few were still in circulation. Even earning a small amount of money delivering newspapers or mowing lawns was enough to start you on your way to building a coin collection.

As a young boy, I always found the trip to the local coin shop to be a highlight and a lot of fun. An important and necessary purchase was a new Whitman blue coin folder in which to store your coins. The folders displayed not only the dates and mintmarks of the coins in that particular series, but also the mintages, which helped me understand why I could find a number of 1909 pennies, but I could never find a 1914-D Lincoln cent from the Denver Mint. We would buy folder after folder for newer-date coins in the series that we collected, or a folder for a series that was brand new for us. All of these coin folders also provided information about the particular series they held, and that was, in great measure, how we learned.

At a midpoint in the 1960s, the U.S. Mint stopped making higher-denomination coins from 90 percent silver, and the hobby changed from finding the coins you needed to fill your album in your pocket change, to having to buy them. As silver prices rose and many coins were being melted for their silver value, coin collecting became a more difficult and more expensive hobby.

By the late 1970s, I proudly was a "vest-pocket" coin dealer, attending coin shows in my local area and buying and selling coins while still maintaining a full-time job. But one thing never changed. While looking through coins went from being a hobby to being a business, the driving force was and still is the thrill of the hunt. The thrill is always there when I'm looking at coins, in the hope of finding something unusual, scarce, or even—rare. I became a full-time dealer the year I got married and never looked back.

In the decades that followed, I ran my own wholesale business and a retail business, traveled to coin shows in 46 different states, and, years later, worked for the largest online retailer of coins and bullion in the United States. Coins and currency were becoming more than just a hobby, and these items were now certified by independent, third-party grading companies that would provide their opinion on the grade of your coin, for a fee. In fact, coin information was now available not only in many different books and printed publications, but also online. I was fortunate enough in my career to have traveled to four continents buying and selling coins and meeting people from world mints, coin dealers, and collectors all around the world.

But while I was just beginning my journey, a gentleman named Ken Bressett was already helping thousands of other people learn about our hobby and, most important, the history behind our coins.

Bressett worked on gathering and editing information for a Whitman Publishing book relating the history of all American coinage—what was then called the *Official Red Book*. It was first published in 1947 by Whitman and edited by Richard S. Yeoman. Bressett did years of editing on this extremely important work. The official title of that book is now *A Guide Book of United States Coins*, and it became an annual purchase for millions of coin collectors who want to find out the most current pricing and the latest information available on our coinage.

Ken Bressett became the official editor of the *Red Book* in 1972, after Yeoman retired. Over the decades, the *Red Book* not only provided pricing and historical information to collectors, but it also became one of the most important books in the entire hobby.

But Bressett did not just edit the *Red Book*. His impact on coin collecting over the last 75 years has been nothing short of monumental. To note that he has written or collaborated on two dozen other numismatic books, received an appointment to the U.S. Assay Commission by President Lyndon Johnson, personally created educational programs for the American Numismatic Association (ANA), served as president of the ANA, and received dozens of awards and citations for expanding the knowledge in the field of numismatics barely scratches the surface of his contributions to our hobby. He truly is a giant in the world of coin collecting.

But helping seasoned coin collectors was only one of his goals. He also recognized that people who were just beginning their coin-collecting journeys desperately needed his guidance as well. Whether one was a novice collector, just starting to study the coins that they had used for decades, or someone who inherited some unusual coins from a friend or relative, there were very few references that truly helped the novice learn the basics.

Twenty-five years ago, the first edition of Whitman's *Guide to Coin Collecting* was published. Known as the *Yellow Book*, due to the color of its cover, it endeavored to help novices understand the fascination millions of us have with our coinage and its history. Now in its fourth edition, it is titled *Coin Collecting: An Introduction to the World of Numismatics*—but it is still the *Yellow Book*.

From the earliest coinage issued when George Washington was president, to the many unusual (for today) denominations of coins that we, as a country, once minted, the *Yellow Book* instructs beginners about the hobby, why people collect, how to safeguard your coins, how to care for your coins, how and why coins are graded, the pricing of coins, and numerous other topics.

The reasons that people collect coins are as many and varied as the people themselves, but the *Yellow Book* has provided guidance to virtually all of them. Whether you are just starting to collect coins, encouraging a young person to learn about them, or are just curious about this topic, the *Yellow Book* will provide you with a great deal of information about this "Hobby of Kings." It is a very important book that will help you begin your journey and learn what is important. It truly is a "must have" when trying to find a good coin book that can help you get off on the right foot.

For someone like me, who has spent the last 60 years collecting and learning about coins, an opportunity to write a foreword for such an important book, written by a numismatic giant like Ken Bressett, is truly one of the highlights of my career. I hope that this small contribution piques your interest. Reading this book will, hopefully, help you learn about coins that you may already own or wish that you did.

But most important of all, I hope that after reading this book, you can truly understand and experience for yourself—the thrill of the hunt.

Michael Garofalo

Mike Garofalo has been a collector of coins and currency since 1963. He became a part-time coin dealer in 1975 and a full-time dealer in 1979. He is a Life Member of the American Numismatic Association and numerous other numismatic organizations. He is the author of *Secrets of the Rare Coin and Bullion Business—By a Lifelong Trader*. He has had more than 60 articles on coins and collecting published in industry publications. In 2008, he joined APMEX as a vice president and was instrumental in the company's growth and expansion. He also was the driving force in obtaining a sales-tax exemption on rare coins and bullion for the state of Oklahoma. He has consulted with numerous coins dealers, with sovereign and private mints, and even with the U.S. Olympic and Paralympic Committee on their commemorative coinage issues. He lives in Oklahoma, with his family, and he still enjoys the thrill of the hunt.

PUBLISHER'S PREFACE

In 1976, at the ripe old age of seven, I attended one of my first coin shows. It was in Hialeah, Florida. My father loved going to these shows, and in those days, you could find one nearly every weekend.

By "show" I mean a gathering of 10 to 50 sellers who'd rent an eight-foot folding table and put out their coins for sale. Coins in this era were typically sold in stapled cardboard flips. These were inserted into plastic pocket-pages that held 20 to a page and were displayed in three-ring binders. The binders were organized by denomination or country. You'd walk up to a table and flip through a dealer's many albums, picking out the ones that interested you, maybe spending an hour or more poring through the tempting array of coins.

Today, nearly 50 years later, the coin hobby has evolved in many ways, with third-party-graded coins taking the lead. But the cardboard flips remain quite popular, and the favored platform for setting up is still an eight-foot table! In other words, attending coin shows is still largely the same experience as it was in the 1970s . . . and I'm guessing the 1950s as well.

In a world of rapid technological change, with cellphones replacing landlines and social media driving our influences, coin collecting offers an island of refuge. Although you might be reading this on a Kindle, you are most likely holding an actual book, which makes you the perfect candidate

—JOE RIMKUS JR. / Miami Herald Staff

John Fiegenbaun
. . . coins attract him

Hope for a Rarity Drives Collectors

And if you were wondering where all the numismatists and philatelists had gone Sunday afternoon, it was probably to a monthly coin and stamp show at the Westland Mall. About 30 dealers set up 47 tables to display their collections at the month exhibit.

The monthly event is a popular one, said Westland promotion director Lisa Doberstyn, and draws a lot of coin collectors (numismatists) and stamp collectors (philatelists) looking for that one great find.

The $15-per-table rental fee is donated to Dade's Operation Reentry drug rehabilitation program, Ms. Doberstyn said.

John Feigenbaum at age seven, Hialeah, Florida.

for budding collector. Coin collectors love holding tactile objects and learning about them. We use a magnifying glass to study the minute details of the object in our hands, and we also love the satisfaction of completing sets.

If you are reading this book, you will also be joining a new community of people. We call ourselves numismatists (try it: "new-*mis*-ma-tists"). You can start your journey with a new blue Whitman folder of Lincoln cents, or with the same folders you inherited from your grandfather. Or you may choose to upgrade to coins in "slabs," like a set of Proof-70 American Silver Eagles graded by one of the major third-party authentication services: NGC (Numismatic Guaranty Company), PCGS (Professional Coin Grading Service), or CACG (Certified Acceptance Corporation Grading).

Your journey in collecting will be incredibly rewarding and lead you in unpredictable directions. You may go from Indian Head cents to Civil War store tokens, or from silver dollars to Spanish 8 reales. Regardless of your direction, your path will be unique to you, your background, and your personal interests. There are no right or wrong ways to collect coins. Even better, take a friend or family member along for the ride.

John Feigenbaum
Virginia Beach, Virginia
August 2024

PREFACE

There are probably as many different reasons and ways to collect coins as there are people who enjoy the hobby. Similarly, there are many people who do not actually collect but simply want to learn more about the nature of coins and money because they are such an integral part of commerce and everyday life. No single book could ever satisfactorily cover all aspects of a topic that expansive, and this one will not attempt to do more than paint a broad picture of what to expect if you have a desire to delve into what some call a hobby, others an investment, others an industry, and still others an academic pursuit. It is only safe to say that a knowledge of coins and the use of money throughout the centuries offers a view of history, art, geography, and social customs unparalleled by any other media, as well as a feeling of being close to those things while holding the tangible evidence in your hand.

Despite the diverse reasons why people are interested in coins, there are a few common threads that seem to be universal. One, of course, is the desire to learn about a subject that is far too often overlooked in traditional academic studies. Another is a quest to find riches in some mysterious treasure like an accumulation of unusual coins obtained as a gift, or to find something in change that may be worth far more than face value. Stories about such things always emphasize the dazzling sums that some coins are worth, while ignoring the reality that chances of finding such a prize of great value are akin to winning a national lottery. A more realistic reason for investing in old coins (if that is your goal) is the proven track record of many pieces that have risen in value over the years and provide a better-than-average return on investment. With careful analysis of the market, prudent purchases, and patience in following price trends you can successfully invest in coins. This book, however, can do no more than acquaint you with the nature of this passion, tell of its many rewards, and share some caveats.

Throughout 60 years of involvement in numismatics on many levels I have encountered a mixture of people who collect for reasons ranging from one who saved coins as a memento of a particular event (like a dime received in change when he had purchased something special) to someone who bought a silver dollar for more than $5,000,000. In between those extremes are those who carefully save coins they find in change and search

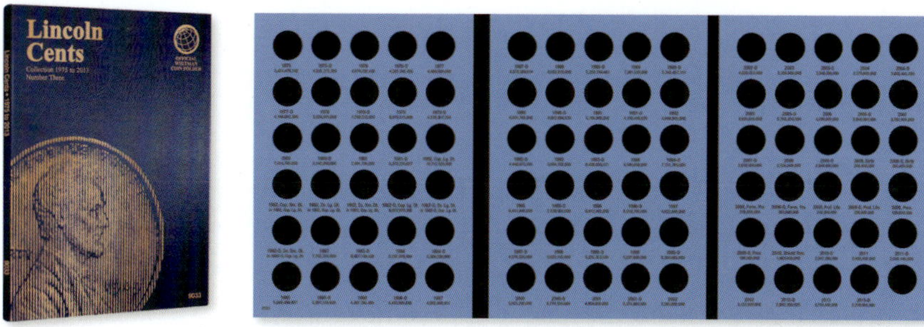

Millions of collectors began their hobby by finding coins in change and saving them in the ubiquitous Whitman blue "penny" boards.

for as many different dates and kinds as possible, to an ever-larger number who purchase coins from dealers or the U.S. Mint and often form collections of remarkable diversity and beauty. Happily, there are no special rules or customs that one must follow to participate in saving coins as a pastime.

Most people begin their quest by learning about United States coins that got their start when the first Mint began operation in 1793. You will probably find it surprising to learn that they were not always able to cope with the nation's needs for "hard money," or that they once made half cents and two-cent and three-cent coins, but therein lies the quest to explore and learn more. The second-most popular endeavor is to collect coins from one's ancestral homeland. Others find great interest in coins saved from their travels abroad or, closer to home, coins from Canada and Mexico.

Hopefully, as you read this overview of what numismatics is all about, you will develop an appreciation of which aspect of the discipline best applies to you and how you can benefit from becoming involved in what has traditionally been called "The King of Hobbies and the Hobby of Kings." Not everyone shares the same drive to collect or save anything. Some dislike the concept, while others aspire to have multiple collections of diverse objects from insects to automobiles. If you are one who might have a latent desire to become a coin collector this book will give you a heads-up chance of being successful. The stories, facts, and recommendations presented here have been carefully vetted to tell an unembellished story of what to expect.

Kenneth Bressett
Colorado Springs, Colorado

Chapter 1

Coin Collecting as a Hobby

Take a survey about hobbies among your friends and you may find some interesting things about their personalities, their likes and dislikes, and probably their outlook on life. A healthy interest in an absorbing hobby or activity seems to be a key indicator of a happy, well-adjusted life, as well as a measure of success and achievement.

Studies have shown that participating in a hobby is beneficial in both physical and psychological ways. People who have hobbies are happier, are more successful, and even live longer than those who do not. There is something about the lifestyle of a collector that is different from others. Collectors are more inquisitive, more outgoing, healthier, and, frankly, more interesting than other friends. The reason why is not well understood.

Given the right motivation and opportunity, nearly everyone has a desire to participate in some kind of activity that is outside their normal daily routine. The accountant who is an evening musician, the policeman who plays baseball every weekend, and the housewife who collects porcelain figurines are examples of the diversity of interests that add another dimension to the lives of active and busy people. The single-minded person who does not extend an outside interest to the world is destined to miss out on some of the most enjoyable moments in life.

It matters little what one chooses for a hobby. What does matter is that it is enjoyable and rewarding to the individual. For some, the thrill of restoring a classic auto to its original form is exhilarating. For others, finding a rare old coin that completes a collection is just as exciting. Some people get the same kick out of finding a special seashell. In every case, it seems to be the achievement, rather than the value, time, or money, that is the rewarding part of each success.

Collectible hobbies are among the most prevalent of all forms of recreation. There seems to be no end to the variety of things that people collect. Some of the things that people save may seem frivolous to others, but it is the challenge that matters. Trying to amass the world's largest ball of string may seem like an odd obsession, but when the ball is mentioned in *Guinness World Records* it has served its purpose of bringing fame and success to the person who made it.

Coin collecting is a rewarding hobby enjoyed by millions of Americans.

Meeting a challenge and doing something that only a few others have been able to accomplish is one of the main goals of a collectible hobby. Owning a rare stamp or coin that is one of only a half dozen in the world gives a sense of pride that brings attention to the lucky holder. For others, the knowledge that buying a rare collectible has been a good investment is doubly rewarding.

The recreational value of any hobby is another aspect that cannot be overlooked. It draws countless people into the arena, and proves time and time again that getting away from a daily routine and into a world the collector can control is therapeutic. But can a hobby actually add years to your life?

Most authorities agree that any absorbing hobby can help, and certainly will not harm one in any way. A study of coin collectors in their 80s and 90s shows that many people do indeed seem to remain more active than others who have not carried on an interest in some similar pastime.

Scientists say people who have hobbies are not just filling time; they may also be extending their life span, increasing their energy level, and living a more rewarding life. There is no question about this in my mind. Those who actively participate in some absorbing activity nearly all live longer, happier lives. And it is never too late to for anyone to begin enjoying hobby benefits.

A longtime friend, Robert H., was a remarkable example of someone who enjoyed his hobby of collecting coins longer than most others. After more than 80 years of actively collecting he was still going strong. Even at the age of 100, he was nearly as alert and spry as many half his age. He enjoyed talking to people and telling them stories of his many experiences during his long life. He also enjoyed "playing with his coins," as he called it, and never missed an opportunity to travel around the country to participate in a gathering of coin buffs.

Did Robert find the secret of eternal youth? To see him in action, you would think so. The first question everyone asked of him was, "How do you stay so active?" His standard answer was that there is no secret. He was blessed with good health, and to keep alert he stayed involved in his favorite hobby of coin collecting. He was absolutely convinced that this was the vital ingredient that kept him going.

Can coin collecting help you live longer? Those who have tried it say it can, and there are many who can back up that claim. Apparently the gods still do not subtract from man's allotted days those hours spent in any peaceful recreation.

With apologies to Izaak Walton.

Many people who embark on hobby interests late in life do so by returning to something that was of significance to them in their youth. This seems to be particularly true of those who take up music again, or try to be more serious about painting, or decide to add to the stamp or coin collection that was put aside when life became filled with college, work, and raising a family. While it often feels like we never have enough time to add to our activities, there usually is some available time that can be devoted to anything that is important enough to enrich our lives. If you already have a hobby or two that by now are habits, you can renew your enthusiasm by exploring new interests that will offer new experiences.

Coins as Money; Coins as Collectibles

Collecting coins and collecting stamps are interests that seem to be related. There are many things about both hobbies that are similar and some people do collect both, but for the most part collectors are usually interested in either one or the other. Philatelists, or stamp collectors, are intrigued by the wide variety of attractive and colorful subjects depicted on stamps. On the other hand, actual artifacts that trace the history and artistry of the world since ancient times fascinate the numismatists, or coin collectors.

One of the greatest differences between stamp collecting and coin collecting is their relation to history. No stamp is much more than 180 years old, whereas some coins are known to have been made over 2,600 years ago. The possibilities of tying coins to history over this vast expanse of time are unlimited, and make the world of coins a treasure house of information about art, history, and technology. A stamp might commemorate some historical event, but a coin could have been present at the actual happening.

One of the first true coins was this ancient Greek electrum piece made in Ionia circa 630 BC.

The first adhesive postage stamp was the famous "penny black" showing a portrait of Queen Victoria and was made in England in 1840.

Very old coins are artifacts that should be preserved in museums like other ancient objects. Many historical museums use coins to augment other displays, and when seen in this context coins are treasured for their educational value. However, coins are unlike most other museum objects in that they were made in great numbers, and many have been preserved over the centuries. The happy result is that many of those same artifacts can actually be owned by private collectors and they can be appreciated and shared by a wide audience. Over the centuries coins have traveled far and wide through trade and commerce, and they are often found in locations not associated with their actual origin. In that, they preserve a record of trade and interaction between countries that might not otherwise be evident. For their role as historical objects all coins deserve to be carefully studied and preserved. Such is the mission of serious numismatic study. (Unfortunately, some 20th-century regulations have now placed restrictions on private ownership of certain very old coins that are considered to be the cultural property of the country of origin, and those coins may be sold commercially only by special permission.)

For many people an interest in collecting coins less than 200 years old can be just as rewarding as searching for ancient artifacts. The procedure is the same. Coins are accumulated, organized, and protected in an orderly manner. In doing this, a mirror-image of history, both current and past, is being preserved for others to learn from in the future. There is a great satisfaction in knowing that your efforts to save a bit of the past in a structured manner might be appreciated by generations to come.

A study of the numismatic history of the world reveals that there have been numerous events and people who would be lost to our knowledge if it were not for records left to us as inscriptions on old coins. Take, for instance, the Roman emperor Regalianus, who ruled for a short time in AD 260, and whose coins offer the only remaining evidence of his full name and image. Similarly, the ancient city of Caulonia would scarcely be known to us today if it were not for a few coins that have survived bearing that name.

In ancient times—before the Internet, radio, or even newspapers—coins were a traditional means of spreading news throughout the land. Their messages can still be read today on pieces that have been handed down to us across the centuries.

Throughout much of recorded history coins have taken part in actual events or have been used as a means of spreading news. Before there were newspapers or other means of mass communications, coins were often used to convey news to people in remote regions. The image of a new emperor, the current favorite god or goddess, and news of a war or victory were prevalent themes on coins for hundreds of years. The panorama of events chronicled on coins that have been used since 640 BC offers a very real connection with those events that can take you on a journey back in time.

Many collectors agree that the large silver dekadrachms of Syracuse, made around 400 BC, are the most beautiful coins of all time. They originally served as prizes in ancient Olympic games.

King Philip II of Macedon (359–336 BC) was so proud of winning an event in 348 BC that he displayed his horse on one of his coins.

Have you ever wondered what Queen Cleopatra of Egypt really looked like? Was she the ravaging beauty we see in movies or read about in novels? Did she actually exist? Those questions can all be answered by looking at one of the many coins she had made for use in her kingdom. Yes, many of those coins still exist today and can be found in museums and private collections. Specimens occasionally come up for sale and can usually be purchased for less than $500. Unfortunately, most of them are somewhat worn from heavy use, but that does not hide the fact that the Queen of Beauty had rather coarse features, and was far from the ideal beauty we have come to expect from movies and literature.

Coins were also present when much of the Bible was written. There are many passages in the Bible that mention coins or the use of money, a very essential part of daily life. Wages for "the laborers in the vineyard," the parable of the "lost coin," and the "coin of tribute" shown to Jesus, are but a few

Queen Cleopatra VII of Egypt, as shown on her coins, appears to be far less beautiful than many believe.

of the many passages that refer to actual coins that can be identified and collected through diligent searching.

Silver tetradrachms of the Phoenician city of Tyre, showing the head of Melcarth, were some of the "30 pieces of silver" paid for the betrayal of Jesus.

Undoubtedly the most famous coins of all that are mentioned in the Bible are referred to as the "30 pieces of silver" that were paid for the betrayal of Jesus. Do they actually exist? Well, perhaps not the same 30 pieces, but coins just like them do. Coins that were used during Jesus' lifetime may very well have been spent by any of the more prominent Biblical figures. Such coins not only still exist, but they are not so rare or expensive that they are all in museums. A nice specimen of a silver tetradrachm of Tyre, the "30 pieces of silver" coin, can be purchased for about $800. The coin is not only an historical treasure, it is also a large and attractive piece that shows the head of Melcarth, the guardian god of Tyre, on one side and an eagle on the other.

The journey through history that coins can provide does not stop with a chronicle of wars, kings, and kingdoms. It also provides an unmatchable link to the artistry of each period of style and mode. Want to see how Queen Elizabeth I looked and dressed? Her coins tell the whole story. Were the Greeks really better artisans than the Romans? It is easy to see the differences in the style and modeling of their coins. Did art works die out during the Dark Ages? Did artists of the Renaissance influence coins of that period? Have modern artists changed the faces of coins today? Answers to all of these questions can be verified by viewing the thousands of such coins that have survived for us to enjoy as collectors. We can actually see what Ferdinand and Isabella looked like because they included their portraits on their gold coins. In Columbus's journal he records how he showed one of these coins to the natives and told them that this was their new king who wanted anything made of this shiny metal.

Ferdinand and Isabella of Spain financed Columbus's voyage of discovery to the New World with some of these large gold coins that show their portraits. No contemporary image of Columbus is known to exist.

Popularity and Growth of Coin Collecting

There are probably hundreds of reasons why people collect coins. Everyone seems to have a slightly different approach to enjoying the hobby, but there are four reasons that are universal:

pride of ownership,

a thirst for knowledge,

a desire to preserve the past, and

profit.

Each of these motivators can be a powerful incentive, but few people collect for only one reason. The most common theme to coin collecting seems to be a desire to form a complete set of one or more kinds of coins. The urge to achieve total completeness and own every possible date, mintmark, or minor variety of some type of coin is probably the most compelling factor for many collectors.

No one knows exactly when coin collecting became a popular hobby. It is certain that there were collectors of old and unusual coins more than 2,400 years ago. Exactly why the ancient Greeks collected coins is uncertain, but it is easy to speculate that they appreciated the superb artistry of those coins, just as we do now. It is also evident that some of the most beautiful older designs were copied from those coins and reused by later coin engravers, who must have been inspired by seeing the old pieces.

The silver tetradrachm of Athens was used as a standard for trade throughout the ancient world for more than 300 years. This piece, showing the goddess Athena and her owl, both symbols of wisdom, was minted around 450 BC.

By the Middle Ages old coins were being saved by many people, and were appreciated for their artistry and as artifacts of past civilizations. They were often collected by the aristocracy in an effort to preserve things that were unusual or of great value. In time, some of their collections became national treasures or part of the national museums of various European countries.

Later, in the seventeenth and eighteenth centuries, it was considered fashionable for wealthy European families to have a curio cabinet that included a selection of old coins. Some of the more aggressive collectors formed extensive collections that thankfully preserved many coins that might have otherwise been lost through attrition or melting.

Thousands of merchants' tokens like this were used to make change by English tradesmen during the late eighteenth century.

Oddly enough, it was the shortage of copper coins in England in the late 1700s that started the interest in coin collecting that endures today. The price of copper kept the British government from making enough coins to accommodate the needs of daily commerce, and to make matters worse, counterfeiters took this opportunity to issue thousands of lightweight imitation coins. Merchants who were desperate for some means of making change were forced to use the false coins for lack of anything better.

The situation changed somewhat in 1792, when a few merchants began making their own coins to give out to customers as change. The homemade coins served a dual purpose: they were a handy means of making change and they also contained an advertising message for the company that issued them. What's more, the tokens eventually had to be returned to the same store to be redeemed. In time thousands of businesses issued private tokens, most of which had unique designs that were attractive and interesting.

A virtual flood of privately made merchants' tokens was put into circulation from 1792 to 1794. It was then that collectors began saving as many different designs as they could find, and a wave of interest in coin collecting began throughout England. To add to the excitement, some manufacturers of the merchants' tokens began making fancy pieces just for collectors. Some of these were made using an obverse die of one token combined with the reverse of a different token. Such combinations were called "mules" because of the unnatural mating.

Over the course of four years an estimated 10,000 different English tokens were made for use in trade or for sale to collectors. The craze was not unlike the modern fascination (which has recently waned) with baseball cards, and all their infinite varieties. Books were written cataloging all of the known issues of merchants' tokens, political tokens, and advertising tokens, and values were established for the rarer pieces. Interest in collecting English merchants' tokens has remained high over the years, and recently has escalated to new heights. Tokens once valued at $1 to $5 now sell for as much as $35 to $100.

President Thomas Jefferson collected many things, including coins.

The craze to collect these amusing tokens in the 1790s and beyond not only took on a life of its own, it also started a wave of interest in collecting all sorts of other coins, both modern and ancient.

Serious coin collecting did not become fashionable in the United States until somewhere around 1830. There were a few collectors as long ago as presidents Thomas Jefferson and John Quincy Adams, both of whom saved coins as part of their other accumulations of interesting objets d'art, but there were only a few wealthy collectors who seriously tried to put together sets of United States coins.

The Civil War, and all of the numismatic innovations that it brought, was the great turning point in the interest of collecting in America. It was in that period of the 1860s that federal paper money was issued for the first time, and along with that, there was an extensive production of small-denomination scrip called "fractional currency." The value of those notes ranged from three cents to fifty cents, and they were made in a variety of designs. Those unusual notes, together with the seemingly endless array of Confederate States paper money, became fertile fields for collecting opportunities.

The introduction of paper currency was but one of the many changes in American money that occurred during or near the Civil War. There was a shortage of small change that could not be met by mint production. To alleviate the problem of making change in daily transactions, merchants resorted to issuing their own coins in the form of token cents. Like the English merchants' tokens of the late 18th century, these displayed advertisements of goods and services provided by the merchants. Some of the Civil War tokens had patriotic themes and others were political, but most of them were little more than advertisements for business firms.

Various innovative forms of money were introduced during the Civil War to alleviate the shortage of hard money caused by hoarding. Privately made copper cents were ubiquitous, and stamps encased in a frame with a mica cover also passed for small change. Paper money was used as an expedient by both the Northern and Southern states. Denominations ranged from cents to $1,000.

A Civil War token privately issued by M.L Marshall of Oswego, New York.

The Civil War also brought about new coins and new coin designs. In 1864 a two-cent coin made its appearance with the religious motto IN GOD WE TRUST, which slowly came into general use and eventually spread to all other U.S. coins. In 1865 a three-cent coin made of nickel was introduced. Later the small-size cent, which had been in use since 1857, was also redesigned and made thinner.

At the end of the conflict most of the currency issued by the Confederacy and the Southern states became worthless. The old saying, "Save your Confederate money; the South will rise again," became a joke that did not come true until the 21st century, when attractive pieces began selling on the numismatic market for more than face value.

With so many numismatic items to choose from, the hobby has grown in popularity over the years and a number of books on the subject have been written to stimulate interest and answer the many questions that concerned collectors. In the beginning there were no published records of how many coins had been made in each year, or even what kinds of coins were issued. There was speculation about some dates of certain denomi-

Two-cent pieces and nickel three-cent pieces were first minted during the Civil War.

nations that could not easily be found, but no one really knew what had or had not been made at any of the United States mints.

The demand for information about coins as a collectible hobby was met by a few of the established collectors who had learned through experience, and who were skillful in writing books and articles on the subject. Others saw opportunity in buying and selling old coins, and established themselves as dealers and auctioneers. Much of the information about coins available to collectors of the time came from editorial comments in auction catalogs, through a few books on the subject, and from sales catalogs and bulletins devoted to the hobby. Some of the available information was a mixture of half-truths and speculation.

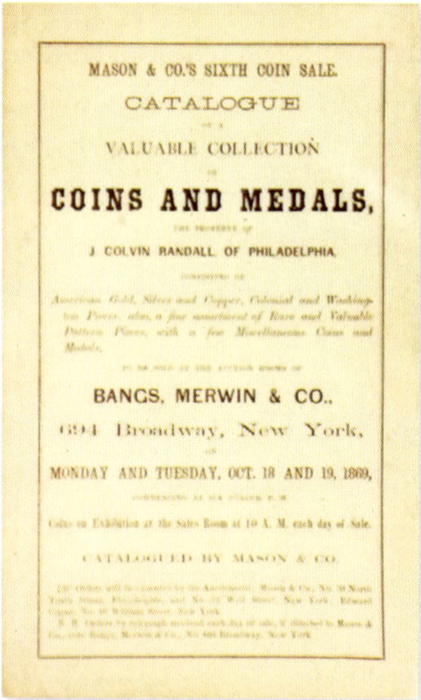
MASON & CO.'S SIXTH COIN SALE.
CATALOGUE
VALUABLE COLLECTION
COINS AND MEDALS,
J. COLVIN RANDALL OF PHILADELPHIA
BANGS, MERWIN & CO.,
694 Broadway, New York,
MONDAY AND TUESDAY, OCT. 18 AND 19, 1869,
CATALOGUED BY MASON & CO.

Early numismatic literature was scarce and often lacking in accurate information. Auction catalogs were some of the most reliable sources of data about which coins actually existed.

The American Numismatic Society (ANS) was founded in 1857 and began preserving coins, information, and reference materials in all areas of numismatics. It published articles and books that were available to its members. It was, and still is, an organization of researchers and students whose objectives are to study, locate, and preserve historical numismatic data. The very similar American Numismatic Association (ANA), which was founded in 1891, took on a slightly different role and became a national organization for coin collectors and hobbyists. In the early days of their existence both groups were not able to give much guidance to newcomers who took up the challenge of coin collecting. In time a flood of high-quality literature from both the

ANA and the ANS caught up with the demand for information, and by 1920 the lure of numismatics was in full swing throughout the country and throughout the world.

Collecting Comes of Age in America

During the Great Depression, from 1929 to 1934, few Americans could afford to collect coins, but those with collections found them to be a resource that was easily converted into the necessities of life. Several large collections were sold, and some others were formed by accumulating coins that were available at bargain prices. Throughout those terrible times a latent interest in coins remained and some people turned to collectible hobbies as a rewarding and enjoyable form of recreation.

When the nation began its recovery from the Great Depression in the mid-1930s, a more intense interest in coin collecting developed. Much of that new activity was due to products that were introduced to the market by the Whitman Publishing Company, a mass-market producer of children's books and games. One of the "games" they produced was a board punched with holes that would hold one each of all the Lincoln cents or one each of the older Indian Head cents. The boards would fit in a standard picture frame. The game was to find all of the coins, put them in the holder, and hang the frame as a wall decoration.

An early Whitman coin board for large cents.

In time the coin boards came to be seen as a basic aid to coin collecting, and they were redesigned to a more convenient size and form that could be folded in thirds for easy storage and to better protect the coins. As interest grew, more coin series and denominations were added to the Whitman selection of "coin folders," and several books were created to answer collectors' questions about the various coins they were saving.

The hobby of coin collecting was further advanced by the introduction of the Whitman coin folder in 1938. It soon took the place of the old coin board that was large and bulky.

Two of the books introduced in the 1940s have continued to be updated and published each year and still serve as standard references for information about U.S. coins. Both of these books, the *Handbook of United States Coins* and *A Guide Book of United States Coins*, were originally authored by R.S. (Richard) Yeoman, and I have continued on as editor of them since 1974. The *Handbook*, usually called the *Blue Book* because of the color of its cover, is a basic reference to all coins used in America from the days of the early English settlers to the present. This book lists every United States coin by date and mintmark, and shows each coin's approximate wholesale value in up to seven grades of condition.

The prices shown in the "Yellow Book" that you are now reading are averages of what dealers usually pay for coins that they want to purchase. It is different from most other coin books that generally list the retail price of coins, or what dealers charge for the items they sell. This book is only a general overview of each basic coin type or design, to acquaint you with the full range of U.S. coins, with basic prices showing which of those coins are of special premium value.

The *Guide Book of United States Coins*, known as the *Red Book*, shows the retail value of all American coins from the time of the early Spanish and English settlers to the present. This book lists every United States coin by date, mintmark, and major variety. It is the single most widely used reference book in the coin-collecting field. It is much more detailed than the *Handbook* and contains useful information about all areas of U.S. coins. Special sections in both the *Red Book* and the *Blue Book* describe the pieces that were used by colonial settlers and those that were made and used during the gold rush in California. Each of these books answer the questions most often asked by beginners and contain information that is useful even for seasoned dealers.

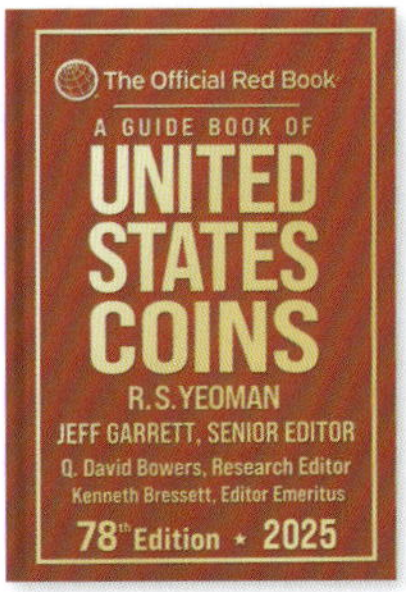

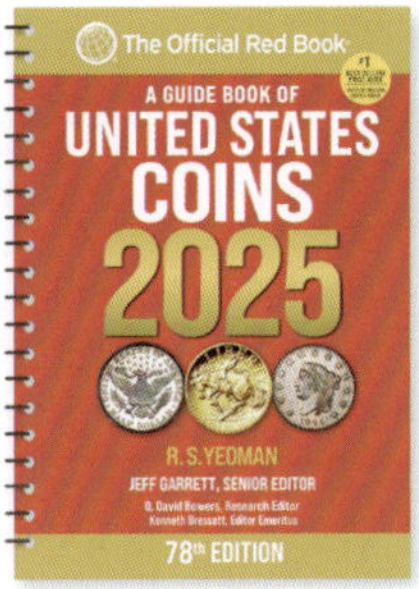

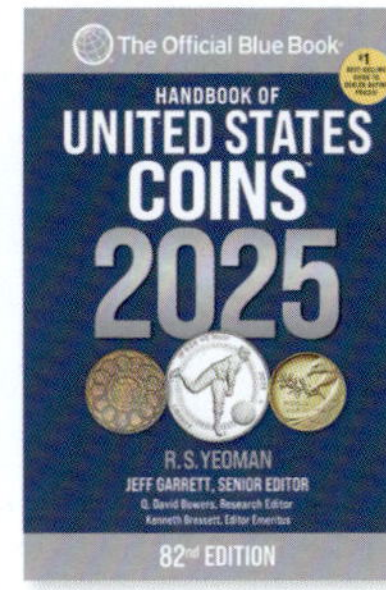

The coin hobby began to blossom again when the economy recovered after World War II. People went back to a more normal way of life, and a new wave of interest in coin collecting arose throughout the country. People tired of war were looking for forms of recreation that would take their minds off the past decade. They began collecting by searching through coins found in circulation and looking for whatever was unusual. At that time it was possible to find just about every date and mint of all U.S. coins going back as far as the Barber issues of the late nineteenth century. It was great fun, but the excitement was just beginning.

It was about that time that my old friend Rudy began saving examples of all the different coins that he could find when sorting through subway

change (he worked as a toll collector in New York City). You can well imagine the variety of dates and mintmarked pieces that passed through his hands, and the unmatched opportunities that came his way. Once in a while he would find an old Liberty Seated coin that had not been made since 1891, but most of what was available were coins of the Barber design introduced in 1892, and later pieces. From around 1935 to 1955 Rudy managed to locate examples of nearly every date and mintmark of all coins from cents to dollars made since 1892. There were a couple of the overdate varieties, like the 1918 nickel and quarter with 8 over 7, that were never found, and of course the rare 1895 dollar and 1894-S dime were not there, but he found everything else. For him it was only a challenge to take up some spare time. Ultimately it became a very valuable collection, and a tribute to what could be achieved through persistence. Unfortunately those halcyon days are long gone, but new opportunities and challenges still await collectors today with a new generation of coins to find.

The current boom in coin collecting got underway around 1960. Coin books and coin-collecting folders and albums were widely distributed through bookstores, novelty shops, coin dealers, clubs, and individuals. The end of finding scarce dates in circulation was in sight, and the hunt was on to see that no valuable coin went unnoticed. Prices paid for those coins were beginning to escalate, and people everywhere were starting to think of old coins as something of value to be treasured and saved.

By the 1960s, collectors were picking older coins—like Liberty Walking half dollars and Standing Liberty quarters—out of their pocket change and saving them.

Over the following two decades, for many people, interest in coins changed from a passive hobby to a form of investment. It was becoming evident that coins had a tendency to go up in value faster than many other investments and that almost every rare coin could be sold for more money than it had cost just a few years earlier. The big winners in this bonanza were those collectors who had put together top-quality collections during the period from 1965 to 1975, and who had saved them as prized possessions without any thought of a profit.

By 1980, when coin dealers and collectors began popping up everywhere, it was almost too late to get in on that phase of the hobby where scarce coins could be found in circulation. It was during this time that the Hunt brothers made their famous move on the futures market in an attempt to drive up the price of silver. The beginning of the decade was also a time of hyperinflation, burgeoning prices for silver and gold, and the demand for all collectibles like coins, old porcelain, stamps, and colored gemstones. People who had made fortunes on the rising market suddenly found that this was not a game that could go on forever. The value of all collectibles is based on supply and demand and when the demand began to waver, prices dropped quickly. By 1983 the rush to invest in rare coins cooled, and people once again began to appreciate coins for their beauty and historical value.

In the ensuing years, from the mid-1980s to the end of the century, participation in coin collecting matured in many ways. It became much more clearly divided into segments of interest that appealed to various types of coin buyers. At one end of the spectrum is a limited number of museums and research students who are principally concerned with the study and preservation of historical treasures. At the other end are the thousands of everyday people who acquire coins in one way or another for the sheer fun of it, without regard for value or anything else other than pride of ownership. In between is a vast array of collectors with every level of interest, from serious investing to searching for the most trivial varieties of current Lincoln cents.

It is not unusual for coin collectors to add coins of all ages to their holdings. A true connoisseur might well enjoy the rugged beauty of this ancient tetradrachm of Macedonia as much as the symbolic representation of Liberty on a Lincoln cent.

Among the many changes in collecting habits of the past decade is the way in which coins are acquired. In the past many different kinds of coins

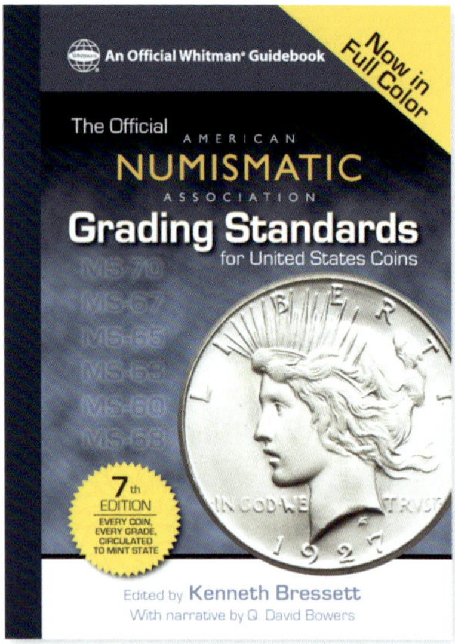

could be found in change or through old household accumulations. Those opportunities all but ended when values of old coins became well known to anyone who had the foresight to purchase a reference book. In the present market, most coins are available only through professional dealers, directly from Mint sales promotions, or through some of the many advertisements that are seen on TV and in newspapers or magazines. The major difference in today's buying habits is found on the Internet with its presentation of numismatic information and sales offerings that were never available in the past. Internet participation by collectors is now at an all-time high. There are literarily thousands of sites that present background information of all kinds of coins, and the opportunity to buy or bid on coins that are available for sale.

A word of extreme caution is necessary concerning coins offered for sale on the Internet from unknown sources. Many of the coins sold through eBay and other electronic venues have turned out to be modern counterfeits that are worthless. The majority of those false coins are made in China as part of a widespread industry and they are extremely well made and deceptive. Some are even cased in counterfeit slabs or counterfeit coin albums and other official-looking holders. All types of world coins have been replicated from common to rare and in all grades of condition. Fortunately for collectors American certification services have kept up with counterfeiting technology and reject any bogus coins sent to them for grading.

Another ever-present concern to collectors is the diversity of opinions about the precise grade of their coins. Those in the highest grade of condition are always more valuable than those that are worn or abused. Official American Numismatic Association grading standards have been established but are not always followed by everyone. It is important for every collector to become familiar with how coins should be graded to better know the true value of coins when buying or selling. Basic rules are given here in chapter 6, but you will need experience and study to become proficient.

While extreme caution is advised in buying coins from any source, it should also be noted that professional coin dealers, especially those who are members of the Professional Numismatists Guild (www.PNGdealers.org) and the ANA (www.money.org), are held to high ethical standards and are a reliable source of quality numismatic items and information about the coin business.

Coin collecting continues to be a rewarding and entertaining hobby, as it has been for the past many hundred years. It is not a simple, passive diversion, but one that kindles the imagination and interest in things historical and beautiful. A well-formed collection of coins and other numismatic items can provide a lifetime of enjoyment and a legacy for future generations. The hobby should not be entered into lightly, but with the fire and conviction of a dedicated curator of a great treasure.

Throughout the years from ancient times when coins were first saved as examples of significant and pleasing designs, to the present where coins are most frequently saved as a recreational hobby, one thing has remained constant: the beauty and lore of those old, rare, and unusual coins hold a fascination for nearly everyone.

Collectors and investors alike will profit by investigating the background and history of the coins they accumulate. These are not just inanimate objects akin to other worldly possessions. They are mirrors of history and art that tell the story of mankind over the past 2,600 years, reflecting the economic struggles, wars, prosperity, and creativity of every major nation on earth. We are but the custodians of these historical relics, and must appreciate them and care for them while they are in our possession. Those who treat rare coins with the consideration and respect they deserve will profit in many ways, not the least of which can be a sound financial return on the investment of time and money.

Chapter 2

Coins Are Where You Find Them

Just about everybody has a few odd coins stashed away somewhere. They might not be collectors, but for one reason or another most people tend to save any coin that does not seem to be ordinary or spendable. It may be a foreign coin that somehow was passed in change, a bus token, or an old penny that looks different because of the wheat ears on the reverse. Whatever the reason for saving those odd pieces, a person almost never just throws them away. They are money, and it takes a lot of courage to destroy any kind of money.

People usually begin collecting by looking at all of the different kinds of coins they can locate, regardless of what they are or where they may be found. That doesn't mean that you will be able to acquire all of those coins, but looking at everything available does give a broad sense of what may be around, and how difficult or easy it is to find such things. You will quickly notice that coins found in pocket change are mostly of recent vintage and probably of little value to building a collection.

Is it worth the effort to check your daily stash of pocket change? Should you inspect every coin that you receive in change at the grocery store? Hasn't someone else already gone over every coin in circulation and pulled out all the good dates? While there is no absolute answer to these questions, it is always a good rule to look at every coin that passes through your hands. There is no telling when or where something unusual will come along, and while there are many other collectors also looking, you could be the lucky one—the first to spot a coin of exceptional value. In recent years many such finds have been reported in coin-collector publications to the delight of those who have taken the time to look carefully at their change.

There was a time when collectors could find nearly every date and mintmark of every kind of coin in circulation. Even old Barber-design coins, dated back to the late nineteenth century, were still in circulation in the 1940s and 1950s, and it was not unusual to occasionally find scarce dates that were worth a considerable premium. Yes, that was a great way to build a collection, and it was something that appealed to young and old alike. Searching for all those different dates was challenging and rewarding, but alas, those days are gone.

One of the things that changed over the years was the trend to keep the same design on United States coins for long periods of time. Coins tend to stay in circulation as long as the design does not change. Take, for instance, the Barber coins that were made from 1892 to 1916. They continued to circulate for 40 years or more because they were familiar and seemingly of no particular worth beyond their face value. They were appreciated only when they were replaced by coins of other designs, or lost through wear and attrition.

Things are not much different today. It seems natural to receive coins as change that are 40, or even 50, years old. They do not look unusual to us because they are of the same design as those we use on a daily basis. If one does not stop to inspect the date, those old coins go unnoticed. However, spot an old coin of an obsolete design, like a Buffalo nickel, and everyone will stop and take a closer look at it. This tendency to ignore what seems commonplace has influenced a generation that does not spend time looking for unusual coins in change, and with that goes lost opportunity.

A good example of the value of carefully inspecting the coins in your pocket is the experience of a Maine collector who always checked change for scarce dates. Most of what he found had little premium value, but one day in 1998 he was rewarded with a 1972 cent that just did not look right. When he got home he studied it carefully and found that the date and letters showed a doubled image, and it was in fact a variety worth over $100.

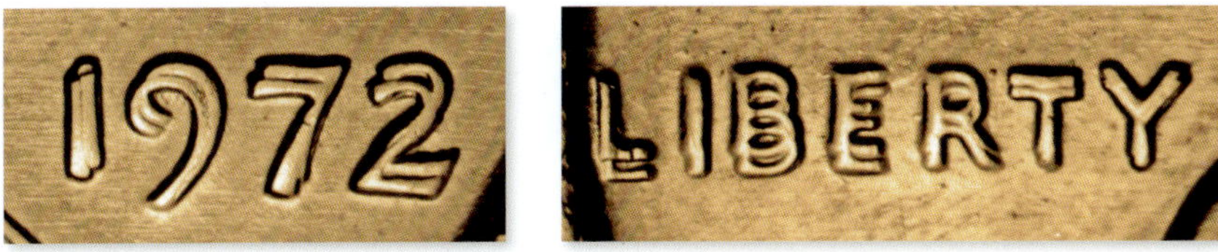

Details of a 1972 doubled-die cent.

It would not be fair to describe the "good old days" of coin collecting without commenting on the fact that while it was possible to find occasional valuable coins in change, most of what was available was worth only face value at the time. The fun in finding those coins was in being able to form sets of all the different dates and kinds of pieces that were in circulation. Most of them became valuable only after they were long out of use and no longer easily available. It seems likely that there may never again be a time quite like the opportunity-rich days before World War II, but it is also wise to consider that there could be similar opportunities today that are going unappreciated.

Most countries used silver in part of their national coinage until as recently as 1964. It was not until the price of silver began to rise beyond the face value of those coins that substitutes had to be made. Now, nearly all coins are merely tokens with no intrinsic value, and thus they have little chance of increasing in worth because of the high cost of the materials from which they are made. That's the unfortunate side of current coins. The good news is that many of the old silver coins are still sitting around in drawers and boxes waiting to be rediscovered by some active collector who can appreciate the value of those old treasures. The coins may be forgotten, but they still exist. There are plenty of them in hiding.

Chances are that you have never found a silver coin in your pocket change. When they went out of use in 1965, many were immediately pulled from circulation by sharp-eyed collectors and anyone well informed about the spiraling cost of silver. Within 10 years nearly all had disappeared from active use as money, and most were shipped off to smelters for melting. Those who were lucky enough to get in on the action found that they could often buy silver coins at face value and sell them for a profit ranging from 3 percent in the early days to 10 times face value (or more) in recent times.

It is no wonder that most of those old silver coins are no longer actively used, but that does not mean that they are not available. Many people never got around to having their accumulation of silver coins melted. Others waited in hopes of even higher profits, and some people wanted to preserve

In years past your pocket change would have included many silver coins.

specimens for the future. Whatever the reasons, there are still many hoards of silver coins hidden away in drawers, boxes, and attics. Some are long forgotten, some are just waiting to be appreciated by a new generation of collectors.

What kinds of coins are in those hoards? The answer to this may amaze you. When silver went out of circulation in the late 1960s it was almost as if time was frozen at that point, and whatever had been in use was set aside without regard to dates, mintmarks, types, or rarity. Many of the old Barber design silver coins were still in circulation at the time, and it was normal to see Mercury dimes, Standing Liberty quarters, or Liberty Walking half dollars in daily change. The Franklin half dollar was, of course, in use everywhere and not uncommon to find in nearly new condition. All of those coins were suddenly taken from circulation and preserved in whatever groups were not sent to the melting pots.

At one point in 1980 the value of silver reached $50 per ounce, and it became profitable to melt many old coins that had some significant numismatic value. Every silver dime at that point was worth $3.60, every silver quarter was worth $9.00, and every half dollar $18.00, just for their precious metal. The pity is that many such coins were melted, but a few did manage to escape a fiery death and were set aside in hopes that they would be worth even more in the future. Old designs, scarce dates, commemorative

coins, and choice-condition United States and foreign silver coins were all suddenly gone from sight, but almost magically preserved in time capsules that today lie hidden and sometimes almost forgotten in the most unlikely places.

Rather than lament the "good old days," when great coins could be found in circulation, it would serve a beginning collector well to go out looking for some of the old hoards of silver, copper, and even gold coins that are now becoming available from a new generation of owners. Those old coins that were set aside 30, 40, or 50 years ago are now being revisited by people who have inherited them, and in many cases they are being offered for sale to anyone interested in them. Searching through some of those accumulations, which are often held by family members and friends, may be a golden opportunity for anyone wanting to fill in a collection or to find rare and valuable dates. Such untapped sources may also yield any number of unusual varieties that went unknown to collectors 30 years ago.

Don't Forget to Check Your Change

It is also true that there are some interesting and scarce coins that are still in circulation and waiting to be found by anyone with enough curiosity to look for them. Every beginning collector starts by checking for unusual coins in their daily change. Make it a habit to scan every handful of coins passed to you. You will soon learn to spot anything that does not look normal, and you can set those coins aside to be studied more carefully later. Anything that is shiny and new should be saved in a special place so that nothing will happen to it before it can be compared to any similar coins in your collection.

You should save at least one specimen of every denomination, design, and date, in the highest quality that you can find. If you do not want to accumulate duplicates of common dates, be sure that the one you save is always the nicest. Do not settle for nicks or marks on any of the common pieces made in recent years. You will almost always find nicer pieces later with enough searching, but in the beginning it will not hurt to save anything that looks different until you can properly classify everything and be sure that you have not missed some important feature.

Some people collect only a few different types of coins, like cents or nickels, while others attempt to save one of each denomination, date, and type. There are no rules or norms, so everyone feels free to do whatever seems best for them. Most people like to start with one series and then build up from there according to available time, money, and interest. All things being equal, a good beginning run would be the Washington quarter series. It is one that can bring hours of pleasure in pursuing, and the reward of being able to complete the collection, either from circulation or through purchase from various sources. A completed collection can be worth anywhere from a few hundred dollars to several thousand dollars depending on the limits you set as to the condition of each coin.

Washington quarters have been made nearly every year from 1932 to the present. That makes it a long and continuous series with lots of dates and mintmarks to look for. The coins are all large and are made of either silver (1932–1964) or copper-nickel (1965 to date), so they are attractive and easy to see and handle. They wear well in circulation, so it is easy to find nice examples of nearly all of the recent dates, and if you are lucky enough to acquire a hoard of old silver coins, you might be able to locate nearly all of the older dates and mintmarks. You may also be able to spot some of the unusual designs that have letters or dates that are slightly doubled, and are of such high interest to collectors today.

Can you tell why this 1969-S Lincoln cent is worth several thousand dollars? It will pay to look for one in your change. Turn the page for a closer look.

The Washington quarter series also has great appeal to those collectors who want to own only the highest-quality pieces available. Each date and mintmark in the Washington series is available in high-grade Uncirculated condition. Finding those pieces may take some time, and they can be expensive, but the completed collection would be a treasure worthy of any connoisseur. In addition to the Washington quarters that were made for circulation, there are also some of most dates that were made as Proof specimens for collectors. These, too, can be added to any collection for interest and value.

In a sense, collecting Washington quarters provides the basic ingredients of training, skills, and knowledge needed to successfully go on to any other area of United States numismatics. The same could be true of Lincoln cents or Jefferson nickels, but the Washington quarter series has so many dates, mintmarks, and minor varieties that it offers some things to look for that are lacking in other series. Thus, they are highly recommended as an ideal starting point.

The quarter series is also unique, and of special interest to collectors because of the continuing series of State quarters that honor each of the 50 states. These were minted in groups of five different states each year,

Various Washington quarters.

starting in 1999 and continuing through 2008. Since that time a new series of quarters made in 2009 honor the District of Columbia and five U.S. territories. Another commemorative quarter series, begun in 2010 for national parks and other historic sites, continues through 2021. If collecting a full set of Washington quarters seems like an overly ambitious quest, you can temper that by beginning with the State designs and gradually work back in time to some of the early dates. It is easy to set your own parameters in this lengthy series, and it is a good starting place that will provide years of fun and satisfaction.

All Coins Are Not Created Equal

Did you ever wonder how we came to use coins as money? Where they are made, or how many different kinds there are? As a collector you will want to know answers to some of these and many other related questions. Once friends and family know of your interest in coins, you will find that you need to be able to answer their questions as well as some of your own. You will also find that there is a great deal of information that will help you understand why some coins are different from others, what makes them different, and how minor differences may affect the value of some of them.

You should also be aware of the history of coins as money, and how and why coins came to be used in trade throughout the world. Did you know that cattle were once used as money? Or that stones, shells, salt, and even teeth have been used in some places around the world? Those items may seem strange to us, but perhaps not as strange as our custom of using paper or a plastic card would seem to the people who put their trust in owning something as valuable as a cow, or as desirable as a decorative string of pig's teeth. And who would not want to have a few cowry shells to brighten up a wardrobe or to use as ornaments and jewelry?

These close-ups of the date and lettering of the 1969-S cent (on page 26) show it to be dramatically doubled. Collectors pay well for such unusual die varieties. In 2008 an Uncirculated example of this coin sold for $130,000.

In the past, livestock such as goats and cows were used as money.

A stone hide scraper, or knife, of a type that might have been the very first item used as barter in Europe over 10,000 years ago.

Anthropologists theorize that some of the first experiments in the use of trade items probably involved scrapers, knives, and cutting implements. Those who where skillful in making such useful items most likely traded them with others who were more adept at hunting or making clothing. In time, a system of trading or barter developed to facilitate the exchange of different kinds of products. Among the most widely accepted and desirable kinds of trade items were livestock. Cattle in particular were always high on the list of things of value. But there was a handicap to owning and trading cattle. They would sometimes die unexpectedly, they were costly to feed and care for, and it was not easy to make change when trading one for something else.

People became troubled by having to take change in the form of three hide scrapers and two chickens when making a trade for sheep or goats. Eventually a few items became universally accepted as being of a standard value that was easily recognizable and divisible, and that could be exchanged for nearly everything else. The most desirable of those early mediums of exchange were metals that could be used in any number of ways. Gold, silver, and copper soon led the way as items that fit the need for facilitating trade.

Once it was discovered that gold had a universal worth, it was easy to convert cattle into gold and gold into goats or grain. In using gold, silver, and copper as handy mediums of exchange, it was possible to take, leave, or ignore all other things that may or may not have appeal to those making the trade. The barter system was never fully abandoned as a way of commerce, and in fact is still used today in some situations. In time most

Many kinds of primitive money can be seen on display in museum exhibits. These are featured at the American Numismatic Association.

major transactions made use of precious metals, and by the seventh century BC small lumps of gold and silver were being stamped with the mark of an overseer who verified the purity and value of each piece. From there, it was a small step to the kinds of coins that have been used throughout the world ever since.

The style, size, and form of most coins have not changed very much from 640 BC to the present. Ancient coins were about as round as could be, considering they were made with primitive equipment. They were similar in size to modern coins, and they had designs that included heads of famous people, birds, and other things still seen on some coins. One big difference is that all older coins contained a full measure of gold or silver. It would probably still be possible to spend an ancient Roman denarius today in place of a United States dime without anyone taking serious notice because of their similarity in design and size.

There is of course a major difference in the way that coins are made today. In the past they were all manufactured one at a time by tedious hand labor. Now they are produced in giant factories with enormous mechanical equipment that can grind out millions of coins every day. Each of those modern coins is an exact duplicate of all others, and each is made to specifications governing size, weight, and design. Or at least they should all be the same, and any that are defective in any way are supposed to be destroyed

Gold and silver coins of King Croesus of Lydia, c. 561–546 BC, were made by the famous king known for his great wealth.

A Roman silver denarius of the first century BC is strikingly similar to many modern-day coins.

Most United States coins are very well made. A few escape the careful eyes of inspectors and enter circulation. Error coins are almost always worth a premium and are worthy of saving for your collection.

before they are released. When something goes wrong with the manufacturing process, and a defective coin does get into circulation, it can make any collector's heart skip a beat, for it is often worth hundreds of dollars. Take for instance a cent that has been struck on a copper-nickel blank intended for a dime coin. Two or three of these show up every year, to the delight of someone who was sharp enough to spot them in change.

The factories that make coins are called mints. In this country there is a central mint located in Philadelphia, Pennsylvania, and branch mints in Denver, Colorado; San Francisco, California; and West Point, New York. There have been several others throughout the country in the past, but only these four are now in operation. It is important to learn about the various mints because each identifies the coins they make by using a distinctive mintmark. This custom has been used throughout the world since ancient Roman times, as a safeguard against corruption or shoddy work on the part of mint workers.

Coins made by the various United States mints operating now or in the past can be identified by a small letter that is included in the design to show where the piece was made. The letter is referred to as a *mintmark*, and one is used on all of the branch-mint coins. The Philadelphia Mint did not use any mark on its coins before 1979, except for the wartime nickels of 1942 to 1945. Starting in 1979 the letter P for Philadelphia was used on the dollar, and thereafter on all other denominations except the cent.

The mintmark is usually on the reverse of coins prior to 1965, and on the obverse after 1967. The Lincoln cent is the major exception to this rule, but there are others. No mintmarks were used on any coins from 1965 to 1967, in an effort to discourage collectors from saving them during a nationwide coin shortage. Although this was a false alarm, it created an abnormal situation that disrupted the sequence of mintmarks for those three years.

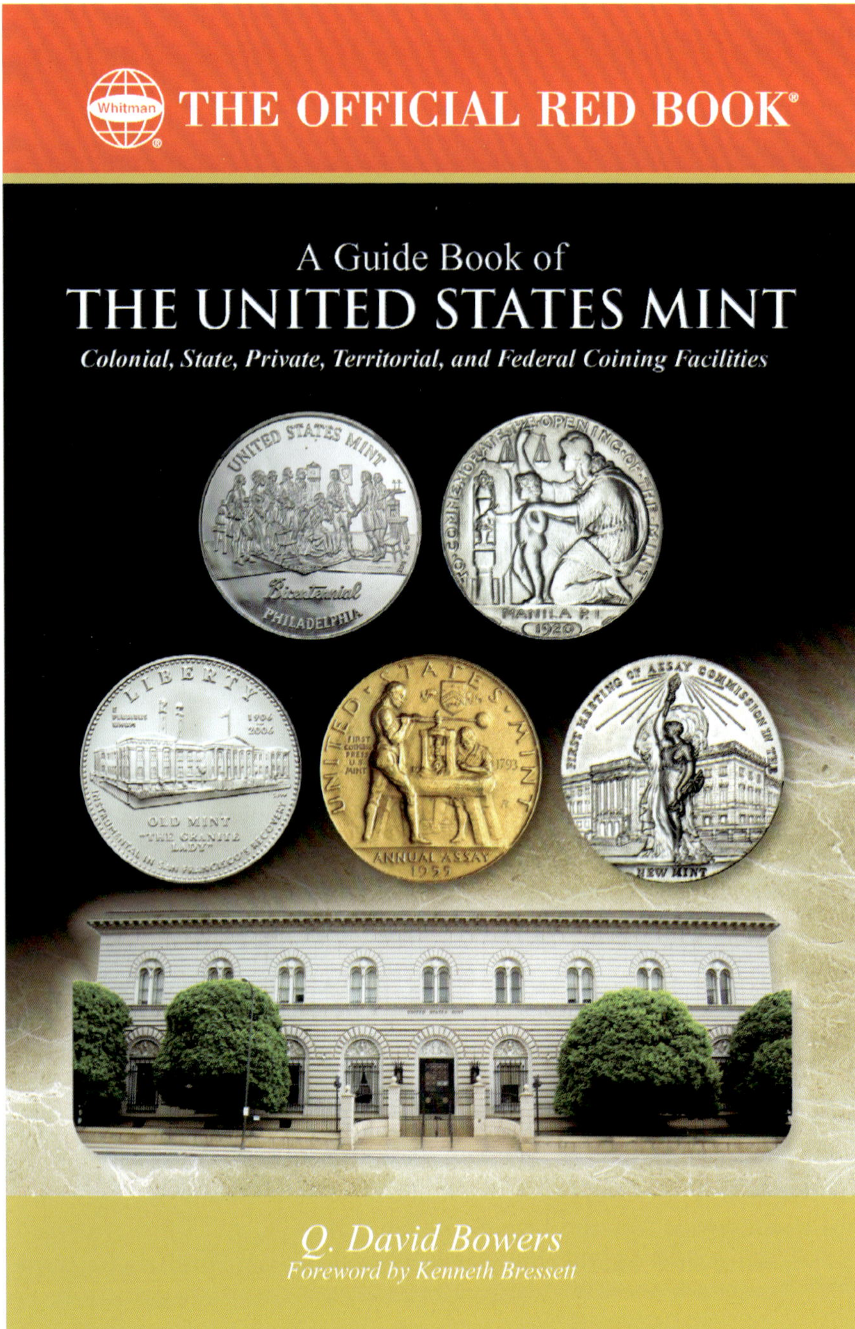
Whitman
THE OFFICIAL RED BOOK®
A Guide Book of
THE UNITED STATES MINT
Colonial, State, Private, Territorial, and Federal Coining Facilities
Q. David Bowers
Foreword by Kenneth Bressett

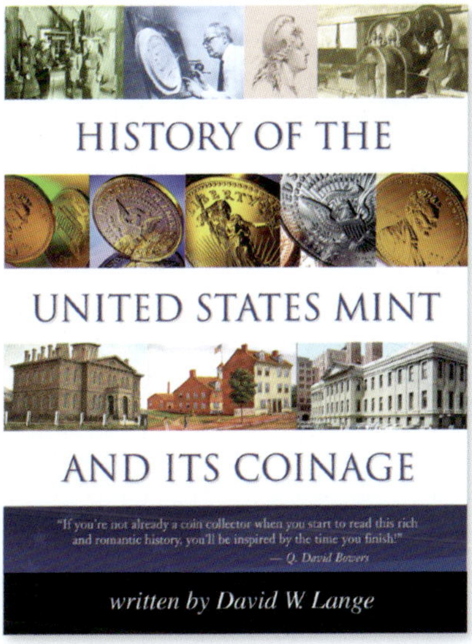

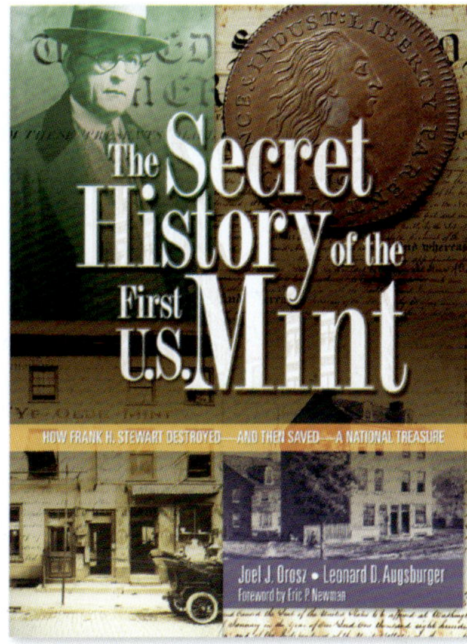

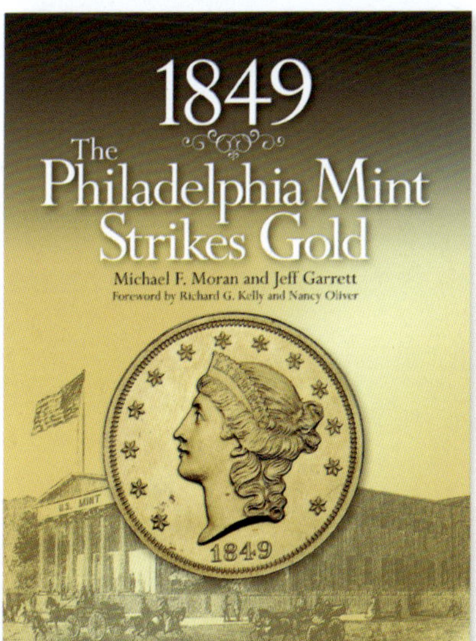

The United States Mint is a big subject—big enough to fill many books. The cover of the *Guide Book of the United States Mint,* seen on the opposite page, shows the impressive Second Renaissance Revival granite structure of the Denver Mint in Colorado. Coinage began there in 1906. Today it is one of Denver's most popular tourist attractions. The coin and medals pictured on the book's cover are collectibles related to the history of the U.S. Mint. Seen on this page are other recent books that tell the stories of the Mint. Q. David Bowers, David W. Lange, Leonard Augsburger, Joel Orosz, Michael Moran, Jeff Garrett, and Roger W. Burdette are among the award-winning writers who have explored this rich history.

Letters used to identify mints are as follows:

C—Charlotte, North Carolina (gold coins only), 1848–1861

CC—Carson City, Nevada, 1870–1893

D—Dahlonega, Georgia (gold coins only), 1838–1861

D—Denver, Colorado, 1906 to date

O—New Orleans, Louisiana, 1838–1909

P—Philadelphia, Pennsylvania, 1793 to date

S—San Francisco, California, 1854 to date

W—West Point, New York, 1984 to date

Mintmarks have been used on coins since ancient times. The Romans made this gold coin called a solidus in the city of Constantinople and identified it by the letters CONOB in the space below the design (called the exergue) on the reverse. In England, King Henry I used mintmarks to identify minters who cheated on the amount of silver they put in his coins. They were punished by having one hand chopped off.

Mintmarks on modern U.S. coins all look very much like those shown below the wreath on this silver dollar from New Orleans.

Charlotte, North Carolina

Carson City, Nevada

Dahlonega, Georgia

Denver, Colorado

New Orleans, Louisiana

Philadelphia, Pennsylvania

San Francisco, California

West Point, New York

Location of Mintmarks

Identifying the mint where a coin was made is important to establishing the value of every coin. Different quantities of coins are made in each of the mints each year, and so it is possible that a coin of any given date may be common from one mint and quite scarce if made at a different mint. An example of this is the silver Barber quarter of 1892: a Very Fine specimen from the Philadelphia Mint is valued around $45; one from the New Orleans Mint, around $60; and an example from the San Francisco Mint, $150.

half cents	All coined at Philadelphia; no mintmark
large cents	All coined at Philadelphia; no mintmark
Flying Eagle cents	All coined at Philadelphia; no mintmark
Indian Head cents	Under the wreath on the reverse (1908 and 1909 only)
Lincoln cents	Under the date, on the obverse
two-cent pieces	All coined at Philadelphia; no mintmark
three-cent pieces made of nickel	All coined at Philadelphia; no mintmark
three-cent pieces made of silver	All coined at Philadelphia, except in 1851 at New Orleans (mintmark on the reverse)
Shield nickels	All coined at Philadelphia; no mintmark
Liberty Head nickels	All coined at Philadelphia except 1912-S and –D (mintmark on the reverse, to the left of CENTS)
Buffalo nickels	Reverse, under the words FIVE CENTS
Jefferson nickels	Reverse, at the right of the building. Silver (1942 to 1945 inclusive): above the dome on the reverse. Starting in 1968: between the date and the shoulder, on the obverse
half dimes	Reverse, either within or below the wreath
dimes	Old types: on the reverse side, below or within the wreath
Mercury dimes	Reverse, to the left of the fasces (the bundle of rods with an ax head)
Roosevelt dimes	1946 to 1964: reverse, at the left of the torch. Starting in 1968: above the date
twenty-cent pieces	Reverse, under the eagle

quarter dollars	Old types: reverse, under the eagle
Standing Liberty quarters	Obverse, at the left bottom of the doorway, near the date
Washington quarters	1932 to 1964: reverse, under the eagle. Starting in 1968: obverse, to the right of the hair ribbon
half dollars	1838 and 1839: O mintmark over the date; other dates through 1915: reverse, under the eagle
Liberty Walking half dollars	1916: obverse, below the motto; 1917: either obverse or reverse; after 1917: reverse, lower left
Franklin half dollars	Reverse, above the Liberty Bell beam
Kennedy half dollars	1964: reverse, to the left of the olive branch. Starting in 1968: above the date
silver dollars	Old types: reverse, under the eagle
Peace dollars	Reverse, near the eagle's wing tip
Eisenhower dollars	Obverse, above the date
Susan B. Anthony dollars	Obverse, at the left, near the shoulder
Sacagawea dollars	Below the date
Native American dollars	Impressed on the edge of the coin
Presidential dollars	Impressed on the edge of the coin
trade dollars	Reverse, under the eagle
gold dollars	Reverse, under the wreath
quarter eagles ($2.50 gold)	1838 and 1839, above the date; others before 1908, reverse, under the eagle; Indian Head type, reverse, at lower left
three-dollar gold pieces	Reverse, under the wreath
half eagles ($5.00 gold)	1839, above the date; others before 1908, reverse, under the eagle; Indian Head type, reverse, at lower left
eagles ($10.00 gold)	Reverse, under the eagle; after 1907: reverse, at the left of the denomination
double eagles ($20.00 gold)	Old types: reverse, under the eagle; Saint-Gaudens type (after 1907): above the date

Other Things to Look for on Your Coins

As important as it is to verify the date and mintmark on a coin, there are also other key features that must not escape your attention. First and foremost is the issuing authority. To qualify as a true coin it must be something officially issued by a sovereign nation and intended to circulate as money. As basic as that sounds, it is a factor that is often overlooked by people who confuse privately made tokens and medals with real coins.

A token is something made as a substitute for a coin. A bus token, for instance, might be made by some private or civic transportation system to be used in place of coins by the public in payment for riding on their line. Tokens used in this fashion make an ideal substitute for coins because they are a deterrent to theft, and are conveniently denominated as one fare to accommodate any odd price or price change in the cost of transportation.

In the past privately issued tokens were made for just about every conceivable use. Bar tokens, good for a drink, are still popular in many parts of the country. Other tokens were exchangeable for bread, ice, milk, a game of pool, or the use of a pay toilet. Today the most prevalent kinds of tokens seen in daily use are those made for arcade games and in gaming casinos. These chips and tokens are all privately made and are not real money. By law they can be used only in the establishment that issued them, and cannot be spent or used like government coins.

At one time tokens were used to pay coal miners their daily wages. Those tokens could only be used at the company store, which was closely controlled by the mine owners. The potential abuses of such a system caused the government to curtail the use of tokens in payment for services. The Coinage Act of April 22, 1864, prohibited the issue of any one- or two-cent coins, tokens, or devices for use as money, and on June 8 of the same year another law was passed that abolished private coinage of every kind.

The paper equivalent of metal tokens is called scrip. Once very widely used in America, scrip is scarcely seen today because of the prohibitions imposed by the laws of 1864. The determining factor that separates legal from illegal tokens and scrip is the matter of where and how it can be spent.

Tokens have been made for just about every kind of goods or services. Transportation tokens, and those used in arcades, are perhaps the best known to everyone today. In the past many were used to pay coal miners for use at the company store. Gaming tokens also fall into this category and are avidly collected by many.

If its circulation is limited to a single transaction or place of redemption, it is an allowable substitute for national money. Prohibited by law are any privately made items that may look like government money or are intended to pass as money in general commerce. When a government issues tokens as a substitute for coins with intrinsic value, those tokens are referred to as fiat money.

The careful wording of government regulations allows the issue and use of private checks. If it were not for the millions of checks used throughout the world, there would not be money enough to satisfy the economy of any of the major nations. Therefore, checks, too, are part of the monetary system we all use daily. Checks are neither coins, nor tokens, nor scrip, but they serve us well as a substitute for government money in many kinds of transactions.

There is also another form of money substitute that has come into widespread use, and which is yet to be defined as to its exact designation and role as money. This is seen in the form of credit cards, debit cards, and electronic transfer cards. In the future these may well become the most dominant forms of money throughout the world. Yet, it does not seem likely that electronic money will ever completely replace coins. One government official said that if we did not already have coins to use in daily transactions, we would have to invent them, and that invention would be seen as a major accomplishment in the world of finance.

Clearly, both coins and tokens have a place in a numismatic collection. It is, however, important to carefully separate the two into distinct categories when attempting to describe and catalog these items. Usually, you will not find tokens listed in a coin reference book and you will not find coins mixed in with listings in a book on tokens. If you are trying to identify some unfamiliar piece and do not find it listed in a standard catalog of coins, you must try to determine if it is indeed a true coin, or if it may be a privately made token, or something else.

Whenever and wherever you find unusual coins or tokens, be sure to take a close look at them and decide if they might fit somewhere in your collection. Perhaps it will be an attractive parking token, or more likely a gaming chip from some casino. Those are some of the most widely saved pseudo-coins. There is a new generation of casino chips that feature distinctive and colorful designs. They appeal to collectors because of their beauty and the almost endless variety of subjects and casinos that issue them. The people who collect casino chips are sometimes bigger winners than those who gamble them away. Some of the scarcer ones are now valued at prices ranging from $5 to $100.

Government-authorized coins share several things in common. This is true of all American coins and nearly all coins from all over the modern world. If an unidentified piece does not have these features, it most likely is not a true coin. Here is what you should be able to find on a federally authorized coin:

> the name of the country issuing the coin,
>
> the date in which it was made, and
>
> a denomination or value.

Money of the future? The use of plastic cards and electronic transfers is a growing phenomenon that may someday replace much of the usefulness of traditional coins, checks, or paper money.

If it does not have these elements, it is probably either a token or a medal.

Medals look like coins or tokens, but they have no monetary value. Medals usually commemorate or honor a significant person, place, or event. Some medals are dated, but usually with the original date of the event being celebrated or the birth date of the person honored. Dual dates like "1850 to 1950" are a common signal that the piece is a commemorative medal and not a coin. Medals sometimes include a country name but they almost never have any indication of a denomination or value. A statement of the weight, for instance "one ounce of pure silver," is a good indicator that the piece is a medal, or a precious-metal ingot, disk, or bar (called a bullion piece) and not a coin.

Medals come in many shapes, sizes, and alloys. Collectors can join clubs such as the Token and Medal Society (www.tokenandmedal.org) and the Medal Collectors of America (www.medalcollectors.org).

OF AMERICA
ONE DOLLAR

Chapter 3

LEARNING ABOUT YOUR COINS

Your first venture into collecting should be searching through all of the loose change that you can find. Perhaps you have never really looked at your money carefully, or even noticed that there are many interesting things to study in the designs and makeup of your coins. Most people are so accustomed to simply counting and spending their change that they fail to appreciate the designs and variations in the coins they are using.

It is important to take a careful look at all of the coins you can find, even the most common and mundane, because that is how you will learn to recognize subtle differences in them. There is no trick to distinguishing the various denominations of United States coins, but do you know where the dates and mintmarks are located? Do you know if the national religious motto can be found somewhere on every coin? Do you know that the motto E PLURIBUS UNUM means "Out of many [states] comes one [nation]"?

While learning about these things, you might like to know that there is no real reason for the tiny letter O in OF AMERICA on the Lincoln Memorial cents and Franklin half dollar. It is simply a matter of artistic license on the part of the coin designer. The same reason is true for the letter V being substituted for U on another coin. Can you identify it? Take a good look at the building on the reverse of a Lincoln cent minted from

1959 to 2008. You knew that it was the Lincoln Memorial, but did you ever see the tiny statue of the president inside the building? Getting to know more about these coins from the past is part of the fun in collecting them.

The Lincoln Memorial on a Lincoln cent.

Do you already know who all the people are who are shown on the various American coins that you use daily? If not, you should take a closer look at the features of each coin. Their portraits are some of the best around and should not go unnoticed. Busts made during the presidents' lifetimes by the master sculptor Jean-Antoine Houdon inspired two of them, on the Washington quarters of 1932 to date, and the Jefferson nickels of 1938 to 2004. You will not find portraits of any living people on circulating American coins, because of restrictions that go back to the time of George Washington and the beginning of coinage in this country.

When the first coins were being considered, President Washington was asked if he wanted his portrait on them as was the tradition throughout Europe. For centuries most kings and rulers had been depicted on their national coinage as a sign of sovereign power and leadership. The president thought better of the custom and declined the honor. In doing so, he began a practice that has been followed ever since.

In 1866 the United States Congress passed a law forbidding the depiction of living people on our currency, but it did not specifically mention coins. Some interpreted that to mean that the restrictions applied only to paper money because some issues had used portraits of living people. Over the years a few coin designs have tried to circumvent the full intention of the law. You will not find the images of any living people on coins in circulation, but there have been several commemorative coins that did attempt to get away with the indiscretion.

Thomas E. Kilby, governor of Alabama in 1921, was one such person. He appears on a commemorative half dollar made in that year to celebrate the centennial of the state. Other living people with their portraits on coins were President Calvin Coolidge in 1926, and Eunice (Kennedy) Shriver in 1995. (A 1936 half dollar commemorating the centennial of Bridgeport, Connecticut, didn't technically violate the law but perhaps skirted the edges of its intent, with a bust of showman P.T. Barnum on the obverse. Barnum, who died in 1891, was not a city founder, though he was perhaps

Our country's first president refused to allow his portrait to appear on any of the nation's coins because he wanted to make a full break with European tradition. Firms that wanted to get the coinage contract tried to influence his decision by showing the president on their sample pieces, but all were refused. Collectors treasure the few proposed coins that still remain showing these portraits, because they never did get into circulation. Pictured is a 1791 Washington "cent."

Alabama governor Thomas Kilby—in his official state portrait, and on a 1921 half dollar commemorating the state's centennial (actually observed in 1919).

Eunice Kennedy Shriver—seen at a family gathering in 1990, and on a silver dollar celebrating the Special Olympic World Games in 1995.

its most famous citizen. Did he have the last laugh on the public for being so gullible? Probably not; his coins originally sold for $2 each when they were issued in 1936, but they are now worth as much as $225 each or more.)

The act of April 7, 1866, against using living portraits was a direct answer to the public's resentment of the portrait of Spencer Clark, the government's Superintendent of Printing, that were featured on the five-cent Fractional Currency notes that were then in circulation. Clark had used his own portrait on a whim when he thought there was no one else more suitable. Representative M. Russell Thayer of Pennsylvania complained about the portrait and introduced a bill to prevent anything like this from happening again in the future.

The bill that passed said: "No man should be immortalized on the public money of the country until the (favorable) verdict of posterity has been made upon his name." This sentiment should have been heeded in more recent years as well, as it seems clear that it was meant to apply to coins as well as currency, and to women as well as men.

The 1864 five-cent Fractional Currency note shows a portrait of Spencer Clark.

Yes, there is much to look for on your coins, and much to learn about the money you use before you can fully know and appreciate the designs and symbols that have been used. Did you realize that the eagle on the back of old American coins is there because of a law that requires it? The first coins of this country used the eagle as a symbol of power and strength. It is a majestic bird, and perhaps well suited to represent our country, but there has always been a group of dissenters who would prefer some other symbol (they say that the eagle is a vicious bird of prey, and not appropriate to our culture). As a symbol, the eagle has been used by more countries than anything else, and it has a history going back more than 2,000 years to when it was used to represent numerous districts in ancient Greece. In recent years several U.S. coin programs have been exempted from the custom, to add a more contemporary aspect to their artistry.

Would you have selected something other than an eagle for our national bird? Benjamin Franklin would have, if given his way. He reasoned that the turkey was a true native American bird, a source of food for our Founding Fathers, and a peaceful creature that was worthy of admiration. Franklin did not get his wish in this matter, and the half dollar coins that were made to honor the great statesman from 1948 through 1963 have an eagle on the reverse. Take a good look at it and you will see that it is not the standard or usual bird shown on all other United States coins. This one is the smallest ever used on any coin and almost seems like an afterthought. Did the artist do this out of respect for old Benjamin's wishes, or did he simply want to feature the Liberty Bell as boldly as possible?

Commemorative coins, and the special circulating issues honoring states, parks, presidents, and others have been exempted by law from having to use the national bird as part of the design.

A 1795 ten-dollar gold coin, and a 1952 Franklin half dollar, each showing an eagle.

Benjamin Franklin would have preferred a wild turkey on U.S. coinage, rather than an eagle. In 2015 one was featured on the America the Beautiful quarter dollar for Louisiana's Kisatchie National Forest.

Expanding Your Knowledge

You will probably soon reach the limit of what you can learn about coins merely by looking at them and studying the different designs. At that point you will be ready to begin reading about them in books and magazines. You may also want to discuss your hobby with some experienced collectors. Both are excellent and necessary ways to advance your interest and expertise in numismatics. There are many different ways to approach this aspect. Some people enjoy the camaraderie of being with others who share similar interests. Others prefer to do things on their own, and to be almost secretive about their hobby. Either way of learning is worthwhile, though there are certainly advantages to being with others who can answer questions and perhaps provide materials for examination.

Many beginning collectors today make their first entry into the hobby by exploring the subject on the Internet. There are hundreds of sites where you can find information about all kinds of coins, tokens, and paper money. It is possible to learn about coins, collecting, and literature through the Internet, and even to buy or bid on coins that are offered for sale. Websites like those maintained by the U.S. Mint (www.USMint.gov) and the American Numismatic Association (www.money.org), are excellent places to start learning about coins and collecting trends.

Another easy way to begin your search for knowledge is through a visit to your public library. Chances are that you will find several books on coins and coin collecting on their shelves. If you do not see exactly what you are seeking, be sure to ask for assistance. Specialty books are sometimes hiding in places you might not think to explore, under headings like *hobbies*, *activities*, or *numismatics*. If you are fortunate enough to use a major library, you might also find copies of a few monthly magazines devoted to coins and paper money.

While at the library be sure to ask about a listing of local clubs dedicated to special interests like coins or stamps. They usually keep such a registry, or they can put you in touch with some group or activity in the area that will have the information you need to locate other local collectors. In time you will want to attend some of the meetings of fellow collectors to test the level of activity and degree of enjoyment that might be found there. Not all coin clubs are the same. Some are better than others, but by and large they all offer some degree of activity that will prove to be helpful to you in your quest for involvement in the hobby.

Coin collectors share their knowledge in local, regional, and national clubs.

There is a general pattern to coin-club activity all over the country and you will probably find it the same in your city. Local collectors who want to get together and talk about things of mutual interest usually form groups or clubs. In the beginning a few people will meet in someone's home or perhaps at a convenient restaurant. Later, as the group grows, a meeting room will be found where they can get together and conduct business or perhaps do things in a more structured way. The meeting place is quite often in a civic center, bank conference room, library, church, or museum.

Nearly all coin clubs have elected officers. They seem to be necessary for running meetings in an orderly manner, but most clubs are rather informal. A good president will start meetings on time, keep the programs flowing swiftly, and stay focused on the subject at hand. A meeting will usually include a bit of club business to be taken care of, a treasurer's report to be read, and some plans to be made concerning future meetings or club events. The formal meeting is then usually adjourned and the evening turned over to a speaker, an auction, or interaction and visiting among the members.

A meeting of the Metropolitan Coin Club of Atlanta (online at www.mccatl.org).

Joining a coin club is a way to meet other collectors, make new friends, and add to your collection.

Club meetings are held once each month in most cities. Some very active areas have two or more coin clubs or hold their meetings every other week. In areas of California there are so many collectors and clubs that it is possible to attend a different meeting every night of the week without traveling more than 100 miles. It is not unusual for an involved collector to attend two or three coin-club meetings each month, and to participate in each of them as an officer, a speaker, or an exhibitor from time to time.

Beginners can have just as much fun at club meetings as any of the regulars. They are always invited, and the older members are always happy to answer questions, offer help in identifying coins, and, believe it or not, often give coins away just to stimulate interest among neophytes. Visitors to club meetings are always welcomed and never pressured to join or to do anything other than simply enjoy the meetings. For the timid or overly cautious, everyone respects the privacy that some people desire and respect their anonymity. If these are not enough reasons to attend a meeting or two, then you should also know that most clubs serve coffee and sweets during their social time . . . and that dues rarely exceed $10 per year for regular activities.

Numismatic Books

There is no end to the number and variety of books that have been written about coins and collecting. The library of the American Numismatic Society, housed in New York City, has a collection of well over 100,000 items. The American Numismatic Association has more than 128,000 books, auction catalogs, periodicals, videos and DVDs on various numismatic topics in its Colorado Springs, Colorado, lending library. A good private library of a serious collector may have more than 500 different titles, and some of them contain a thousand or more. Most hobbyists like to have, and use, about a dozen general books to guide them through basic information about several different topics.

In time you will find it important to have at least a few books to kindle your interest in the various possibilities of collecting. Perhaps you will want to learn more about the coinages of ancient Rome, or explore the money that may have been used by some of your ancestors in a foreign country. A book about medals or tokens or commemorative coins could open a whole new field of collecting interest for you, and in time you will want to know more about the background of all United States coins and the role they played in forming this country.

Some of the more serious book collectors find as much enjoyment in locating and owning rare books as they do in saving coins. Not only that,

American Numismatic Association headquarters, in Colorado Springs.

but over the years it has become evident that owning quality numismatic books is a rewarding investment as well as a means of learning about the hobby. Many collectors have been able to sell their books for many times the price that they paid for them originally. Take, for instance, a clean, undamaged copy of the classic book on early American coppers, *The Coins of New Jersey*, by Edward Maris. The original 1881 edition that sold for $350 or so 30 years ago is now valued at $2,500. The reprint version made in 1987 originally cost $75, and is now trading for almost double that. Even some old *Red Book*s (Whitman Publishing's *Guide Book of United States Coins*) which originally sold for $2 or $3 each are now valued at more than $300 because of heavy collector demand.

Collectors can join hobby groups such as the Numismatic Bibliomania Society (online at www.coinbooks.org), whose members support and promote the use and collecting of numismatic books, periodicals, catalogs, and other written or printed material relating to coins, medals, tokens, or paper money, ancient or modern, U.S. or worldwide. The NBS publishes an excellent journal, *The Asylum*, and also an award-winning free weekly magazine called *The E-Sylum*, distributed by email and also available on its website. On the other side of the written page, membership in the Numismatic Literary Guild (www.nlgonline.org) is open to authors, publishers, and editors of recognized numismatic books and publications.

Kenneth Bressett with a small portion of his home numismatic library.

You will not need an entire library of books to begin your literary journey into coin collecting. Two or three well-chosen titles will probably suit your needs for quite some time. The most essential tool is a book that lists all of the various coins that have been made by the United States over the years. You will also soon want to know how to grade coins, what all the markings on them mean, and, like everyone else, you will want to know what each of your coins is worth.

One of the most useful books you can own is *A Guide Book of United States Coins*, which is mentioned on page 14. Most collectors simply call it the *Red Book* because of its bright red cover. It contains factual information on all of the coins that have been used in America since the early settlers of the 1600s, shows actual-size pictures of every coin, and gives historical data and statistics about each item. In addition, perhaps most important of all, it lists the current values of everything in up to nine grades of condition.

The *Red Book* was originally written by R.S. Yeoman and was first produced in 1946 by the Whitman Publishing Company. Each year since then a revised edition of the book has been published, updating the information and including all of the changes in United States coinage. New editions of the standard *Red Book* and the *Deluxe Edition Red Book* (known as *Mega Red*) are published each year, using price information gathered from a panel of nearly 100 of the country's leading coin dealers. The average prices shown in the books are considered an accurate and unbiased representation of what coins are currently selling for throughout the country.

In addition to the basic information you will find in *A Guide Book of United States Coins*, you will probably also want to have a book that will tell you more about how to properly grade your coins. You should be able to do a pretty good job of grading after reading the *Guide Book* and using the instructions given in this book, but there is more to it than that. In time you will want to learn about other kinds of coins and the intricacies of rare pieces that could be exceptions to the usual rules.

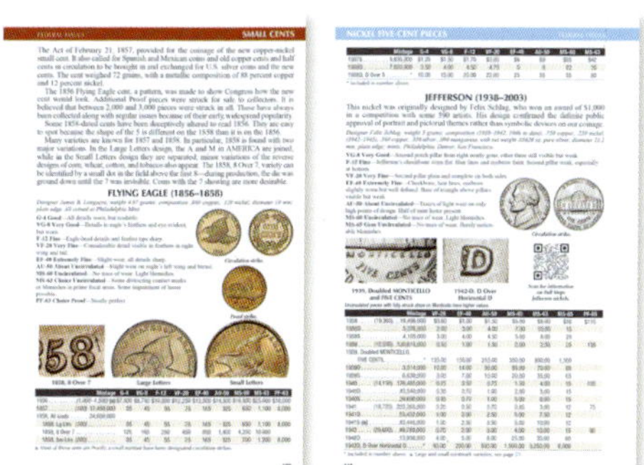

The *Red Book* includes grading instructions, photographs, technical specifications, pricing, and other information for every U.S. coin series.

Numismatist Bill Fivaz marveling at the 1,504-page *Deluxe Edition* of the *Red Book*, popularly known as *Mega Red*.

There are several books on the subject of grading. The most widely used is the *Official American Numismatic Association Grading Standards for United States Coins*. As its name implies, this is the officially designated system of grading sanctioned by the ANA. This book contains both pictures and detailed descriptions for each grade of every United States coin type from 1793 to the present. Special sections discuss grading techniques, the care of coins, grading terms, and what to look for in investment-grade pieces. Many of the coins are enlarged and shown in full color.

Another very popular grading book is called *Photograde*. This is similar to other grading books, but it has slightly different descriptions of the coins, and a different series of photographs.

A recent addition to the hobby is *Grading Coins by Photographs*, by Q. David Bowers, which has enlarged full-color images and easy-to-follow text.

Many collectors find it helpful to use two or more books in order to gain a more complete understanding of grading. Any or all of the more popular grading books will provide most of the information you will ever need to successfully grade your coins, but there are other books available, and each of them contains useful information on the subject. You will find it important to learn all you can about grading because it is impossible to determine accurately the value of any coin without knowing the exact grade of the piece.

The system of grading used in this country has evolved over many years and uniform standards have been established that can be used and understood by everyone. Thus, a good book on the subject is essential for all collectors. Grading has been discussed more than any other in the field of collecting and is a subject that you will find coming up often in conversation with other collectors. This topic is covered in greater detail in chapter 6 of this book.

Most beginning collectors, especially those in the United States, are primarily interested in their national coinage. For that reason, the abovementioned books will be of greatest use to nearly everyone just getting started. However, they are not just beginner's books. The average collector buys a new edition of the *Guide Book* every other year to keep up-to-date on all the changes in prices and new issues. Grading *standards* never change, but perceptions, commercial trends, and individual tastes do, so several books on coin grading will be a benefit in keeping up to date on market adjustments. You will probably also want to own a copy of the

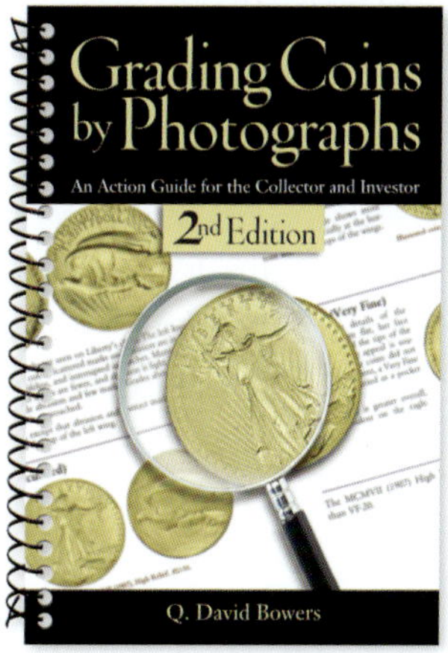

Handbook of United States Coins, which lists the average wholesale values of all U.S. coins, or how much dealers will pay you for them.

If you have an interest in world coins you will need special books to learn about them. Here you have even more choices of available books. Many of them give an overview of modern world coins and show pictures and values of most of the coins that you are likely to own or might want to purchase. Also available are books covering in detail all the coins that have been made worldwide in the seventeenth, eighteenth, nineteenth, and twentieth centuries. Usually, each century is covered in a different book, which may be purchased separately or as part of a set.

Another approach to learning about world coins is through specialized catalogs and books on individual countries. The most popular for Americans are the coins of Canada, Mexico, and England. There are several books that cover coinage of these countries in detail. Some of these references will be found in your public library and may be borrowed so that you can get a taste of what they contain before purchasing them. Members of the American Numismatic Association can borrow all of these, and many other books, without cost through the mail from the ANA lending library.

The American Numismatic Association's Dwight N. Manley Numismatic Library in Colorado Springs welcomes students from all over the country, and assists them in research work.

Building your home library of numismatic reference material can be almost as much fun as collecting coins. There is an old adage that advises, "Buy the book before the coin." It is as true now as at any time in the past. The investment you make in books will repay itself many times over in the knowledge you will gain, the enjoyment you will find, and the advantage you will have in selecting just the right coins for your collection.

Clubs, Associations, and Museums

Getting started in coin collecting can seem challenging and a little overwhelming to the beginner. It is a large field and full of strange words, customs, and practices that can be learned only with time. There is, however, a quick route for coming up to speed without spending a great deal of time learning the basics. Books are essential, but beyond that a membership in some coin club can be your best investment. It may be a local club where you can meet one-on-one with other members on a regular basis, or it may be one of the many regional or national organizations that usually meet less frequently.

Regional organizations operate somewhat differently than the local clubs described earlier in this chapter. Regional clubs are much larger and they are the support group for any number of local clubs. A regional group like the Michigan State Numismatic Society (www.michigancoinclub.org) serves clubs and members throughout Michigan. The Central States Numismatic Society (www.centralstates.info) includes Illinois, Kentucky, Wisconsin, and nearly a dozen other states throughout the entire upper Midwest. Florida United Numismatists (www.funtopics.com) supports clubs throughout the Sunshine State. These and other larger groups are able to offer members the benefits of a periodical magazine, and they frequently put on conventions and shows within their districts.

There are some definite advantages to belonging to both a regional group and a local club. Regional magazines have a reputation for being informative and of high quality. They often contain articles by members, news of coming events in the area, locations and information about local club activities, and general stories about members and things that are of interest to collectors. The calendar of events published in each issue tells when and where you can find meetings, exhibits, and shows close to you that will be worth attending. Knowing that you belong to an organization of collectors with interests similar to yours is also a benefit because you are supporting a common objective.

Regional groups also sponsor coin shows and conventions. They are usually held once or twice a year in some city that is convenient to the members. Some clubs try to rotate the place where their conventions are held in order to make them accessible to everyone. The major conventions are supported and often run by member clubs who share in the profits from such an endeavor. Quite often the money a club makes from putting on a show will more than pay for all of their other expenses for the year. In that

Some of the larger shows, like the Whitman Expos (held in Baltimore three times a year), draw collectors not only with coins for sale but with amazing educational exhibits and displays, along with major coin auctions.

Amazing educational exhibits and displays are a highlight of the larger coin shows.

way they are able to keep membership dues in local clubs at an absolute minimum. Any surplus is often used to sponsor junior members and to encourage them to participate in the fun of coin collecting. It is not unusual for a club to offer a free or very inexpensive membership to any junior who attends. In many cases they are even given coins, books, or albums to spark their interest.

There are also national and international organizations that act as umbrella groups for all of the other clubs. In this country there are two: the American Numismatic Society (ANS; online at www.numismatics.org) and the American Numismatic Association (ANA; www.money.org). The ANS is a scholarly group primarily concerned with academic research and the study of coins from all periods of time. They maintain the largest collection of coins in the country in their museum in New York City. Their library is a world-renowned resource for students, but unfortunately it is not a lending library and may be used only by members who visit the New York facility. The ANS also provides research information through their website at www.numismatics.org without charge, and they frequently publish scholarly books and conduct seminars and lectures.

The other national organization, the American Numismatic Association (ANA), with headquarters in Colorado Springs, Colorado, is geared more toward collectors, and is a little less academic than the ANS. The focus of the ANA is on U.S. coins, but both organizations are concerned with coins of all countries and periods of time. An advantage of the ANA is its magnificent library, which allows members to borrow books on just

Coin exhibits at the American Numismatic Association's Edward C. Rochette Money Museum, Colorado Springs.

about any numismatic topic. To request books, a member needs only to consult the list of available titles, or telephone (719-482-9821) or email (library@money.org) the librarian for assistance. Books are sent by mail, and the borrower has to pay only for postage each way.

The ANA library also has an extensive assortment of DVDs, video tapes, slides, and audio programs that may be borrowed in the same way as their books. These aids are used most often by clubs for their monthly programs, but they are also available to individuals. The ANA Resource Center encourages research projects, and their experienced staff offers help in locating books and information to help answer numismatic questions.

In addition to the countless books and other resources that are available to those who want to learn more about coins and paper money, there are a number of museums around the country featuring permanent exhibits of coins. These can be a source of information and entertainment for anyone with even a passing interest in numismatics. Many are located in popular vacation sites and are easily accessible. See if some of these fit in with your future travel plans:

American Antiquarian Society. 185 Salisbury Street, Worcester, Massachusetts. U.S. coins and paper money.

American Numismatic Society. 75 Varick Street, New York, New York. Large exhibit of all numismatic items.

Museum of Art. Rhode Island School of Design, 20 North Main Street, Providence, Rhode Island. Ancient Greek coins.

The Newark Museum. 49 Washington Street, Newark, New Jersey. Coins, medals, tokens, and paper money.

Philadelphia Mint. Fifth and Arch Streets, Philadelphia, Pennsylvania. Coin presses and artifacts, U.S. coins and medals, guided and self tours.

National Numismatic Collection. Smithsonian Institution, National Museum of American History. Constitution Avenue between 12th and 14th Streets NW, Washington, DC. Broad exhibits of all numismatic items.

Mint Museum of Art, Charlotte, North Carolina. Mint Museum Uptown: 500 South Tryon Street; Mint Museum Randolph: 2730 Randolph Road. State bank notes, bonds, and Bechtler gold coins.

Mel Fisher Maritime Heritage Society Museum. 200 Greene Street, Key West, Florida. Gold and silver bars, coins, and other artifacts of sunken treasure.

Texas Memorial Museum. 2400 Trinity Street, Austin Texas. Ancient to modern coins, paper money, and medals.

Magnes Collection of Jewish Art and Life. 2121 Allston Way, Berkeley, California. Medals and coins related to Jewish heritage.

Denver Mint. 320 West Colfax Avenue, Denver, Colorado. U.S. coins, medals, paper money, and mint equipment; public tours.

American Numismatic Association Money Museum. 818 North Cascade Avenue, Colorado Springs, Colorado. Extensive array of coins, medals, tokens, and paper money from all cultures and periods of time.

The Durham Museum. 801 South Tenth Street, Omaha, Nebraska. U.S. coins, patterns, and related items.

Higgins Museum of National Bank Notes. Airport Road, Lake Okoboji, Iowa. National bank notes and other U.S. paper money.

Cleveland Museum of Art. 11150 East Boulevard, Cleveland, Ohio. Ancient and modern coins, Renaissance medals, and British gold.

Other museums and exhibits can be found by consulting the Internet, local telephone directories, chambers of commerce, or information bureaus. And you might find the award-winning book *The Numismatourist* useful. Billing it as "the only worldwide travel guide to museums, mints, and other places of interest for the numismatist," author Howard Berlin describes more than 175 places in 75 countries that are open to the public, with almost 100 covered in detail with pictures. While traveling you may also want to visit coin dealers along the way. You will find their places of business listed online and in the local resources mentioned above. Sometimes they are indexed under "Stamp and Coin Dealers." The ANA maintains a list of its member dealers at www.money.org/ANADealers. And the Professional Numismatists Guild keeps a searchable list of its more than 300 members online at www.pngdealers.org.

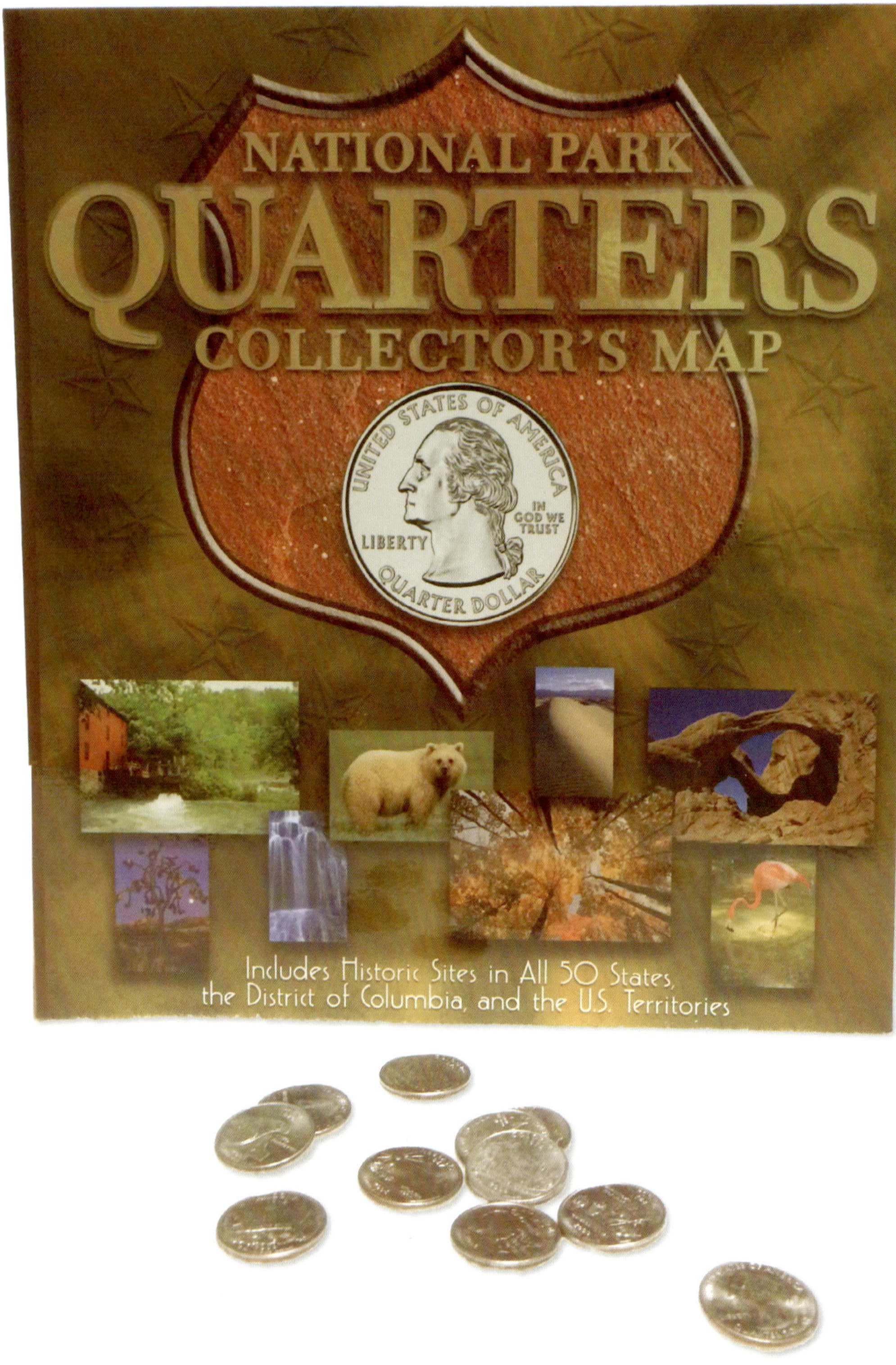
NATIONAL PARK
QUARTERS
COLLECTOR'S MAP
UNITED STATES OF AMERICA
IN GOD WE TRUST
LIBERTY
QUARTER DOLLAR
Includes Historic Sites in All 50 States,
the District of Columbia, and the U.S. Territories

Chapter 4

How to Get Started

There are no special requirements for getting started as a coin collector. Just about everyone is a collector of one sort or another. Few households do not have some old or unusual coins tucked away in a drawer, and because all coins have some intrinsic value, few if any, are ever discarded, whether they are rare or common. Even the lowly lost pennies that many pass by on the ground are eventually retrieved and tossed into a jar to be saved for the future.

To become a coin collector you need only to organize those coins that you already have and supplement them with whatever else can be found by searching through your pocket change, from helpful friends, or through your local banks. In every case you should be sure to select the coins in the finest possible condition so that they will not have to be constantly upgraded with better pieces.

A few months of searching could produce an acceptable specimen of each different type and denomination of United States coin currently in use. If you wish to extend your collection beyond those basic coin types, you should try to secure one coin of each date for any or all of the different series of denominations. Soon you will have enough different dates to need some sort of organized method of storage. The most convenient and inexpensive way to take care of your new collection is to place the coins in a specially made album or folder. There are many different kinds of

A Whitman Classic® coin album for U.S. type coins (one example of each coin type from the 1900s and 2000s).

A Whitman folder for Buffalo nickels.

storage systems on the market that hold every series of U.S. denominations by date and mintmark classification.

The advantages of using custom-made holders are that they will protect your coins from damage or improper handling, and that all of the coins are identified by date and mintmark so that it is easy to see at a glance what you have in your collection, and what dates are still missing. Albums are somewhat better than coin folders because each coin is protected by a clear plastic sleeve that covers both sides and allows easy viewing.

Visit with a coin dealer or fellow collector to see how they store their coins. Sometimes bookstores carry supplies of different coin-storage folders and albums. It is usually best to see what is available on the market before buying several holders. Most collectors like to have a uniform series of albums, and it could be costly to make the wrong choices before deciding on what kind of holders will look best for your collection.

You will find coin stores in just about every major city. They can be very helpful in getting a collector started by supplying the books and other things needed to successfully work with your coins. Look for dealers on the Internet or in your telephone directory. They are sometimes listed under "Hobby Supplies" or "Stamps and Coins."

Coins in cardboard holders, four inches long by two inches wide, with an interior sheet of Mylar® film creating a protected window. These are folded over and stapled with a coin inside, creating a "two by two" (2x2) holder.

An 1883 Liberty Head nickel in a protective hard-plastic case.

Some collectors prefer to store their coins in individual holders rather than in albums. This is a more tedious method but it allows for greater flexibility in organizing a large or varied collection. The most common individual holders are small paper envelopes, or cardboard mounts. Plastic holders offer even greater protection, but at a somewhat higher cost.

You will also need at least one basic coin reference book to provide information about what coins you should be looking for while forming your collection. As the old saying goes, you can't tell one player from another without a program. It is nearly impossible to successfully collect one of each U.S. coin without having a catalog listing of what exists in each series. Basic references like the *Handbook of United States Coins* (the *Blue Book*) or *A Guide Book of United States Coins* (the *Red Book*) provide the necessary information, as well as helpful tips on how to collect, exactly what to look for, and what each coin is worth. While I strongly recommend these, there are several others on the market that are also worthwhile.

Once you have a good book and a means of organizing and protecting your collection you will be ready to start hunting for as many different coins as you can find. In the beginning it is wise to accumulate, or at least take a close look at, every coin. You may not want to save all kinds of coins, but you can make that decision later. Getting into the habit of studying every coin that comes your way is good practice for recognizing those minute differences that might separate a common coin from something of value.

You can identify foreign coins by comparing them to illustrations in a reference book like the 15th edition of R.S. Yeoman and Arthur L. Friedberg's *Catalog of Modern World Coins, 1850–1964.*

In the beginning most collectors save one each of all common coins and, of course, put aside all others that have a premium value. These can be used later in trading with other collectors for hard-to-get dates that are not easy to find in circulation. Values listed in the *Handbook of United States Coins* can be used to establish the worth of each coin and enable collectors to make equitable exchanges. Trading a 1933-D Lincoln cent for a 1923-S could be a good deal for both parties if such a coin were lacking in one collection and a duplicate for someone else. This sort of trading goes on frequently at coin-club meetings and can be a very enjoyable part of the hobby. The best exchange is when both parties feel satisfied.

Once a collection has been started there are no rules or boundaries covering what current coins a person can or should collect. Many collectors confine their activities to one particular series, such as United States cents, and literally spend a lifetime trying to obtain one choice coin of each date from each mint; or in the case of the old large cents, one specimen of all of the minor die differences or varieties.

The allure of old coins appeals to collectors of all ages.

Other collectors attempt to form sets of every available United States coin, but that is a very ambitious goal. A growing number of hobbyists are now content with only one coin of each date, regardless of mintmark. Those who use coins both as an investment and as a hobby often buy only selected coins in the highest grade of condition and sometimes spend as much on a single coin as others would pay for a complete set of pieces in a more average grade.

The most popular and enjoyable kind of collection seems to be a type set of different designs, in which one coin of any date or mint is used to show the design that is used throughout an entire series. In the case of the Buffalo nickel, a single piece could represent all of the others because they all look essentially the same. A variation on that kind of collecting would be to also include the Buffalo nickel dated 1913 that has a slightly different reverse showing the animal on a raised mound. Assembling a full type set of all U.S. coin designs can be as challenging as you wish to make it, depending on just what is included in the collection, and its condition.

Whitman coin folders and Whitman Classic® albums are designed to hold not only the date and mint series, but also type sets and other specialty collecting formats. They each have individually labeled spaces for the kinds of coins that will be needed to complete each series. For those collectors who want to organize their own arrangements there are folders and albums with blank pages, as well as envelopes and mounts that can be stored in special plastic boxes.

Collectors identify two varieties of Buffalo nickels: one with FIVE CENTS on raised ground, and the other with a recessed area.

Many new collectors become interested in the hobby because they have been fortunate enough to inherit an accumulation of coins. Often these coins are thrown together in a cigar box or small container. The first step in managing such a group is to separate everything into groups of similar coins. The United States pieces will be easy to identify because they will all have the country name on them. It should also be fairly easy to tell which are made of silver, copper, nickel, or gold. Foreign coins, and anything that is not immediately recognizable as a United States issue, can be set aside for future investigation. There will probably also be a few pieces of paper money in an old accumulation. Those, too, should be carefully sorted out and stored as flat as possible until more attention can be paid to them.

An accumulation of old Barber half dollars.

Anyone not fortunate enough to inherit a beginning group of coins might find some success in asking relatives and friends if they have coins set aside that can be looked at or purchased. Use the *Blue Book* to establish equitable prices when you are able to buy things that you might need for your collection. Be cautious, however, about the condition of the pieces you intend to buy. If you are not sure how to grade them, you must use a grading guide and study each piece carefully.

The number of household accumulations of odd coins that exist will probably amaze you. They will include coins that have been brought back home as souvenirs by soldiers, coins that were never spent on trips abroad, coins of Canada or Mexico that could not be spent in the United States, and coins that just looked different and were tossed aside. Any and all of them might have a place in your collection and all will be worthy of investigation.

Collectors appreciate a wide variety of coins ranging from the very common coin of India shown here to the rare colonial copper piece from Vermont dated 1785.

In your search for unusual coins you will find that many of the items available are silver pieces that have been set aside since they were withdrawn from circulation when the copper-nickel–clad coins were substituted in 1965. Accumulations of old silver coins can prove to be a bonanza for finding dates and older designs that would not otherwise be available. And you will find that they probably will not cost as much as you might think. Most old silver coins can be purchased for only a little over their bullion value. In the trade they are referred to as "junk silver." That does not mean that they are worthless; it is just a holdover term that has been used in the coin hobby for many years.

If you get the opportunity to purchase any of those common silver pieces you will need to know the current bullion trading price of silver in order to calculate a fair value. You can easily find that figure (called the "spot" price) on the Internet, or in any daily newspaper in the financial section. Look under "Futures" and you will find the daily (or even hourly) quotations for most precious metals. The figures shown for silver and gold tell how much is being bid for those raw metals. It does not mean that you can buy or sell at exactly those prices, but it is a good indication of approximately what an ounce of gold or silver is worth anywhere in the world.

To figure the value of common silver coins you can multiply the spot price of silver per ounce times the amount of silver in each coin and arrive at the average bullion value. Here are some calculations that will help to make the exercise easy to figure what common silver coins are worth in terms of bullion value. Keep in mind that these are a little less than the exact spot price because of refining costs and the difference in what dealers actually pay in order to make a profit. These should be considered fair prices for any non-premium U.S. and similarly sized foreign coins that you purchase:

Silver Bullion†	Dime 0.07234 oz.	Quarter 0.18084 oz.	Silver Half Dollar 0.36169 oz.	Silver-Clad Half Dollar* 0.14792 oz.	Silver Dollar** 0.77344 oz.
$15.00	$1.09	$2.71	$5.43	$2.22	$11.60
16.00	1.16	2.89	5.79	2.37	12.38
17.00	1.23	3.07	6.15	2.51	13.15
18.00	1.30	3.26	6.51	2.66	13.92
19.00	1.37	3.44	6.87	2.81	14.70
20.00	1.45	3.62	7.23	2.96	15.47

† Spot price of silver, per ounce. * Dated 1965–1970. ** Dated 1878–1935.

"Junk silver"—common-date 90 percent silver coins in circulated condition.

In any accumulation you buy there are bound to be a number of unusual items that seem to have no proper place in your collection. These might include tokens, medals, privately issued chits, or even an occasional Civil War token, or a foreign or ancient coin. All of these should be carefully preserved. They can be stored in paper envelopes or mounts in a special section of your holdings. Their future importance to a well-balanced collection will be recognized after they have been properly classified and their historical background studied.

Various tokens.

When You Are Ready to Purchase Other Coins

At one point or another, we all reach that time when no other coins can be located in change or through lucky finds. It's then that you must decide where and how to go about buying coins from other sources. Most of your coins will have to be acquired by purchase. It simply is not possible to fill any set or collection entirely from circulation or old household hoards. If you are fortunate enough to have a coin club or a few coin dealers in your city, they should be your first stop in looking for sources of supply.

A local coin club is often an ideal place for buying, selling, or trading coins but eventually even that resource may become exhausted in the quest for appropriate specimens. An experienced coin dealer is one source that

Meeting other coin collectors gives you opportunities to buy, sell, and trade, to build up your collection. Pictured: Retired *Coin World* editor Beth Deisher speaking to the Bluegrass Coin Club at its 2016 Christmas banquet.

generally will have most of the pieces you will want, and even very rare coins for you to study and admire. Dealers in many major cities can offer a large selection of coins for your consideration, and if you do some comparison shopping you will be able to find the most favorable prices.

When buying coins from a dealer or fellow collector, you should follow the same rules you used in selecting coins from circulation. Always choose the best that you can find or can afford. If you settle for second best there is a good chance that you will want to replace it with a better specimen later, and you will probably lose money in the transaction. Any coin that seems less than ideal to you will undoubtedly look the same to others, and may be difficult to trade or sell later.

The names of grades used by most collectors are simple terms that have been used throughout the world for at least the past 200 years. Listed from highest to lowest they are Uncirculated, Extremely Fine, Very Fine, Fine, Very Good, and Good. In recent times a few in-between grades have been added for better delineation of condition and to reflect any valuation differences. Information about grading standards is presented in chapter 6.

It will not always be possible to buy coins in perfectly new condition, but you should aim for the best pieces that your funds will permit. The nicest collections are those that contain coins of a uniform grade. Whether they are all in choice Uncirculated grade, or all Fine or Extremely Fine, it will be to your advantage to select a grade that suits your budget and try to match all of your coins to that standard. Any coin in high-grade condition, usually Extremely Fine or better, will always be a joy to own and will always command top value at time of resale.

If you do not have ready access to any dealers' shops, you can consider purchasing coins through the mail or from dozens of offerings on the Internet. This is a very common practice, and is usually quite reliable. There are, however, rules and cautions that should be followed. It is possible to purchase just about any coin you would ever want directly by mail

A coin in nice condition will always please you, while a similar one that is worn may soon need to be replaced in your collection.

through advertisements. You can also bid on such coins at mail-in or Internet auctions. Either method of purchase can be rewarding and fun. But they also present some risks because you may not have a chance to see the coins before purchasing them.

Buying coins through the mail can be relatively trouble-free if you follow a few commonsense rules. Most important is to select a reliable dealer who can serve your requirements. It is not always easy to make that selection, but you will have the best chance by picking someone who is a member of one or more of the major numismatic organizations, and who has pledged to provide quality service. The American Numismatic Association and the Professional Numismatists Guild (PNG) require their dealer members to follow a code of ethics and to treat customers fairly. Any member may be expelled for failure to comply with association rules. Dealers who belong to the ANA or PNG have established their reliability and willingness to serve customers in a businesslike manner.

Buying through the mail gives you the convenience of home or office delivery.

AMERICAN NUMISMATIC ASSOCIATION

P·N·G
Knowledge. Integrity. Responsibility.

A second clue to the reliability and quality of a dealer can be learned from where they advertise their coins and services. All of the major coin publications enforce regulations that govern sales policies. If a buyer is not satisfied with a purchase, or does not receive exactly what has been advertised, the publication will not accept further ads from the offending dealer. Considering these regulations, the length of time that a dealer has been an advertiser in major publications and a member of the ANA or PNG is a good indication of reliability.

Following are the most widely read numismatic publications that contain advertisements of coin dealers and offer coins and supplies for sale. They also contain quality articles and news stories about all kinds of coins and paper money. Reading one or more of these publications each month is highly recommended, and almost a necessity for anyone who wants to be truly involved in the hobby. You are invited to contact each of them for samples and information about subscriptions to their publications. Some of them can also be purchased at newsstands.

CPG Coin & Currency Market Review
1702 Laskin Road, Suite 202
Virginia Beach, VA 23451
Online: www.greysheet.com

COINage (monthly magazine)
3622 Lyckan Parkway, Suite 3003
Durham, NC 27707
Online: www.CoinageMag.com

Coin World (weekly newspaper)
PO Box 150
Sidney, Ohio 45367
Online: www.CoinWorld.com

The Numismatist
(monthly journal of the ANA)
818 North Cascade Avenue
Colorado Springs, Colorado 80903
Online: www.money.org

An alternative to buying through the mail or online is shopping at a coin show or convention. This is by far the most satisfying way to purchase coins because they can be inspected right on the spot and sometimes even compared to similar coins that other dealers have at the show. There is also a big advantage to dealing one-on-one and getting to know the person from whom you are buying. At a convention where there are often hundreds of dealers all competing for business, it is considered part of the fun

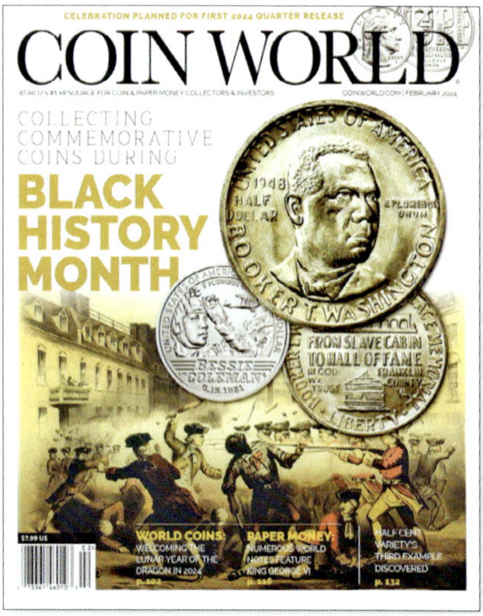

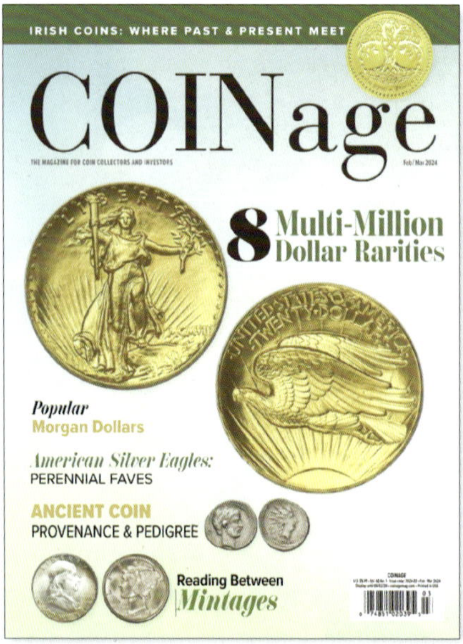

Weekly and monthly collector newspapers and magazines are important for keeping up with the hobby. *Coin & Currency Market Review* has been published since 2018, *Coin World* since 1960, *COINage* since 1964, and *The Numismatist* (magazine of the ANA) since 1888.

to bargain for the best price possible. Haggling about prices is not uncommon at coin shows, but is not an acceptable practice when responding to an advertisement.

Other Sources for Buying Coins

It is not easy to find perfect Uncirculated examples of current coins. They will not be found in circulation because once coins are touched by any sort of friction they are technically circulated or worn and no longer qualify as being in strictly Uncirculated condition. Once in a while you will be able to find rolls of brand-new coins at a bank, and you can select brilliant Uncirculated pieces from them, but that is not a way that you can find choice examples from all current dates and mints.

The reason is that banks really do not want collectors searching through rolls and then returning the unwanted pieces to them. It is just too much work to count and re-roll the coins and put them back into circulation. Many times old and new coins are mixed together to discourage anyone from searching or saving rolls of new coins. It is good to keep this in mind if you are fortunate enough to find a friendly bank that will allow you to buy and search rolls. Be sure that you always roll the pieces you return,

Your local bank can be a source of rolls of coins.

and substitute other coins for any that you remove. It is also a good practice to mark each roll that you search in some way so that you will never go through the same coins again.

A few new coins can usually be found in rolls or in change each year, but it is frustrating to try to locate all of the different dates, mintmarks, and denominations. The distribution system used in banking channels keeps money localized so that new coins from the Philadelphia Mint usually stay in the east, while coins from the Denver Mint are more apt to be

An official United States Mint Uncirculated Coin Set.

The U.S. Mint also offers annual Proof sets.

used in the western parts of the country. Unless you travel a lot, you may not get to see all of the new coins each year, even if you try to get them directly from a bank.

As a means of encouraging collectors to save new coins, the U.S. Mint has a special sales division that allows Uncirculated coins to be purchased at a reasonable cost. These are specially selected pieces, struck on special presses under higher-than-normal pressure, that are packaged in protective holders for collectors. They also make nice presents, especially for youngsters or anyone new to the hobby. If you are lucky enough to live near the mint in Denver, Philadelphia, or San Francisco, or near U.S. Mint headquarters on 9th Street in Washington, DC, you can visit their gift store and see the various items that are offered for sale. Otherwise, you can order through a sales catalog that may be obtained by calling 1-800-USA-MINT or from their website at www.USMint.gov.

Uncirculated Government Mint Sets consist of one new coin of each denomination and mintmark made in a given year. They are assembled in Mylar film packages. One packet contains a Lincoln cent, Jefferson nickel, Roosevelt dime, Washington quarters, and a Kennedy half dollar from the Philadelphia Mint, while another package has the same kind of coins from Denver. Together they form what is known as a Mint set.

Uncirculated Mint sets can be purchased directly from the Mint only during the original year of issue. Older sets are never available from the Mint, but often can be purchased from coin dealers and through special promotions. Cost of these sets varies with the number and kinds of coins made each year. For information, current prices, and ordering instructions the Mint can be contacted at 1-800-USA-MINT, or online at catalog.USMint.gov.

It is fun to contact other new collectors on the Internet. There are many chat rooms and other places where you can get together to talk about coins or to trade mintmarked coins from your part of the country for theirs. Check under *coins, numismatics, coin clubs,* and *hobbies* to find websites.

Tools of the Trade

What do you see when you look at your coins? Do you really see all that is there, or only part of what they have to offer? Many coins are admired for their beauty and the fine details in the design, but some of that is lost if it cannot be seen clearly. For those who want to get the most out of viewing their coins there is one very important tool that is absolutely necessary: a good magnifying glass, or perhaps a couple of different kinds to help with grading and authentication.

Magnifiers come in all shapes, sizes, and qualities. To get the most out of looking at your coins, use a glass that seems best suited to you and the way you want to view your coins. A glass that is too powerful will show only a small portion of the coin in its field, while one that is low-powered will not bring out the fine details. Chances are that eventually you will want to have several different kinds of glasses for use in different situations.

A typical reading glass of the kind that is used mostly for magnifying print may be too weak to be efficient for looking at coins. Those glasses are usually rated as 2+, or 2 power, and while they magnify things to twice their actual size, that is not enough to bring out the kinds of details that should be seen on small coins. An inexpensive reading glass will usually be made of plastic, rather than glass, which will also limit the clarity of what can be seen through it.

The magnifier known as a jeweler's loupe is a precision instrument made for close scrutiny of tiny objects. They are made of special glass and often constructed of two or three pairs of magnifying optics that correct the image so there is no distortion at the outer edges. Some are color corrected so that the clarity and brilliance of a diamond can be fully appreciated. Loupes come in a variety of powers from about 7+ to as high as 20+. These are fine for examining gems, but are usually far too powerful for looking at coins. The problem with them is that the field of view is so small that only a portion of the coin can be seen.

An experienced coin dealer will often use a loupe of 7+ to 10+ to detect counterfeit coins, or to carefully grade a rare coin. However, for general viewing that kind of power borders on overkill. A good rule of thumb is to leave the powerful and expensive magnifier to the professionals, and to work with a modest glass better suited to your needs.

One of the best values is a 3+ lens made by Bausch & Lomb. It is powerful enough to clearly show all details of a silver-dollar–size coin. The optics are good, and there is very little distortion, but they are apt to have fuzzy images at the outer edges of a large coin. These glasses are convenient because they slide into a self-contained plastic case for protection and storage, making them easy to carry in a pocket at all times.

Other low-priced lenses are usually made of plastic instead of glass. There is nothing wrong with a plastic lens, but they are not as optically perfect as glass. In the low-power range of 2+ to 3+ this is hardly perceptible. Another advantage of inexpensive lenses is that you can have several of them on hand so you and your friends can use them to enjoy looking at your beautiful coins. Some glasses are even equipped with a self-contained light source that can help you see in rooms with low light. Magnifying glasses can usually be found for sale in jewelry stores or ordered through catalog houses.

An H.E. Harris & Co. 10x ("ten-power") loupe.

Chapter 5

Caring for Your Collection

Building a valuable coin collection is fun, but it can also become a nightmare when something untoward happens to your coins. As sturdy as coins may seem, they are actually very fragile and can be easily damaged by improper handling or storage.

One of the most common errors is in believing the myth that well-cleaned, shiny coins are more desirable than those that are old and tarnished. Yes, shiny coins seem much more attractive, but when coins are improperly cleaned they can easily be scratched and damaged. A harshly cleaned coin is always worth less than a similar one that is natural and untouched. The best advice is *never attempt to clean a valuable coin*. You can always have a coin cleaned professionally if it absolutely needs it, but you can never undo the harm that inexperienced cleaning may do to your coins.

You should also take precautions to make sure that your coins are handled carefully by anyone who inspects them. Friends who do not know the value of old coins can be careless when viewing your treasures, so do not hesitate to tell them how important it is to keep them free from marks and abrasions. Dropping onto a hard surface is one of the worst things that can happen to a coin.

It is also important to make sure that your valuable coins are stored in a secure place. A bank storage box is ideal. If that is not an option, be sure that they are kept in an inconspicuous place where they will be missed by

To minimize damage if you accidentally drop your coins, examine them over a padded surface. This could be as simple and "homemade" as a soft cloth laid over a notepad or magazine.

any intruder. Also be sure that coins are stored in a place that is at a constant room temperature and free from excessive humidity. Your attic and basement, which are the two most common hiding places, are without doubt the worst possible choices.

I once met a collector who told me that he had never dropped a coin. He was just too careful to do anything like that, and felt that he did not have to be particularly careful about his coin-handling habits because he did not see that as a problem. He believed that others who spent time carefully making sure they never damaged their coins in any way were only asking for trouble.

Needless to say, he eventually regretted his cavalier attitude, and admitted to me that he had indeed dropped more than his share of coins over the years. One of them was damaged to a degree that it lost much of its value. By then it was too late to do anything about the abused piece, but he wanted to know the tricks of avoiding anything like that happening again. In a way he was lucky, because he had only ruined one coin. It did not take much in the way of instruction to help him avoid further problems.

The rule that everyone must follow is to always hold every coin by the edge, and never touch the face, or flat surface, of the piece. This is essential. There is no excuse for anyone ever holding coin in a way that could impress a fingerprint on the surface. To be even safer, you can, and should, use white cotton gloves while handling valuable Uncirculated coins. Some people substitute thin Latex gloves and think them safer because they are not as slippery as linen. Others find them awkward and harder to use. Both offer a degree of safety that is better than taking a chance of "fingering" a valuable coin.

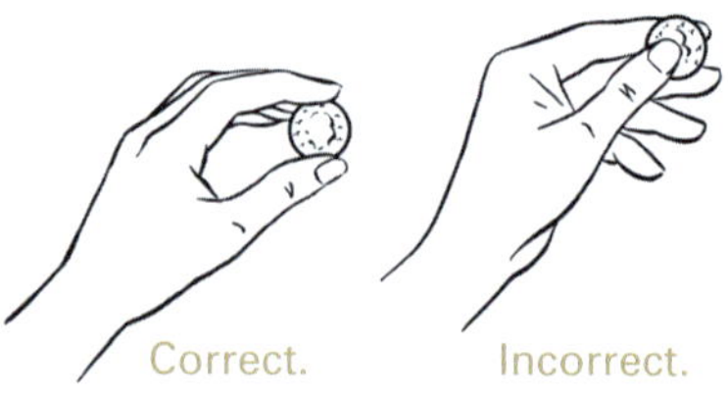

Don't take chances. There is a correct way to hold a coin. It's the mark of a competent and wise collector to do so with utmost care.

A fingerprint on a coin's surface might not seem like such a terrible thing, but it can be severely damaging to an otherwise uncirculated piece. The oils, acids, and salts on a person's skin easily attack the delicate surface of a new coin. Simply touching an Uncirculated coin will leave traces of those contaminants on the surface that will eat into the finish. The "fingerprint" will not be seen at first, but in a few weeks it will begin to blossom and become clear in every minor detail. The tragedy of these marks is that they are unsightly, and they will never go away except when worn off by circulation or harsh abrasive cleaning.

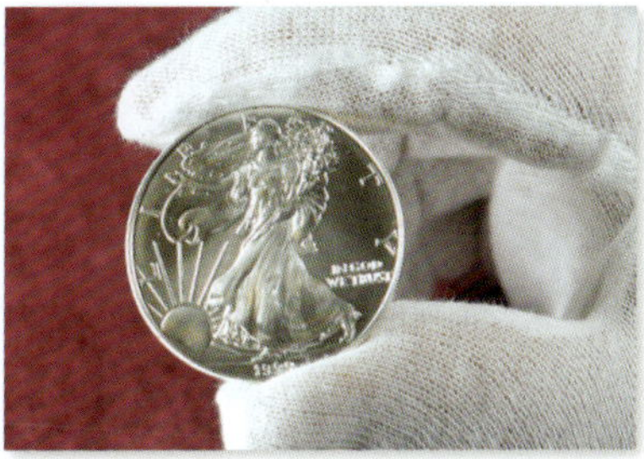

This collector is properly holding her coin by its edges, wearing cotton gloves, with a padded surface below.

Notice the fingerprint at the bottom on the reverse of this coin. It will stay there forever. Moisture spots can also be seen scattered about the reverse. Perhaps someone sneezed!

Also important to the proper handling of coins is to always work over a padded surface. A jeweler's tray is ideal, but not always convenient or available. The next best thing is using a cloth pad or folded towel. Remind yourself that no one is exempt from occasionally dropping a coin. It happens to the best numismatists and seems inevitable. Dropping a coin on a padded surface will do little or no harm and it may save lots of aggravation. For added protection, it is always prudent to view coins over a carpeted floor.

If the coin you are inspecting is in a secure holder, it is usually best not to remove it. There may be reasons to take a coin out of its holder, but often this is inviting danger. Never touch or rub the surface of a coin with your hands or anything abrasive. Even some paper and plastic holders can harm an Uncirculated coin if not used properly.

For some reason there is a natural tendency to rub the surface of a coin with the thumb to make it clearer and shinier. This is one of the worst things anyone could ever do. The trick is to treat all coins as if they are extremely fragile. They are!

A collector's desk set up for studying coins. Note the padded surface, gloves, magnifying glass, good light source, and various coin holders.

Have you ever seen an Uncirculated coin with tiny black spots on the surface? Those are moisture spots, and they are caused by someone coughing or breathing on the coin. Wear a surgical mask if you have a cold and just can't wait to look at your coins. Those spots can also be caused by moisture condensation if coins are moved from a cold place to a warm room.

Be especially vigilant when handling other people's coins. I have seen rim nicks that have lessened the value of the coins by hundreds of dollars—all due to careless handling or being dropped on a hard surface. It only takes a few extra minutes to be safe rather than sorry.

Albums and Holders

The importance of building your collection with coins in the finest possible condition cannot be overemphasized, but preserving them is equally important. Coins should not be abused, mishandled, or stored loosely with other coins, which can cause nicks, dents, or scratches. Careful storage in specially made holders, albums, or folders is essential to preserving high-quality coins. When handling coins you should always hold them between two fingers on the rim, and only remove them from holders and albums when necessary.

No matter how well preserved, coins are susceptible to oxidation and tarnishing. If you live in a community where the air is polluted by factories, near salt water, or with excessive humidity, you must constantly protect your coins from these harmful elements. The only sure way to preserve a coin's natural condition is to seal it in an airtight container. This, however, is generally impractical, as is embedding a coin in plastic or sealing it in aluminum or tin foil. The chief drawback to this kind of protection is that you are not able to get to the coin when you wish to examine or display it.

Modern technology has produced a variety of plastics that are suitable for protecting coins. The popular 2" x 2" coin holder made of polystyrene plastic with an airtight seal is the most practical container for a single coin. The Whitman Snap Lock plastic holder made of inert polystyrene is one of the best. These holders are suitable for display purposes, are a convenient size for storage, and allow coins to be easily removed when desired. The special construction of these holders offers nearly complete protection for an indefinite period of storage.

2" x 2" coin holders.

Less valuable coins can be stored in 2" x 2" cardboard coin mounts, or in paper coin envelopes. All of these items may be purchased through coin dealers or hobby supply stores. One of the major advantages of using 2" x 2" paper envelopes is that any information about the coin may be written on the outside of each envelope. It is also possible, and fun, to use computer-generated printed labels to identify coins in any of these holders. One computer program is designed to catalog and inventory your collection, and to print labels whenever needed.

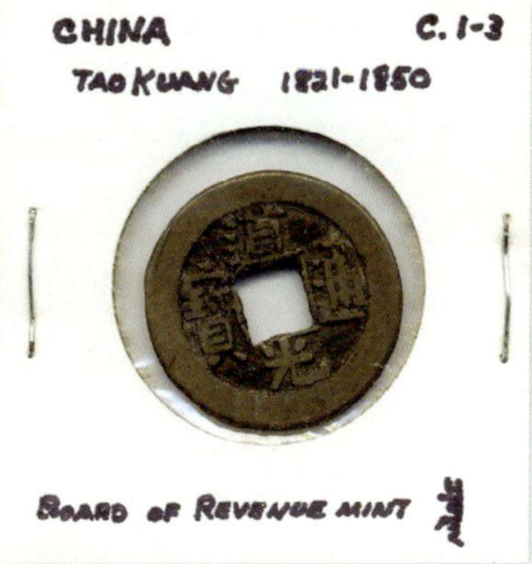

An old Chinese coin in a 2" x 2" cardboard holder, with its information written on it.

A variety of containers is available for storing individual envelopes or plastic holders. Many of the trays and storage boxes used for storing photographic slides may be adapted for storing coins. Coin dealers generally offer specially constructed cardboard or plastic storage boxes made specifically for coin use. Be careful to select one that is as nearly airtight as possible. If you plan to store your coins for a long period of time in one of these containers, it should be sealed with tape to add further protection. You should also examine your coins periodically to see that no harmful tarnish has developed; but of course, you will want to look at your coins from time to time anyway.

There are many types of holders and albums that will hold complete sets or series of coins. Plastic pages, similar to plastic 2" x 2" individual coin holders, are available for complete sets of each denomination. They are by far the most attractive and protective, but also the most expensive. Polystyrene coin holders for Proof sets or Mint sets are also available, and offer a convenient method of storing all the coins of a single year.

Plastic sheets protect the Morgan dollars in this coin album.

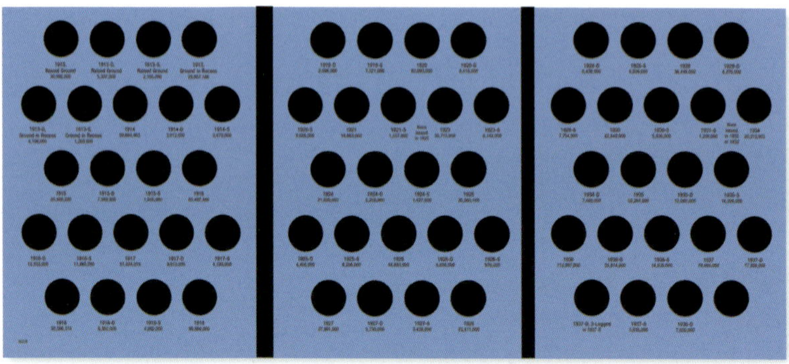

A classic Whitman blue folder, with openings for each coin in the Buffalo nickel series.

Coin folders and albums are the most commonly used storage holders for coin sets. The Whitman Classic® Album consists of individual pages with openings for one date or mint of each coin in the series. Specialty holders are also available for type sets and older coins. The openings in these albums are covered on both sides with removable plastic slides. This arrangement provides not only great protection to the coins, but it is also a convenient way to display them, as both sides of all coins are visible. It is also easy to remove individual pages for exhibition and display. A simple screw post holds pages in place so that they can be removed, replaced, or added to the basic album.

A less expensive but still practical means of storing sets of United States coins is the Whitman blue coin folder. Most collectors begin by purchasing folders for a set of current Lincoln cents, Jefferson nickels, or higher denominations if their funds permit. One coin of each date and mint can be inserted into the openings of these folders. A brief history of each coin series and an indication of the number of coins issued each year are included in this convenient method of organizing and storing a collection.

Tarnish and Corrosion

This 1876 half dollar has much of its detail intact, but is marred by unattractive tarnish and corrosion on the reverse. Collectors will prefer a uniformly clean specimen with light, even toning.

Each year an alarming number of Mint State and Proof coins are irreparably damaged through improper storage. In addition to causing huge losses in value, this phenomenon has a significant impact on the availability of desirable high-grade coins. Often it is you, the unsuspecting collector, who suffers when assuming that a coin will be immune from harm as long as it is stored in a popular type of coin holder, such as an album, roll tube, or single coin container, then placed in a safe or vault. This is a very dangerous and naïve misconception. The fact is anyone who does not seek to understand the proper methods of coin preservation runs a high risk of serious damage and loss of value. Such damage can actually begin in a matter of months from the time a coin is improperly stored.

Metals are found in their natural ore state in combination with other elements, and include oxides, the chemical compounds formed by the reaction of metal with oxygen in the air. Before the coining process can begin, the metal is refined and purified, thus removing the oxides. This pure metal is chemically unstable and tends to revert to its former natural ore state by recombining with oxygen and reforming the oxides. Newly minted coins immediately start to acquire an oxide layer, which begins at a thickness of millionths of a millimeter and is invisible to the naked eye. In the early stages, oxides on coins aid in protection against other forms of corrosion and do not hide the luster of the coin surface.

As time passes, the oxide layers increase in thickness and are added to by various types of contaminants, forming uneven coatings. Often called *tarnish*, these layers become visible with time and can lead to the formation of dark spots and other discoloration. Later, actual pitting of the metal surface may take place. Naturally, such advanced forms of corrosion are not always removable and may substantially lower the numismatic value of a coin. It is important to protect coins from all forms of corrosion, and this may be accomplished by giving careful attention to proper storage in a humidity-controlled environment and with the use of coin containers that form a barrier between the coin and any outside elements.

Whether coins are stored in your home or in a safe deposit box, care must be taken to ensure that the environment is suitable. Moisture and heat are enemies of coin metals because they promote oxidation and corrosion. If coins are kept at home, they should be kept in a room that is comfortable for you—namely, one that is cool, not humid, and within the normal range of room temperatures.

Tarnish can take the form of colorful toning on a coin.

The same precautions apply when a safe is used for home storage. Despite the perceived strength of a cement floor, never put a safe in a basement that is not protected against dampness or flooding. Never keep coins in an attic where the heat can build up to extreme temperatures during the summer. If coins are stored in a bank, select a vault room where it is cool and dry and preferably air-conditioned in the summer, because air conditioning also removes humidity from the air.

Additional Protection

Some of the problems with humidity could be reduced by storing coins in a place with relative humidity controls, but few of us have that luxury available either at home or in a bank vault. A compound known as silica gel offers a partial solution to this dilemma. Silica gel is a porous, granular, non-crystalline form of silica that is commonly used in many situations to help create a dry storage environment. It is cheap and easy to use, and fits easily into nearly all kinds of cases and boxes in a home or bank vault.

If there is a downside to silica gel, it is that it needs constant attention. Silica gel will continue to absorb atmospheric moisture until it becomes saturated, but at that point it stops, and becomes potentially detrimental to your coins—like placing a wet sponge near them. If you use silica gel, it is important that you monitor it on a regular basis, and change it when it

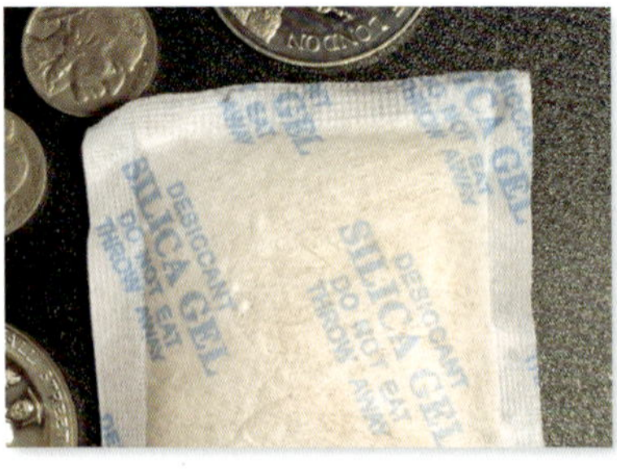

A bag of silica gel with the standard warning: "Do Not Eat."

becomes saturated. You may have to do this on a monthly basis, or somewhat less frequently, depending on the situation. Some forms of silica gel will change color from blue to pink to indicate that it is time to change or refresh the gel. Silica gel can be rejuvenated by heating it in a 250-degree oven for several hours. A microwave oven also works but is not as efficient. Silica gel is relatively inexpensive and can be a good investment for anyone who takes the time to properly monitor its use.

It is not always convenient to check on the silica gel stored with your coins. If they are in a bank vault, you may forget to look in on them for weeks at a time. A secondary consideration is that if you store paper money along with your coins, the silica may do more harm than good by drying out the paper. Be sure to read and follow all instructions that come with the product you choose.

Insurance and Record Keeping

Insurance is as essential for protection of your valuable coins as proper storage methods. This might not be necessary for a small collection of coins with minimal value, but if the value is significant to you, it's time to think about risk insurance. If you store your coins in a bank vault, insurance that covers all risks such as theft, fire, water damage, and other perils should be purchased because the normal bank vault insurance covers only dishonesty, negligence, and a few other risks.

Low-cost vault insurance is widely available from most major carriers. However, such insurance policies usually cover coins only when in the vault, not outside or in transport to and from the bank. Coverage outside the vault is generally costly, often as much as 10 percent of the value insured per year.

If your coins are stored at home they can be insured through a special rider to your home policy. The cost of this will vary according to where and how the coins are stored and protected. Do not assume that your home policy will protect coins under the same terms as your other property. They are considered cash and may be appraised at face value. Check with your insurance agent to learn more

Collectible coins and bullion, like any other valuables, deserve insurance coverage for your peace of mind.

about terms and conditions that may apply to coins and other collectibles that you store at home. Obviously, you must determine if the cost of such protection is warranted, but in all cases, some form of insurance is highly recommended. In addition, each year you should appraise your coins and update the insurance coverage for them as needed.

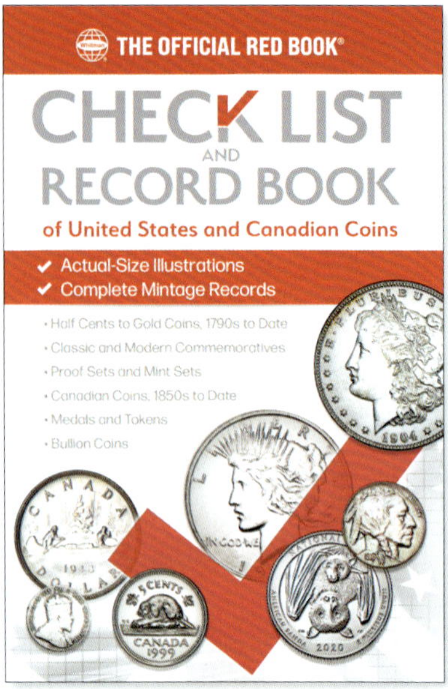

You can keep track of your collection in an electronic spreadsheet, on paper, using an app, in an inventory book—whatever is most convenient for you.

Keeping track of the value of your collection means that you will have to have a complete inventory of what you own. Making a list is easy, and it will not be an arduous task if you keep it up-to-date with each new purchase. You can use your computer to great advantage in making such lists, and a few special coin inventory programs (often advertised in coin publications) are available for your convenience. It is extremely important to always have an inventory available in case of theft, damage, or even death. You will also need such records for tax purposes when it comes time to sell your collection or pass it on to someone else. You should be sure to include mention of your collection in your will so that all of your wishes are followed at the time of death. Taking care of this kind of paperwork is just as important as protecting a collection in all other ways.

When inventorying your collection you should keep a record of exactly what each item is, when and where you purchased it, the original cost, the current value, and where it is stored. A proper description of each piece would include the date, mintmark, metal, denomination, any special features, a catalog number if that is known, the condition or grade, and the country or issuing authority. If the piece is a token, medal, or some other numismatic item, that, too, should be noted. A typical entry might look something like this:

United States. Five cents 1942-P. Silver wartime composition. Uncirculated. Purchased 1996 from Ace Coin Co. for $5.00. Current value $10.00.

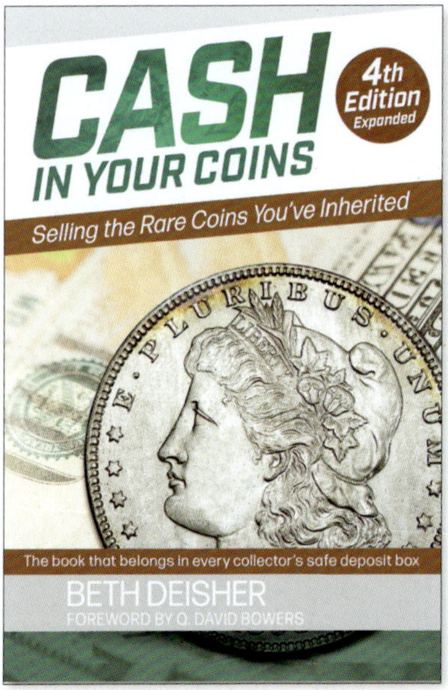

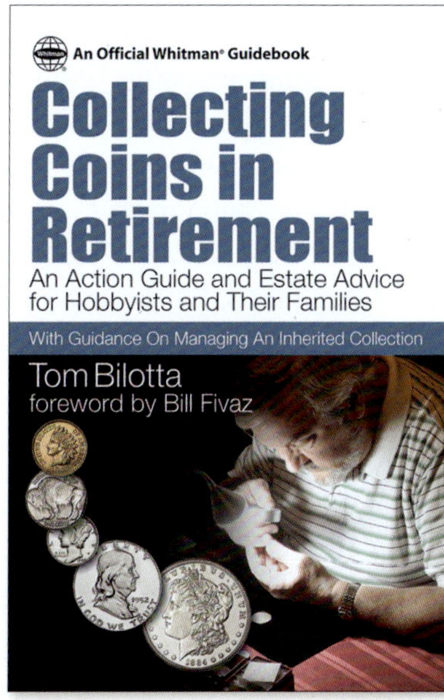

Beth Deisher's book *Cash In Your Coins: Selling the Rare Coins You've Inherited,* and Tom Bilotta's *Collecting Coins in Retirement,* both emphasize the importance of keeping an inventory of your collection.

Storing Your Coins

There are many surface contaminants that can find their way onto a coin and harm the metal if not removed. The most common are dirt, grease, oils, dust, and dandruff, all of which are often invisible to the naked eye. The minting process itself may leave deposits of grease from the dies or from other related tools and machinery used to prepare the coins. Individuals may mishandle coins and deposit skin oils, or leave fingerprints on them. In addition, some kinds of plastic holders can be a major source of contamination because of migrating chemical compounds from the plastic film.

If a coin has been improperly stored in the past or is corroded, it is important to remove any harmful surface contaminants before storing the coin. Coins purchased from a dealer will probably have been treated already if there were any problems. Common solvents, such as alcohol and acetone, may be safely used for this purpose, but even that kind of a bath is best left to more experienced professionals. Silver dips, consisting of thiourea and dilute nitric acid, are sometimes used by dealers to remove any surface pollution. However, the dips will also remove toning and oxide layers and expose the metal to atmospheric attack. Improperly used, dips can leave stains on coins.

Unless you have some unique concerns about surface contaminants on the coins you intend to store, it is best to avoid handling them or attempting to cleanse them in any way before storage. Questions about problem coins are best left to the judgment of experienced collectors or dealers. Consult with one before attempting to cleans or improve your coins.

Don't take chances with your valuable coins. All PVC (polyvinyl chloride) holders can release harmful gases and chemicals that can damage rare coins beyond repair. Soft, pliable, clear plastic called PVC is unlike other hard, stable plastics. Be sure that the holders you use are either rigid or cloudy. Ask a trusted collector or dealer for advice about non-PVC holders.

You may also be unaware that certain types of coin-housing products specifically designed to protect coins can actually cause serious damage. In the past some coin holders were made of polyvinyl chloride (PVC), a type of soft plastic film with a tendency to release harmful gases under heat and pressure. Coins stored in these vinyl holders often suffer damage caused by contact with PVC. There are very few such holders on the market today, but collectors should avoid using any product known to contain polyvinyl plastic.

PVC damage on a British crown.

Popular Coin Holders

The following is an examination of the most popular holders available, with ratings for safety and utility.

Coin Albums—There are two main types of coin albums that have been marketed for many years. This first is of cardboard construction, with holes punched for coin insertion. Some designs leave one side of the coin directly exposed to the air and are more suitable for beginning collectors who use them mainly for coins taken from circulation, or inexpensive duplicate pieces. Others have moveable plastic slides designed to protect both sides of the coin. Here, care must be taken not to abrade the high points of coins when the slides are moved in or out. This album design provides good physical protection and when kept dry is quite suitable for coins that already have layers of oxides on them.

A Whitman album for American Women quarters.

A second type of popular coin album is made of clear vinyl pages mounted in a plastic binder. Each page consists of long, horizontal pockets and slide strips that fit into them. Coins are inserted into the openings of the slide strips that are then inserted into the pockets of the page. In the past these pages and slides have been made from PVC plastic, but most manufacturers are now using an "un-plasticized" vinyl that seems to be relatively safe for short-term coin storage, as long as they are carefully watched for any signs of deterioration.

2" x 2" Holders—These inexpensive holders consist of two identical 2" square cardboard sections, hinged in the middle, with round windows covered by a thin layer of clear Mylar® or cellophane plastic. The coin is placed between the windows, and the halves are then folded together and stapled shut.

Holders of this type are not recommended for long-term storage of any coins of high value, as they do not offer protection from many forms of harm. First, the thin, clear windows can be torn easily by the staples of an adjacent holder when stored in rows in a box. A tear would allow air to attach the coin directly. Second, it is easy to scratch a coin in a 2" x 2" because there is practically no physical protection offered by the thin windows.

2" x 2" holders are available for nearly every coin size.

Third, the cardboard itself may accumulate moisture. Some staples can rust and iron oxide particles can cause severe stains if they touch coin metal. Finally, microscopic dust particles migrate to the clear window by static electricity and are held against the coin, where they may cause black "flyspecks." This spotting is virtually impossible to remove without incurring a significant loss of the protective oxide layering.

Plexiglas™ and Styrene—These clear plastics are very popular for use in many rigid coin holders. They are inert when made from pure source materials. The thick three-ply Plexiglas (acrylic) type, in which individual coins or entire sets can be housed, provides excellent physical protection. However, this material is subject to cracking and allows air inside, resulting in conspicuous toning lines on the coin where any openings exist. Perhaps the greatest disadvantage of these holders is their bulky size and relatively high cost of storage per coin.

The single coin or mint set snap-together polystyrene holders will not harm coins chemically and are relatively airtight, providing a good measure of protection without having risk of impurities. The two halves of square or rectangular plastic have a matte exterior finish with clear centers to fit the particular coin. After the coin is placed in the opening, the halves are squeezed together. They are made in sizes to fit all modern U.S. coins and are available at a modest cost per coin.

A second style of styrene holder, the coin capsule, combines two round sections of clear styrene with a neoprene spacer that surrounds the coin. The coin fits between the two halves that snap-lock together. These holders are chemically inert, provide excellent physical protection, and are relatively airtight. They are also costly on a per-coin basis, and somewhat bulky. Special housing components are available for this style of holder, including frames and boxes.

An individual coin holder.

Another similar coin capsule consists of two round cups that fit snugly together. They are available in various sizes so that coins fit tightly within the bottom cup, and the cap side fits on top of that. These holders are made of thin triacetate, a clear inert plastic that provides a relatively airtight container for individual coins. For better storage convenience these holders generally require an outside holder such as a 2" x 2" cardboard mount or standard paper coin envelope.

Flips—In the past PVC was used in the manufacture of a convenient holder known as a flip. It is a simple double-sided envelope of soft plastic that can be folded over to a convenient 2" x 2" size. A single coin could be stored in the pocket on one side of the flip, and an identification tag in the other. Dealers often use flips because they are soft, clear, flexible, and inexpensive. In addition, coins can be seen from both sides without removing them from the holders. Unfortunately, some of these old flips are still being used for coin storage, even though there is a new, and much safer, generation of Mylar® plastic flips that are available.

The long-term effect of PVC plastic on coins was not known at the time the original flips were marketed. Several years after its introduction, collectors began to notice green or blue flecks of sticky matter on coins stored in PVC holders. It was later learned that the chemicals and gases from PVC leak out of the film under certain conditions and can attack the surface of a coin. Chemical stabilizers that are added to the PVC formula have a tendency to break down and cause further damage to coins. This occurs when hydrogen chloride gas escapes from the film. The gas readily combines with moisture to become hydrochloric acid, which can be

A coin in a plastic flip, with its information written on an inserted card.

extremely damaging to the delicate surface of a coin, and even more so to paper money. Extreme heat and moisture tend to speed the adverse reaction of PVC, and it is now known that there is no way to reverse or clean away the damage caused by storage in these kinds of holders.

The new generation of flips made from Mylar film is chemically inert and safe for long-term storage. They are not as soft and flexible as the older version, but they are convenient and practical. If you intend to store coins in flips, be sure that you use the kind made of Mylar film and not vinyl. If you have questions about any of the holders that your coins are currently stored in, be sure to ask for the advice of an experienced collector or dealer.

While Mylar flips are a big improvement over the older PVC holders, they are by no means airtight. Airborne contaminants can still enter the pockets unimpeded and this fact must be considered when selecting holders for your coins.

Roll Tubes—Tubes for storage of coin rolls have been made from many types of plastic. Round polystyrene (clear) tubes with polyethylene caps have enjoyed wide popularity among dealers, collectors, and investors. They offer relatively safe storage for coins in all grades as long as the caps are securely tightened and care is exercised when handling the filled tubes. A full styrene tube can crack and even shatter upon impact with a hard surface if accidentally dropped from a distance of only a few feet. The strongest types available are also the most expensive. They are made of polyethylene, a very durable plastic, easily recognized by its milky opaque color and square-edge design.

Unfortunately, there is no single "perfect" way to store coins. Most collectors use a variety of different holders and protective containers to house their valuable items. I have seen them all, and I have come to understand that whatever pleases each individual may be what is best for that person. Some like to show their coins to friends and need holders that protect the coins from handling but are easy to see. Others have their most valuable coins sealed in plastic "slabs" and store them in a bank vault. The single most important consideration is that coins should be shielded from moisture, air, and extremes of temperature. For maximum protection, I would recommend that coins be sealed in plastic holders and stored in an airtight plastic box that is kept in a bank vault. Even then they should be inspected two or three times each year to be sure that they have not deteriorated in any way.

Square-edged polyethylene coin tubes.

Flyspecks on the obverse of an 1865 copper-nickel three-cent piece.

PVC exposure caused the green haze on the surfaces of this coin.

Fingerprints on an Eisenhower dollar.

A Lincoln cent damaged by exposure to seawater.

Environmental damage on an Indian Head cent.

2002

Chapter 6

Grading Techniques and Standards

Grade, the condition or state of wear of a coin, is one of the main factors affecting a coin's value. Until the last few decades, most grading was done by instinct. Based on knowledge and personal observations, one seller might have one system, while another seller with varying observations, experiences, and opinions would use a somewhat different system. There was little standardization. Minor differences in opinion about grade were of little consequence where there was only a slight difference in the value of a coin. The need for stricter, more descriptive, standards developed when coin prices began to escalate in the mid-twentieth century.

Within the short period of time from 1950 to 1965, many coins that were trading at $10 became worth $200 or more. A very small difference in grade seemed to make a very large difference in the price that a serious collector was willing to pay. The precise grade of each coin suddenly became extremely important and acceptable standards were needed to ensure that one person's opinion about grade was as close as possible to another's.

In 1977 the American Numismatic Association undertook the task of reviewing all of the various grading options then in use, and combined them into a unified set of standards that could be used by everyone on an equal basis. These were then published as *The Official A.N.A. Grading*

Standards for United States Coins. Those standards, with only a few slight refinements, have been used ever since by most of the coin fraternity to settle disputes and to establish the grades of all U.S. coins. Use of this book, in its seventh edition as of 2017, is highly recommended for all collectors. It has information about grading techniques, why some coins are graded differently than others, and how to accurately grade each level of condition for every U.S. coin. The book is fully illustrated with pictures of each grade, all of which are in full color to show important details and differences.

The concept of grading coins has always been important to collectors. Part of their quest is to find and preserve the best available specimens of each issue, and the finer the condition, the more valuable the coins because of the demand for perfection. It is not difficult to understand why collectors want their cherished coins to look as nice as possible for study and display. New coins are beautiful, with their shiny luster and crisp details. Unfortunately, few coins are still available in fresh, unblemished condition because by their very nature they were made to pass from hand to hand for use as money.

Even those coins that have been preserved in fresh, new condition are rarely perfect in every respect. The rigors of time take their toll on coins as with everything else, and old coins become dull, tarnished, or marred even if they were never placed in circulation. Abuse occurs even in the mint where coins are made, for these are merely a commercial product, intended not to satisfy a collector's taste, but to serve as a circulation medium. The manufacturing, transportation, and storage processes all contribute to the less-than-perfect condition of a coin even before it can be selected and saved by a collector. It is a wonder that any coins ever survive in a really high state of preservation.

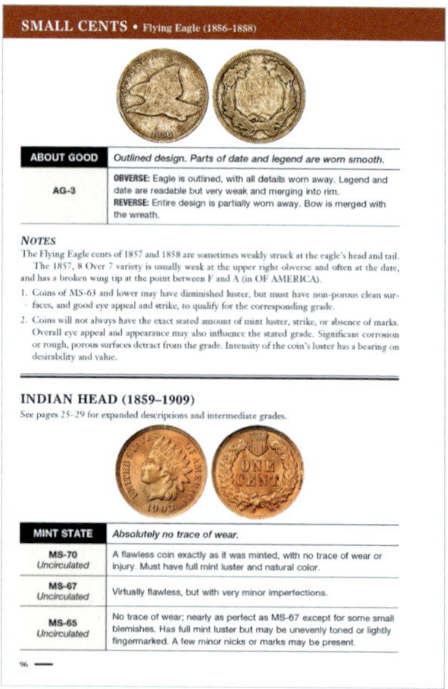
SMALL CENTS • Flying Eagle (1856–1858)

ABOUT GOOD	*Outlined design. Parts of date and legend are worn smooth.*
AG-3	**OBVERSE:** Eagle is outlined, with all details worn away. Legend and date are readable but very weak and merging into rim. **REVERSE:** Entire design is partially worn away. Bow is merged with the wreath.

NOTES

The Flying Eagle cents of 1857 and 1858 are sometimes weakly struck at the eagle's head and tail.

The 1857, 8 Over 7 variety is usually weak at the upper right obverse and often at the date, and has a broken wing tip at the point between F and A (in OF AMERICA).

1. Coins of MS-63 and lower may have diminished luster, but must have non-porous clean surfaces, and good eye appeal and strike, to qualify for the corresponding grade.
2. Coins will not always have the exact stated amount of mint luster, strike, or absence of marks. Overall eye appeal and appearance may also influence the stated grade. Significant corrosion or rough, porous surfaces detract from the grade. Intensity of the coin's luster has a bearing on desirability and value.

INDIAN HEAD (1859–1909)

See pages 25–29 for expanded descriptions and intermediate grades.

MINT STATE	*Absolutely no trace of wear.*
MS-70 *Uncirculated*	A flawless coin exactly as it was minted, with no trace of wear or injury. Must have full mint luster and natural color.
MS-67 *Uncirculated*	Virtually flawless, but with very minor imperfections.
MS-65 *Uncirculated*	No trace of wear; nearly as perfect as MS-67 except for some small blemishes. Has full mint luster but may be unevenly toned or lightly fingermarked. A few minor nicks or marks may be present.

96

A sample page from the *Official American Numismatic Association Grading Standards for United States Coins,* seventh edition.

Planchets in the Denver Mint, waiting to be coined into America the Beautiful quarters.

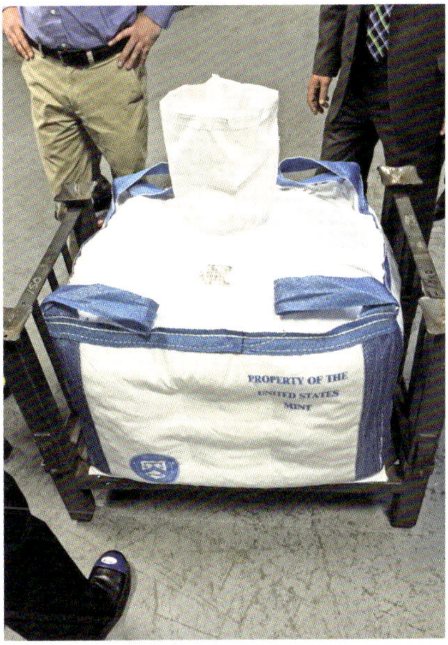

A bag of 200,000 quarters in the Denver Mint.

A view inside one bag's $50,000 face value of freshly struck 2015 Kisatchie National Forest quarters—each one in lustrous original Mint State.

Hundreds of bags of Uncirculated quarters, each bag holding 200,000 coins, temporarily stored in the Denver Mint.

The pieces that do manage to escape damage from automatic counting or weighing machines, the trip from the Mint to the Federal Reserve and on through the banking system, and every other peril from the coinage press to the wrapping machine, are even then faced with the remote chance of being saved by caring hands. Then they need someone to give them proper and careful attention to safeguard their original condition and prevent any further damage from careless handling or even from the atmosphere.

These problematical chances of survival for even a modern coin are compounded manifold for coins of the past. They were rarely given any consideration as future collectors' items, and few were ever saved for any reason. Thus the chance of survivors in exceptionally high grade of condition is literally one in a million.

A Look at Uncirculated Coins

Despite their rarity, Uncirculated coins do exist for nearly all issues and dates of United States coins. Available quantities are small, and a few of the older pieces do not seem to have survived in the Uncirculated grade. The really amazing fact is that examples of perfectly preserved coins have been found that record the history of coinage back to its origin, and bright, unworn specimens of ancient Greek and Roman coins still exist, as do coins of nearly all times, nations, and cultures throughout history.

Any coin that has survived for more than 50 years and is still in bright new Uncirculated condition is an exception to the probability of survival, and should be preserved for the enjoyment of future generations. Such coins are the pride and joy of collectors, students, and museums. The competition to own those rarities has created a demand that has made choice old coins very valuable. Prices for such items vary with the scarcity of each coin and the degree of perfection in its state of preservation. These factors, coupled with the demand from an ever-growing group of collectors, speculators, and investors, are what establish the value of all coins.

An Uncirculated dime.

The term "Uncirculated" refers to any coin that has never been used as money or abused in any way so as to cause wear or abrasion on the surface of the piece. A true Mint State, or Uncirculated, coin must be as fresh and new as the moment it was coined at the mint. It may have suffered some nicks and marks from the minting process, or when it was bagged and stored, and if the coin is old enough it may have become tarnished, but if it has never been worn from handling it is considered to be Uncirculated. Once such a coin is slipped into someone's pocket or purse the chances are that it will encounter enough friction to take it out of the Mint State category. The damage may be so minimal that it can only be detected under strong magnification, but to a numismatist the coin can then only be graded "About Uncirculated."

The circular groove on this silver wartime nickel is damage caused by a coin-wrapping machine. The coin is otherwise in attractive Uncirculated condition.

Coins in true Mint State are further rated as to their degree of perfection on a point scale that ranges from MS-60 to MS-70. The lower number, Mint State–60, describes a coin with no trace of wear but does have a number of other imperfections, abrasions, or marks that make it the lowest acceptable coin in that category. The highest number, MS-70, is a theoretical state of perfection that is rarely achieved by any coin other than a specially minted presentation piece. Modern bullion and specialty coins made for collectors often approach perfection thanks to state-of-the art coining equipment. Such coins are not intended for circulation. They are encased in plastic and sold by the Mint at premium prices.

Unlikely as it may seem, even some ancient Greek and Roman coins have survived the centuries in their original new condition. Such coins must have been buried shortly after the time they were minted and were never touched thereafter. Under the right conditions coins can last for many years without being harmed. But store them near moisture, acids, or sulfur and they will begin to disintegrate rapidly.

Within the range of Uncirculated coins are pieces that fit a standard description of each type of coin for each point value from 60 through 70. While the higher ranges of condition hold great appeal to everyone, it is generally only the investors and wealthy

Modern collector coins of the United States Mint, such as this five-ounce .999 fine silver coin of the America the Beautiful series (shown at actual size), are nearly always in high-end Uncirculated condition, as originally made. In fact, a *circulated* specimen, or even one graded less than MS-68, would be a rarity!

collectors who are seriously interested in owning coins graded at the levels from MS-66 through MS-68. Collectors, who are often content with attractive, more affordable material, find older coins in the range of MS-60 through MS-65 very acceptable. The term "investor grade" is sometimes applied to older coin types that are graded as MS-65 or higher, because those pieces have traditionally appealed to investors and have proven to be high-quality items with excellent potential for appreciation in value. The difference in price for such coins is sometimes astounding. A coin that sells for $300 in MS-63 condition might cost as much as $15,000 in MS-66 grade.

The quality of mint luster is another factor of eye appeal that has much to do with the value of an Uncirculated coin. Mint luster is the characteristic flashy brilliance that is seen on a new coin. It is imparted at the moment the metal blank is struck. Mint luster is fragile and will start to fade as soon as a coin enters circulation. Once gone, there is no way to restore it. The original mint luster on a coin is very different from any artificial polish, but it takes a bit of experience to tell them apart. Study the way a new coin flashes when you twist it in the light, and learn to distinguish the look of that coin from another that has been worn by gentle circulation.

The Morgan dollar at left is in its natural Uncirculated state, with mint luster. The one at right has been cleaned, resulting in a flat, artificial look.

The physical differences in the various grade point levels for most coins are slight, and difficult for non-collectors to discern. Trained numismatists and experienced collectors agree that Uncirculated coins can be divided into different categories on the basis of marks and eye appeal, but they also readily admit that part of the evaluation process is subjective and prone to human error or personal opinion. Written descriptions of the differences in Mint State grades are vague at best and subject to interpretation. Even very experienced dealers sometimes find difficulty in determining the exact grade of coins that are borderline cases and may swing one way or the other.

Many dealers and collectors rely on independent services to establish the grade of their coins. There are several such services that do this for a reasonable fee. They are referred to as "third-party" grading services because they are neither the buyer nor the seller of any particular coin they grade. Their opinions are generally accepted as being accurate and consistent. Coins that they examine are encapsulated, or sealed, in plastic and certified. Professional grading services that are employed for establishing the grades of encapsulated and certified coins use specially trained numismatists who, because of their experience and skills, are remarkably precise in their determinations. The opinions rendered by the third-party grading services are a consensus of views by three or more of their staff members and are usually very consistent and accurate. Unfortunately, even the best of human opinion is subject to occasional error in such a subjective exercise.

A slight difference of opinion as to the severity of a small mark on an otherwise nearly perfect Uncirculated coin would seem to be of little consequence to most people. In the case of a rare coin, though, it might determine the difference between a quite normal MS-65 specimen, valued at one price, and an MS-68 coin worth two to four times as much. That difference in value can be, and often is, a matter of thousands of dollars, while

"Slabs" of several of the most popular third-party grading services.

the difference in the physical appearance of the coin is so slight as to be unnoticed by the untrained or unaided eye. In an extreme case, the difference of a full grade point might depend upon the location of a tiny blemish that seems more distracting on one coin than it might on another, even though the marks are of equal severity. Yet another difference, equally slight, might take a coin out of the "finest known" category, and make a difference of tens of thousands of dollars in its value as a collectible.

When experts grade coins they must take into consideration many factors that go into determining the evaluation. There are fairly well defined guidelines for determining the number and severity of marks, scuffs, or blemishes that could plague an Uncirculated coin, but beyond that there are other factors that are quite subjective. Eye appeal is one of the considerations that can add or subtract from the grade level of a coin that might otherwise meet the standard criteria for a given grade. The severity and location of blemishes, the coin's brilliance and color, and even the sharpness of design can all influence a grader's opinion.

It has often been said facetiously that ownership of a coin adds at least one point to its grade. There certainly is some truth to that as a perception, but in actuality the difference is probably something tied to the bargaining and pricing process, or pride of ownership. Whatever the reason, the ownership syndrome is responsible for many of the differences of opinion that occur in coin grading by people other than those of the independent grading services.

Other differences in opinion, or errors in grading, occur when one grader simply is not as skillful as another or does not take the same care in making determinations. An experienced grader will, whenever possible, use standard magnification and lighting to view each coin so that they are all seen under the same ideal conditions. The experts also often consider a second opinion, and are careful not to work with coins when they are tired or distracted. They realize that grading is an inexact science at best, based to a degree on skill and subjective opinion. To give the matter anything less than full attention and devotion could mean the difference of thousands of dollars to a coin's value and destroy the profitability of someone's investment. For these reasons, grading investment-level coins is best left up to the experts, especially those professionals of the independent third-party grading services, unless you plan to devote years of study and practice to honing your skills.

Notice the differences in the condition of these two 1886-O dollars. The one at left is graded MS-61 because of the nicks and scratches. The other graded MS-64 has a smooth, nearly blemish-free surface.

Those collectors who do spend years learning how to grade accurately have a great advantage over others, including some dealers, who have not taken the time to study and practice grading skills. These people are able to purchase raw, or non-encapsulated, coins with the knowledge that what they buy is accurately graded and priced at the lowest possible level. Their ability to make a profit from their grading skill often motivates some to become professional dealers. Yet most collectors are content simply to use their skills to add high-quality pieces to their sets on their own terms, rather than relying on the opinion of others.

For these and other reasons the vast majority of collectors do not care for "investment" or certified coins, do not collect them, and would far prefer to select their own pieces and house them in uniform holders to match the other coins they own. This difference in attitude between collectors, who want to do their own work in selecting coins, and investors, who need the assurance and protection of certified coins, has caused a marked division between the two groups. It has also been the main reason for the rather substantial price difference between raw and certified coins, and the preference by the collector group for lower-quality Uncirculated coins that are often priced at a fraction of the prices charged for investor-grade pieces.

What Makes Coins Valuable

Just about anything can be, and has been, used as money. Everything from rocks to elephant tails have been put to use at one time or another in societies where the people have decided by mutual consent to use those objects as a medium of exchange for other items. In today's world the value of whatever is used as money still depends more on consent than on actual intrinsic worth. There was a time when each coin had to contain a full measure of precious metal to make it acceptable, but now nearly every country in the world uses some form of a token substitute for its money. Our paper dollars and copper-nickel–clad coins are examples of how we arbitrarily assign value to nearly worthless items. The fact that our five-cent coins contain metal that is more valuable than our dime does not seem to bother anyone.

Yes, the process of establishing value for coins as money is strange, but it gets even more complex when we think about some of the other interesting facets of a coin's value. Consider an old American silver dollar, such as the 1921 Morgan dollar. Millions were made; they are probably the most common of all silver dollars and can generally be found in almost any accumulation of old United States coins. Chances are that you have one in your collection. What is it worth? Well, when these pieces were issued for circulation, they had a face value of $1. You could walk into just about any bank and pick up all you wanted for $1 each, not only in 1921, but also for the next 40 years. So this is a dollar coin; but beyond that it was also equal to a day's pay in the early years, and later became equal to an hour's pay. In a sense it originally had a purchasing power ranging from $10 to $50 or more.

A 1921 Morgan dollar.

When these dollars were current, they were also worth about 40¢ in silver bullion value. Just about the time they were all taken out of circulation around 1965, they were still dollar coins, but the silver content had risen in value to slightly over $1. If you were to melt one of these in coins in 1980, it would have been worth around $30 because of the high price of silver bullion, and now, years later, if silver is valued at $18 per ounce, the silver bullion content in the old Morgan is about $14. However, these dollar coins have a premium for their convenient and recognizable source of silver bullion so they actually sell for closer to $16.

That rather lengthy observation should explain what the coin sells for, but it does not even address some of the other elements that give the piece its extraordinary worth. There is the matter of its historical value, which is significant considering that these silver Morgan dollars are among the most colorful and treasured relics of the old West, that they helped to build this country and keep it strong, and that the almighty American dollar is world-renowned. It is difficult to put a historical value on this coin; it is easier to establish its value as a collector's piece.

For that we have some guides as to exactly what numerous buyers are willing to pay for the 1921 Morgan dollars in various grades of condition.

We find that a specimen worn from years of service is worth about $16, and one that shows little wear is worth less than double that amount. Surprises start when we see that a piece in minimal (MS-60) Uncirculated condition sells for $25, and one in MS-63 for $40. Then we learn that a specimen graded MS-65 will cost over $100, and if it is much better than that, or has an exceptionally brilliant surface, it could be worth as much as $1,000! Just what is the 1921 Morgan dollar worth? Who can say? The answer depends on which kind of an evaluation is used, which time period is being considered, and whether it is destined for the historian, bullion dealer, collector, or investor.

Morgan dollars evoke the rich history of the American Old West.

This scenario of values for an American dollar, the kind that were called "cartwheels" when they were in daily use, is meant only to point out the differences that come from various points of view. In at least one sense it can be related to the problems that arise in pricing all rare coins for the numismatic market, for these are not a necessary commodity and the value is mostly in the eye of the beholder. To say that such a coin is not worth $1,000 is no more accurate than to think that it could never have been worth 40¢ or a day's wage, or any of the other values that it claimed during its lifetime. Value is a factor of demand, and as long as there are people who appreciate the rarity of this coin in extraordinarily high-grade condition, it can be worth any amount that a willing buyer is ready to pay in order to acquire a specimen.

Both dealers and investors are faced with difficulties in trying to establish a fair value for excessively rare coins. The market is usually led by prices realized at public auction for rare items that would not normally be found in any dealer's inventory. In many cases dealers bid on those coins for their customers, who usually set price limits for a particular coin that is on the auction block. It is then the dealer's responsibility to determine that the coin is genuine and properly graded, and to bid on it in the hopes of getting it at the lowest possible price for the client. This process is fairly straightforward when coins have been pre-graded by an independent service, but it becomes rather chancy when the coins are "raw," and their value is left up to the skill of the buyer.

Serious problems can arise when coin sales are negotiated at conventions or between dealers or collectors, where there are disagreements about the precise grade of a coin. This is especially true when the differences in value are on the order of 10 to 30 times for each point level of condition. It is here where skill and conviction pay off for the experienced buyer, and where a newcomer can make a costly mistake.

It is a fickle market and even if several experts agree on the grade and value of a coin on one day, they may reverse that opinion on the very next day and send the price off in a different direction. I remember an incident where a certain rare gold U.S. coin was sold to a dealer during a coin show for $20,000. He later resold it to another dealer for $23,000, and that dealer sold it to a customer for $25,000. Two days later at the same show, the collector was offered only $17,000 for it by the same dealer who had originally paid $20,000. In this case the collector kept it for a couple of years and eventually sold it to someone else for more than he had paid for it.

A coin auction in progress: auctioneer Chris Karstedt welcomes bidders to the 2005 Eliasberg sale.

Whatever the reasons may be for the volatility of the rare-coin market, none are easy to predict or understand. It is safe only to observe that even though certain coins are extremely rare, the total number of willing buyers is often just as limited, and the market reacts in a direct response to supply and demand, regardless of the worth of any coin.

Piles of common-date Barber quarters displayed for sale at an American Numismatic Association World's Fair of Money in Chicago.

Fortunately for the beginning collector, most of the problems associated with buying rare and high-grade coins do not apply to the kinds of coins that are most often available on the market. Collectors rarely sell or trade high-priced coins with each other, they are not found very often in old household accumulations, and they are almost never seen in circulation. Most coin dealers specialize in the kinds of coins that will appeal to the greatest number of collectors, and it is rare to find extremely valuable coins in a dealer's stock. Almost all high-end coins are seen only in the inventory of specialty dealers or at public auctions.

Collectors can usually buy with confidence from dealers and through advertisements if they follow the simple rules of checking to see that the dealers are members of the Professional Numismatists Guild (www.PNGdealers.org) or the American Numismatic Association (www.money.org) and that they are using official ANA grading standards. A telephone call to the dealer can usually verify these points if they are not stated in an advertisement. Once your grading skills are sufficiently honed, you will also be able to successfully buy coins at conventions and from other sources. It takes a bit of practice and skill, but that goes with the hobby, and many people find grading one of the most rewarding parts of collecting.

As stated before, you will need a book for full guidance, but you can learn the basics with ease. Here are some of the major characteristics of a coin's surface that you must learn to recognize before you can begin to grade like an expert. It is well to keep in mind that all coins are individual, and one may wear and look slightly different than any other.

Bag marks. The terms "bag mark" and "contact mark" are used interchangeably. The first is more common, the latter more accurate. They refer to any nicks, small cuts, or other similar marks on a coin's surface. These marks usually occur during the minting process or when the coins come into contact with each other in mint bags while in storage in the Treasury Department, or in bank vaults. It is usual for nearly all Uncirculated coins to have some contact marks. The larger and heavier a coin is, the more contact marks it may have. In time, the effects of circulation may wear away all evidence of such marks.

The contact marks and blemishes on these Liberty Head gold double eagles diminish their grades, but they are still considered Uncirculated.

Older coins were often affected by peculiarities of the striking mint. For example, double eagles struck at Carson City, Nevada (a remote location), nearly always have very heavy bag marks. This is attributable to the rigors of transportation from the Carson City Mint, and also to the somewhat more primitive conditions (when compared with Philadelphia) that existed at the time the coins were made.

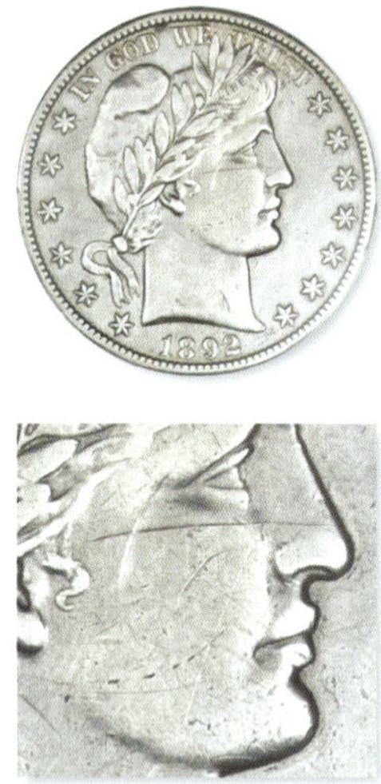

Scratches on a Barber half dollar.

Scratches. Scratches are small grooves or marks on a coin's surface that result from either careless handling or normal circulation. Scratches, if prominent and conspicuously visible, merit consideration because they detract from the eye appeal and value of a coin. Many coins below Very Good condition will show some small non-detracting scratches that can be disregarded.

Edge bumps (nicks or dents). A coin, particularly a heavy one, dropped inadvertently and impacting with a hard surface against its rim, will usually acquire an edge bump. Like surface injuries, edge bumps reduce the value of a coin to some extent, depending more or less upon severity. Rim nicks that can barely be seen from the obverse side of a coin are not considered particularly damaging.

Edge bumps on a gold double eagle and various silver dollar coins.

Die weakness. Die weakness originates from several causes. After extensive use, certain design features on a coinage die tend to become worn, resulting in weak areas on the struck coins. Often when a die became worn it was polished, dressed, or re-engraved and put back into service. Such dies are apt to have weak spots or missing features.

Another cause of weak-appearing coins occurred when some areas of the die were weak to begin with. At times, portions of the central design were only lightly impressed into the die, thus causing a weakness in the coin design, usually on the areas in lower relief. Further, improperly hardened dies had a tendency to sink in certain areas, which imparted a noticeable weakness to the coins struck by that particular die.

Striking weakness. Most weaknesses on modern coins are a result of striking. Striking weaknesses take many different forms. Several times throughout United States' coinage history, a design was used that had directly opposing areas of high relief on both the obverse and reverse dies. When this occurred, striking pressure was often inadequate, or not enough metal was available in the blank coinage disk to be pushed up fully into the recesses of both dies. The result was a weakness in the design on one or both sides of the coin.

Most weaknesses in design make a coin worth less than a better-struck piece. Quite the opposite is true of the famous three-legged Buffalo nickel of 1937-D, where excessive polishing of the die created a modern rarity that is very much in demand by all collectors for its novel appearance.

A weakly struck 1920-S Buffalo nickel (left) compared to a strongly struck 1938-D.

Grading Circulated Coins

You can begin learning to grade by studying common coins taken from circulation. Use a grading book to determine what number best fits the amount of wear on each coin. Begin by sorting the circulated coins into piles according to wear. You will soon notice a pattern to what the various grades look like. You should be able to see some clear differences between pieces that are Good, Fine, or Extremely Fine. The in-between pieces will be Very Good, Very Fine, and About Uncirculated.

After you have practiced with circulated coins and your reference book for some time, you will be ready to grade the coins in your collection. The next step will be to look at some professionally graded coins in a coin store, at a club meeting, or at a coin show. Try to guess what grade will be assigned by a dealer, and see how close you come to agreeing with the grade.

Discuss your grading attempts with a dealer or experienced collector. They will help you to get a better understanding of and feeling for your ability. Don't be surprised if your skills are soon better than those of others. Many longtime collectors never bother to learn good grading skills. They think it is too time-consuming and would rather just buy coins that appeal to them, regardless of grade. Do not make that costly mistake. Learning to grade is well worth the effort and will pay off in many ways.

The numeric grading scale is divided into two major groups. Coins that are worn in any way are assigned numbers from 1 to 58. Number 59 is not used because it is considered too difficult to judge. Coins in new condition (Uncirculated or Mint State) have numbers from 60 to 70. Such coins are graded according to their state of perfection and attractiveness.

Coins showing any signs of wear are graded according to the amount of the design that is affected. The more features that are worn away, the lower its grade and number will be. Coins also become less desirable once they get dark and shabby looking. High-grade coins are always in demand, but unless a piece is exceptionally rare, it will have very little value once it is worn smooth, marred, or otherwise damaged.

Start grading with common coins from your pocket change or from your local bank.

STANDARD GRADING GUIDELINES

Uncirculated (MS-65)—Above-average new coin that has never been handled, abused, or worn in any way. May have a few small contact marks or blemishes.

Uncirculated (MS-63)—Choice Uncirculated, but has several obvious marks and nicks from contact with other coins.

Uncirculated (MS-60)—No trace of wear, but has numerous marks and blemishes from rough handling while in storage.

About Uncirculated (AU-50)—Shows only the slightest trace of rub on the highest points of the design. Still retains nearly full mint luster and brilliance.

Extremely Fine (EF-40)—Design is lightly worn throughout, but still retains full sharpness in every detail. Some mint luster remains.

Very Fine (VF-20)—
A moderate amount of wear is noticeable on the high points of the design. Main features are very bold.

Fine (F-12)—Shows moderate to considerable wear throughout. Entire design is bold with an overall pleasing appearance.

Very Good (VG-8)—
Well worn, with main features clear and easily seen although rather flat.

Good (G-4)—Heavily worn, with design visible but faint in some spots. Some details are worn smooth.

About Good (AG-3)—Very heavily worn, with portions of the lettering, date, and design worn away. The date may be barely readable.

Coins in any condition lower than About Good are rarely collected unless they are very rare. Low-grade coins and those that have been holed, or severely damaged, have very little value because they are unattractive and are not wanted by serious collectors. Even the rarest of coins in poor condition are discounted heavily when they are sold, and are not considered a good investment.

Uncirculated coins must be graded very carefully because of the vast difference in value for each grade level. Values quoted in price guides for coins in MS-65 condition or better usually refer to pieces that have been certified by professional grading services.

Holed and otherwise damaged coins have tales to tell, but are worth very little to collectors.

Third-Party Grading

As discussed above, several professional grading services grade and encapsulate coins for a fee. Beginning collectors, investors, and anyone unskilled in grading can rely on these services to offer expert opinions about grades and, in effect, the value of their coins. Third-party grading is of the greatest importance when rare or very valuable coins are involved, and is almost a necessity for establishing an accurate grade for coins in MS-65 or better condition. In addition to the reassurance factor of knowing that a coin is genuine and has been professionally graded, the "slab" or plastic encapsulation is also of value to collectors because of the protection it offers for long-term storage.

Grading services are known by various acronyms: PCGS, NGC, ANACS, PCI, NCI, etc. Their advertisements, qualifications, and unique services can be found in most numismatic publications. The cost of these services is fairly uniform, as is the quality of their work. Collectors often prefer one over the other because they want all of their coins to be housed in the same kind of holder.

Coins valued at under $50, or in low grade, are seldom "slabbed" because of the cost of the service, which can be $15 to $25 or more per coin.

THE UNITED STATES OF AMERICA
WE TRUST
20
THIS CERTIFIES THAT THERE IS ON DEPOSIT IN
THE UNITED STATES
FIVE CENTS
1903
ONE CENT

Chapter 7

COIN PRICES AND VALUES

The growth in demand for coins as an investment rather than as collectibles or objets d'art has become characterized by different groups being interested in different kinds of coins.

Collectors by nature generally want to have complete collections and are often more concerned with the acquisition of new types, dates, or varieties than in trying to obtain coins in absolutely perfect condition. Even though collectors appreciate the rarity and beauty of high-grade coins, they often pass those by because of price considerations.

Investors do quite the opposite. They are accustomed to buying the finest quality in all of their purchases and expect no less of their coins. They are also keenly aware that coins in high grade are hundreds of times rarer than their counterparts in a lower state of preservation.

In the growing split between coins that appeal primarily to collectors and those in demand by investors, two quite different markets have developed. For the average collector there is virtually a world full of coins ranging from the most ancient made in the seventh century BC to modern Proof and collector sets made for their enjoyment each year by many countries. Collector coins have continued to appreciate in value over the years at a fairly steady rate, and the hobby has been a rewarding investment for its followers who formed collections of carefully selected pieces of reasonably high quality. It is accurate to state that nearly all collectors would like to own the choicest specimens possible, but many are content to settle for something less when faced with a tremendous price difference.

An example of just how vast this difference in value can be is the case of the 1880-O Morgan silver dollar that at one time was selling to collectors in the very acceptable basic Uncirculated grade of MS-60 for approximately $100. At the same time a similar specimen in the relatively high grade of MS-64 was selling for nearly $2,000. In the superior Uncirculated "investor" grade of MS-65, the 1880-O had a price tag of more than $25,000, with practically no specimens available through any dealer. In many other cases the difference in value between average Uncirculated coins, and those in investment grade, is tenfold.

1880-O Morgan dollars in MS-60 and MS-65 grades.

Are those coins worth the difference? Most collectors do not seem to think so. Investors are equally convinced that in the long run it is the super coins that will show the greatest appreciation in value. Historically the high-grade pieces have proven to be the best suited for investment purposes and have gone up in value at a faster rate than the more common lower-grade pieces. In the case of the 1880-O Morgan dollar, the speculators who purchased top-grade pieces at any price in the past could have profited immensely, while there has been no significant price movement for any of the coins in lower grade. There is a danger, however, in that any investment that goes up in value quickly can drop out of favor just as fast and lose its value.

The difference in demand and value for normal and investor coins has become even more divergent with the widespread use of plastic encapsulation for certified third-party grading. "Slabbed" coins, as certified coins are called, have become a near necessity for the investor to ensure that coins are properly graded and will be acceptable to others at their time of liquidation. On average the cost of third-party grading is approximately $25. It can be as much as $125 for the express service that is sometimes used to cinch a quick sale. These costs are included in the price of the coin and passed on to the investor. Collectors able to form their own judgment about grade and authenticity do not want their coins sealed in plastic, and do not want to pay the added cost of a third-party opinion. Obviously it would not be cost-effective to slab a $50 collector coin and add the $25 to its price for no particular purpose.

Many of the rare and valuable coins in high grade have now been committed to plastic and serve the investor community well by being actively traded through networks where dealers accept them sight unseen on the basis of the stated grade. There are, however, many similar coins that have not as yet been through any grading service. These "raw" coins are more the domain of collectors and dealers than of the investors, who seldom get to see such coins before they are slabbed. As might be expected, there is an entirely different price structure for raw coins than that used to sell investment-tailored coins. Some of that difference is in the cost of slabbing, and some of it has to do with the basic difference between wholesale and retail pricing, but the major hedge lies in the uncertainty of exactly how any given coin will grade when it is sent to the grading service.

Consider again the 1880-O Morgan dollar. The difference in value for a single grade point was as much as $23,000. That means that if a borderline coin of this type were being traded at a coin show, the value could swing that much in either direction. People being people, the owner will always value and grade the piece somewhat higher than the way a potential buyer sees the coin. Beyond that, any of the top grading services could at any time grade such a coin one way or the other by a single point. For those reasons many raw coins trade at coin shows to dealers and collectors for prices far less than what is eventually charged to investors. Both are getting good value, but there is a difference in price that is related to the risk-taking. It is quite likely that any given coin will be priced very differently depending on whether it is raw or slabbed, and destined for the collector or investor market.

If speculators and investors could learn to purchase coins the way that collectors do, and select only top-quality pieces that are properly graded and priced, their chances of making money would be vastly improved. Unfortunately, learning to act like a collector takes more time and effort than most non-hobbyists care to spend. As one investor aptly put it, "If I devoted my time to learning how to trade in the coin market, I would not be able to conduct my own business which provides the money I spend on coins."

Even with that practical approach there is an attitude that can be adopted to add to the chance of successful investing. That is to *think* like a collector when making decisions about which coins would be best to own. A true collector is never rushed into purchasing anything that he knows could come along again some other time at a better price. He or she always looks for the highest affordable quality, is not overly swayed by what others are buying, and has a knack for finding bargains.

Even more importantly, collectors tend to select coins from the heart and to buy the coins that appeal to them emotionally. These are the kinds of coins that will always appeal to others as well, and will always be in demand. Such coins are the classics of numismatics and constantly appreciate in value. The proven rule of thumb is that if a coin holds great appeal for you as a thoughtful connoisseur, then it most likely will appeal to others. Whatever seems of marginal interest or quality to you will probably look the same to others and have little interest to future buyers.

Collectors have another admirable trait: They are patient and seldom rushed into selling their coins. They purchased them in order to form and enjoy a collection. The hours spent studying and working with their pieces is considered part of the reward of owning fine coins, and holding them for a minimum of three to five years is normal. Some collectors make a lifetime commitment to the hobby and are richly rewarded when the collection is sold after 30 or 40 years of appreciating values. These are the people who have been successful at coin buying and who have inspired others to attempt to do the same. Unfortunately there are many others who often approach the hobby with only minimal effort and perseverance.

Traditional collectors are not the only ones with limits to the amount of money that they will spend for any given coin. Most investors have their personal guidelines and limits for each purchase. There are exceptions to both categories of buyers, of course, but as a rule the unseasoned investor gets a little nervous about spending more than $3,000 for any single coin. The amount is generally increased with confidence gained through profitable purchases, and tops out at around $20,000, or wherever the budget will allow. A consideration of these buying habits is important in selecting investment coins because it sets the stage for where the demand will be for those same kinds of coins when it is time to sell them.

There are also lower limits to which coins are best suited for the investor market. Few people are interested in buying bulk quantities of inexpensive coins. Serious investors far prefer a limited number of more expensive pieces. This gives them the opportunity to better control their portfolio and watch the price performance of individual items. It also provides a better opportunity for diversification, and in buying quality pieces at higher price levels, one tends to avoid the common coins that will always be available in quantity.

A good rule for investors to follow is to concentrate on purchasing coins in a price range of $300 to $10,000. There will be exceptions worthy of consideration, but within this perimeter are the coins that assuredly are not common, and not priced so high as to be out of the reach of most investors, or even many collectors. Coins in this price bracket also stand a good chance of doubling in value in a shorter period of time than those priced much higher or lower.

It is a well-known axiom that coins can go down in value as quickly and as easily as they go up. There are no guarantees in coin investments.

It seems axiomatic to stress the importance of investing only in coins that are properly graded and priced, but failing in this respect has been the downfall of most buyers who have been unsuccessful with their purchases. Getting this important edge is not as difficult as it may seem and must not be overlooked. It mostly takes the same assertive and demanding attitude that one might exercise in purchasing a new car. The buyer is, after all, in charge of the transaction, and should not be intimidated by the seller or rushed into a purchase. It is true that some coins come along only once in a lifetime, but for the most part other specimens of equal rarity or value will surface from time to time. It is usually better to make a considered purchase than to rush into something that may turn out to be less than what was expected.

Coin collectors explore the Sunday Collectible Market in the Plaza Mayor, Madrid, Spain—a weekly market that is one of most popular of its kind in Europe.

The problems of purchasing improperly graded coins have been vastly lessened with the availability of third-party certified slabs. No serious investor should attempt to do without them, as they assure the purchaser that coins have been graded by an impartial service that has no vested interest in the transaction or the grade. Such coins are guaranteed to be genuine and are usually salable at or near the assigned grade any time in the future.

Most slabbed coins can be resold easily at auction, by mail, or by telephone without being inspected by the purchaser, as long as they are sealed in the original plastic encapsulation. There are many dealers who will purchase such coins at competitive prices, and the risk of acquiring coins that are counterfeit, are improperly graded, or cannot be resold in the future is vastly lessened through this option. The cost of the slabbing safeguard is minimal and in fact not so very much more than one would expect to pay for the sturdy plastic storage holder that is provided to protect the coins.

Finding the Right Dealer

Making sure that the coins you buy are fairly priced can be a real challenge. There is no way to guarantee that the coins you buy for your collection or as an investment will be competitively priced or that they are even at reasonable levels that will give you a fighting chance to make a profit on them when it is time to liquidate. You can, however, increase your odds of success by using a few simple techniques. First, remember that there is no single source for any kind of coins. You are dealing with a free market, and one that is fiercely competitive at the dealer level. It is perfectly acceptable conduct for any coin buyer to consider purchasing coins from several sources. By doing so or at least by getting bids from more than one dealer the buyer can compare the prices that are being asked for similar coins in the same grade of condition.

A friend once asked me if I thought that the price he had been quoted for a certain coin was fair. I advised him to shop around a bit and see if some other dealer might be able to sell him the same kind of coin at a lower price. A few telephone calls later, he found that he could indeed buy one for nearly $3,000 less from a different dealer.

It is also fair to inquire about the pricing policy of each company. Many will disclose their standard profit margin, or at least give an indication of their usual markup over the prices published in the weekly industry guide known as the *Coin Dealer Newsletter* or, more popularly, the *Greysheet* (www.greysheet.com). This can be useful for making an assessment of the prices charged by each seller, but do not expect to buy your coins at the prices reported in the *Greysheet*. This is merely a tool intended for use by dealers to keep in touch with market conditions. It is not an offer to buy or sell any of the coins listed, and is not intended for use by anyone other than professional dealers.

The *Greysheet* has been the standard reference for U.S. coin dealers since the 1960s. Since that time the company's offerings have expanded to include several print and digital products.

Even though you may have access to this confidential report through a trusted friend, you must remember that the values shown do not reflect market demand, and it is sometimes impossible for dealers to purchase coins without paying a percentage over the "bid" price. At other times the market may be such that dealers are happy to sell their coins at less than the "ask" price. Do not be afraid to ask questions about the prices being charged for the coins that you want to purchase. A little comparison shopping over the telephone just might save you many dollars, especially when you are considering generic coins graded by the same grading service. This technique works whether you are buying a few basic inexpensive coins for your collection, or investing in pieces worth thousands.

Once you have found a competent dealer or firm in which you have confidence, you will probably want to do most of your business with that company. There is no harm in testing the prices, quality, and variety of material once in a while. One good test is to attempt to resell some of your coins to the same dealer who sold them to you. A signal that you are using the wrong dealer could be if the price does not seem right, or the coins are not wanted. It is best to find this out before you have made a major investment and then learn that you cannot easily dispose of your holdings.

After you find a friendly and trustworthy dealer, sticking with a single source has its advantages. One of the most important considerations is that you may be given the first opportunity to purchase new material or special one-of-a-kind coins. Building a rapport with a favorite dealer will also make the negotiating process much easier, and most important of all, it will give you access to information about market conditions that will be invaluable when you wish to consider liquidation or additional purchases.

Your next question may well be, "How do I find that trustworthy dealer in the first place?" Again, there is no easy answer, but a little effort and consideration of what is needed will help immensely. Do you know any friends who have a favorite dealer who has helped them with coin purchases? If so, that would be an ideal place to start your investigation. If not, you may have to experiment a little, and that can be somewhat risky. It will be especially vexing if you have been contacted by a telephone solicitation, or take a chance with an unknown company selected from an open advertisement in a non-numismatic publication.

You can increase your chances of locating a reputable dealer by selecting someone from one of the monthly or weekly hobby publications. Check to see if the one you pick is a member of the American Numismatic Association (www.money.org) and the Professional Numismatists Guild (www.PNGdealers.org). You can obtain a city listing of all PNG members, and their numismatic specialties, by contacting them through their website. Other listings and advertisements by a variety of dealers can be found in the publications listed in chapter 4.

Dealers who are members of the ANA and PNG, or who advertise in well-established publications, have agreed to abide by a strict code of ethics and their actions are monitored by the organizations to which they belong. Any company or dealer not affiliated with at least one of these groups may have a good reason for not belonging, but it would be in your best interest to find out exactly why. Perhaps they are new to the field, or refuse to abide by the regulations. Worst of all, they may have been expelled for some past misconduct. Whatever the reason, you should satisfy yourself that there is a valid excuse before doing business with anyone who is not committed to standard industry regulations.

A call to your local Better Business Bureau (www.bbb.org) will sometimes provide information on a company that has been subjected to numerous complaints from dissatisfied customers. You will not receive a recommendation, or any information on the worthiness of any company, as that is not a function of the Better Business Bureau. It would not be proper for the ANA, the PNG, or any agency to recommend a specific individual or company, so do not expect that a call to them will provide any different answers. They are only allowed to give information about whether an individual is or is not a member of their organization, and in some cases they will be able to state why a former member may have been expelled.

Your selection process should also include a personal meeting with the numismatic sales representative if possible, or at least a telephone call, to answer a few more questions and to determine if you are comfortable working with that person. You will want to know what kinds of services the company provides in addition to just selling coins. Will they still be around when you need help in determining when and how to sell your coins? Are they experts who know about numismatics and the market well enough to provide answers to all of your questions? Are they experienced?

How long have they been in business? What exactly is covered in their sales policy, return privilege, and guarantees? Get satisfactory answers to all of these questions before spending any money, and remember the old adage, "An oral agreement isn't worth the paper it's written on."

It is not uncommon to receive unsolicited telephone calls from marketers selling coins as an investment. Many of these have no numismatic experience beyond buying low-grade raw coins and selling them at inflated prices to unsuspecting buyers. Asking a few incisive questions will usually expose them as frauds to be avoided at all costs. One common ploy is to offer certain silver dollars or gold coins at seemingly bargain prices, and then convince the client that they would do better by buying other higher-priced similar items. The old "bait and switch" gambit is a sure signal to resist any of their offers.

Advertising in non-numismatic magazines and newspapers is yet another area to carefully consider before believing in their offers of rare-coin bargains. Many such advertisements offer look-alike tokens or medals that are simply gold- or silver-plated and not genuine coins. Others offer real coins at bargain prices—but only one to a customer. You will probably have to pay much higher prices once they cinch you as a customer.

All professional coin firms and dealers should have a stated policy covering the length of time that a buyer will have to examine a coin before it is committed to purchase, and they will guarantee that all coins sold by them are genuine and as represented. Most will agree to repurchase any coins that they sell, and value them on the basis of the grade at which they were originally sold. Any other claims or promises may add to your incentive to patronize a particular dealer, but none will be as essential as those just stated, so let's consider them in detail.

An examination policy is critical to your satisfaction with the quality and appearance of each coin. However, do not expect that every dealer will immediately send you coins just to look at. An examination policy is not meant to provide someone with a source for coins on approval. Dealers are well aware of schemes by buyers to obtain coins from them for the sole purpose of offering them for sale to others, or to shop around for a slightly better coin or higher grade of condition. Dealers must also guard against the risk of coins being switched, damaged, or lost while out for examination, and of course, they often lose the opportunity to sell the piece to another customer. Sometimes they lose money by tying up their funds during a fast-rising or falling market.

There are dealers who do run approval services and who are willing to send coins to collectors for consideration. In these cases the coins may be purchased or returned at the discretion of the buyer. The rules of approval consignments must be clearly understood by both parties before the coins are sent. Many of the newspaper advertisements that sell coins by mail also offer approval services for the convenience of their customers.

It is reasonable to expect a 14-day examination period for most coins. This would not hold true for coins that have been specifically acquired by a dealer on commission from a client, and it does not apply to any bullion items or coins purchased at public auction. When coins are examined by a customer prior to sale, as in the case of transactions in a store or at a convention, it is up to the buyer to make a firm commitment to purchase the pieces unless specified otherwise by special written agreement with the seller.

Trust is important when you're buying and selling coins.

In some cases a seller will agree to allow a buyer to submit a coin to a third-party grading service, and will extend the return privilege to the time necessary for certification, with the sale contingent upon their decision about the grade. This arrangement is particularly useful in the case of raw coins, but it is unnecessary where coins have already been examined and encapsulated by one of the major independent grading services. In that case, the buyer may be given only a few days to examine the coin because it will be accurately graded, and therefore if the collector decides not to buy, it must be returned to the dealer immediately, so that he or she can sell it to someone else.

Every coin dealer should guarantee that the coins he sells are genuine and as represented in every way. No reputable dealer will knowingly sell counterfeit coins, as they are considered the bane of the industry and are the object of severe penalties for fraud. These guarantees are without time limitation as long as clear ownership and possession of a particular coin can be established. Problems arise when a buyer does not discover that a coin is counterfeit until it is time to sell it many years after it was purchased. At that time it will be up to the owner to prove that the bad coin is indeed the identical one sold to him years earlier. Questions will also be asked by the seller about the reason for an unreasonably long delay in establishing that the coin is false.

When a collector in Ohio found that he had purchased a counterfeit $20 gold coin, he tried to return it to the dealer where he had purchased it. The dealer resisted, saying that he had no knowledge of ever selling such a coin. Fortunately for the collector, he had a good description of the coin on his sales receipt and solid evidence of where he had purchased the piece. The complaint eventually went to the American Numismatic Association Mediation Service for consideration. Their ruling was that the coin was indeed bad, and the collector had proof of where it was purchased. The money was returned, and the coin was donated to the ANA for study. The ANA eventually determined that the fake was part of a series of coins that had been made by a California counterfeiter who had gone out of business by then because so many of his products had been detected by observant dealers and collectors.

It is a rare occurrence when an experienced coin dealer purchases or sells a counterfeit or altered coin, but it has happened, and is a risk that no collector need incur. The possibility can be avoided by obtaining a written guarantee of authenticity for all coin purchases, and by recording the serial number of each encapsulated coin on the sales receipt. For coins that are not certified, a good-quality photograph, or sometimes even a good copy-machine image, can be documented as proof of identity. These safeguards will give complete protection as long as the dealer remains in business. The chances of any of the top certifying services overlooking a false coin are practically nil but even if that should happen the loss would be covered by insurance.

An honest dealer will guarantee the authenticity of the coins he sells. Pictured is a counterfeit gold double eagle that could fool an unwary collector.

Re-purchase agreements are much less likely to provide the security found in the other guarantees that dealers offer. In the first place, a dealer or firm must still be in business at the time you wish to liquidate, or the agreement will be meaningless regardless of the original good intention. This can be partially guarded against by doing business with a firm that has been in existence for a reasonable length of time, and which seems dedicated to remaining in business in the future. Unfortunately, there are a few fly-by-night operations that have no intention of ever honoring their agreements. They often close their doors and reopen under a new name to avoid their responsibility.

Even in the best of circumstances it is difficult to find protection and assurance of a profit in any agreement that merely guarantees that a dealer will re-purchase coins from a customer at the same grade level as when they were sold. There is no way to predict the state of the market at any future date, and the coins could be worth less than the original cost at any given time. Even in a strong market when the value of coins has risen, a dealer may be "cash poor" and unable to offer a reasonable price to re-purchase large quantities of coins at the exact time that several customers want to liquidate their holdings.

A client intent on selling all or even part of a portfolio can be faced with having to accept only a fraction of the coin's worth if the buyer determines that is all that he can pay. It does not matter what the coins are worth according to any of the published reports, or if they are accepted by the dealer as being accurately graded. There simply are no guarantees that the coins will be fairly priced at the time of sale or repurchase. Here again, buying only coins that are properly graded and slabbed by a third-party service will help to ensure a larger number of marketing options and demand for the coins, and will make the selling process easier. The protective plastic will also ensure that the coin remains in the same condition as when it was graded and sealed.

If the market is soft, or for some reason a dealer does not wish to purchase a particular group of coins, he or she may suggest that the coins be placed in an auction. This method of selling is perfectly satisfactory, and in many instances is the most advantageous way to sell very rare coins at

Read hobby newspapers, magazines, and journals to keep up to date on the collecting scene.

top prices. The disadvantages are that the selling commissions are equal to around 20 percent of the value, and there is usually a delay of four months or more before the final reckoning and payment to the owner. If the seller's consignment consists of raw coins that were over-graded at the time of purchase, they will be cataloged, bid on, and sold only for their actual grade and value.

Another consideration when selling an investment portfolio is finding a time when the market will be at a high point, with strong demand for the types of material that is to be offered. A dealer's guarantee to assist you with liquidation is of little value if you do not receive guidance about when the time is right to sell. Many dealers are too busy selling coins in a hot market to concern themselves with their clients' profits. If the market should soften to the point where obvious downward price adjustments are on the way, few dealers have the resources to purchase their client's coins at pre-slump highs. These are points that are rarely addressed in any buy-back agreement, and they are certainly not covered in a simple statement that says "the dealer will re-purchase coins at a guaranteed grade." What is needed is a frank and open discussion with the coin seller about policy and past performance. If possible, meet or talk with some other customers who have been through the process with the company that you plan to use and ask about their experiences.

Successful coin buyers don't just rely on a few carefully chosen dealers for advice and counsel—they are a part of the process themselves. Information gained through reading some of the weekly or monthly numismatic publications will prove to be invaluable when making decisions about which coins to hold, which to sell, and which to buy on speculation for future appreciation. In addition to giving one a winning edge in the market, this kind of participation provides a measure of self-satisfaction and confidence. Collectors who take an interest in playing the market are usually very successful, and investors who take time to learn a bit about the coins that they are buying sometimes turn into serious collectors.

There are no guarantees that any coins can eventually be sold at a profit, no matter how desirable they may be. Coin collecting should be viewed as a hobby, not as a sure-fire investment. People who buy choice coins and hold them for a reasonable period of time usually find they are worth much more than their original cost when they are sold, but the laws of supply and demand ultimately control prices.

I remember talking to one investor who became so enchanted with the history of some of the old coins that he had purchased on speculation that he bought a second identical group to keep at home and show to his friends as his "collection." He continued to add to each group, but when the investment portfolio was sold years later, he kept the collection that had been a source of pride and enjoyment for him for such a long time. The knowledge gained from his more personal consideration of the collection gave him an insight into the coin market that provided him with a knack for knowing just what and when to buy and sell.

Those who collect coins purely for the enjoyment of the hobby, and beginners of all levels of interest, are usually not overly concerned about making money on their investment. By its very nature a hobby is intended to be a time-filling, relaxing, and diversionary activity. People who enjoy owning tropical fish do not usually anticipate making a profit on them. There is no reason to consider coin collecting any differently. Perhaps because coins are money people tend to think that they should somehow show a profit over time. Or perhaps it is because coins have traditionally been a stable and good investment. There are many reasons that people are attracted to numismatics as a hobby, but an appreciation of the rewards one finds in the artistry, history, and pride of ownership should far outweigh any consideration of financial gain.

When purchasing coins for reasons other than investment, it is relatively safe to rely on local dealers and the offerings that will be found in numismatic publications and at coin shows.

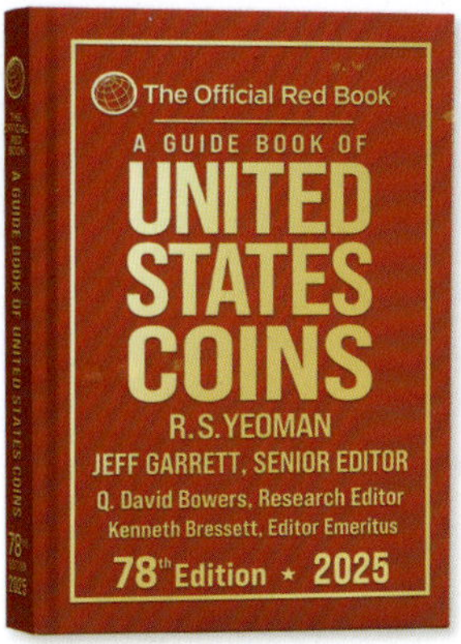

The *Red Book* is the hobby's annual guide to prices you can expect to pay for U.S. coins.

An important reference for collectors who are ready to buy coins is *A Guide Book of United States Coins* (more popularly known as the *Red Book*). In print and updated annually since it first went to press in 1946, it lists retail prices for American coins from the colonial era to date, and covers important related series as well.

The demand for moderately priced collector coins is always high, and competition is usually keener than for the rarer items, for which buyers are often scarcer than the coins. Everyone from the beginner to the most experienced investor is entitled to the same kind of service and assurance from any professional dealer. Sometimes it takes a bit of trial and error to locate the exact kind of coins that you want, at the right price, and from someone you will enjoy doing business with, but finding that happy combination is well worth the effort.

A concluding bit of advice about buying coins for any reason must include the admonition to buy only with discretionary money. The vagaries of the coin market and frequent swings in the popularity of certain coins leave us with no way to know just how salable they may be at any time in the future. Those investors who can hold on to their coins through periods of declining prices are usually rewarded by a full recovery of value and even higher prices at a later date. When coins are purchased with little opportunity to hold on to the investment through troubled times, or if the money is needed quickly for some other purpose, the collection may have to be sold at depressed prices and at a loss to the owner. Coins, or any speculative items, should only be purchased with money that one could afford to lose and still maintain their same lifestyle.

When It's Time to Sell Your Coins

Eventually everyone is faced with the prospect of selling or giving away his or her collection. If it has been properly cared for and thoroughly inventoried and is full of interesting, choice items in high-grade condition, there will be few problems. Unfortunately, many of us are not always careful with our records. Many times the decision to sell is based on a need for quick cash, or in the event of death. Neither circumstance can be foreseen, and that usually means that hasty decisions may have to be made. Sometimes a totally uninformed relative will be assigned to make arrangements to sell a loved one's collection. A careful and thoughtful collector can help to avoid these problems.

The most essential element in proper coin custodianship is keeping an up-to-date inventory. That listing should record the date of every purchase as well as the cost, condition, and dealer name for each coin. It should be kept current with the latest values at least every two to three years. Many collectors also make notes about where individual coins should be sold in order to take advantage of the best market. A copy of your current inventory should be kept with your will, along with any instructions you may have about who can be contacted to appraise or purchase the collection, or if you want to donate the collection or put it up for auction.

There are several options for selling coins. The first you have probably already experienced through buying, trading, and selling to friends and fellow collectors. This can usually be done at club meetings and shows and through local dealers. These are good resources and are often all that is needed to accommodate your wishes. But problems can arise when someone is forced to settle an estate quickly, and with little knowledge of the coin market. If a person is limited to selling locally and dealing with only a few people, and if the collection is large and valuable, it may be difficult to find someone who can, or wants to, buy it all at once. Fortunately, there are other options.

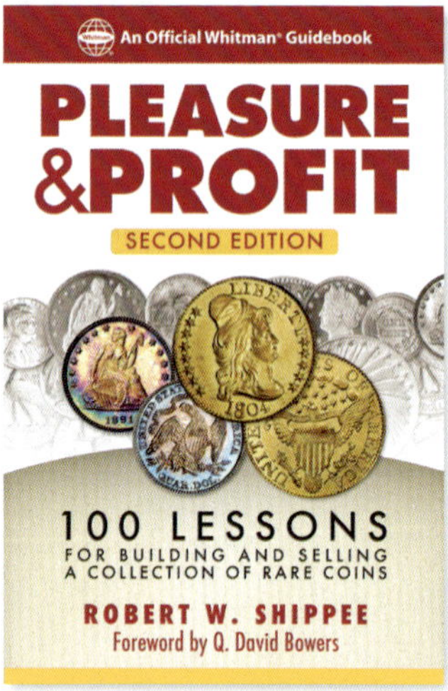

Robert W. Shippee's book *Pleasure and Profit* gives practical advice and real-world examples of the author's successes—and occasional failures—in selling rare coins from his collection.

The first and most essential tool needed for selling coins is a good reference book that lists the current values for the kinds of coins that you have. In some cases it may take several books to cover all categories of United States and foreign coins, paper money, and whatever else is in the collection. Do not skimp on buying and using these books. They not only tell what to expect in way of return when you sell your coins, they are also the key to learning the background of each item, and telling how and why each is valuable.

You will next want to make a special listing of exactly what you expect to sell and what a fair market price would be.

A good way to start this process is to write a clear description of each item on a legal-size pad of paper. Begin with United States coins and list each piece from the lowest denomination to the highest. Describe each coin by date, mintmark, and condition, and indicate how many of each are to be sold. State your estimated value for each coin, or the value shown in some coin book. After listing the individual U.S. coins, continue on with sets, foreign coins, medals, and paper money. Make more than one copy of your inventory so that you can give them to interested buyers, and always keep a copy for yourself.

Many collectors I know have instructed their family to contact a trusted friend to oversee the sale of their coins at the time of their death. These are usually family members or fellow collectors who know something about the collection and the coin marketplace.

Unless there is an emergency situation, do not plan on selling your coins quickly. Hold them for a reasonable amount of time and enjoy them to the fullest. Perhaps you will even want to will them to someone else at the time of your death. That can be a good option for tax purposes, and make someone else very happy with the gift. You must work with a tax consultant to determine exactly how using your coins as a gift or donation will affect your taxes. There may also be a local museum that would welcome such a gift. The American Numismatic Association and the American Numismatic Society have not-for-profit numismatic museums that are always receptive to donations. Contact either of them for details about how you can become a donor.

Most collectors have an objective in saving coins. It might be with the thought of eventually selling them for a profit, passing them on to their children, or using the money for some special purpose. Everyone has a slightly different reason for saving coins and for eventually selling them. I have known many collectors who simply enjoy the thrill and challenge of accumulating a significant collection or set of beautiful and interesting coins. They often have no interest in selling their treasures, and may hold

The museum of the American Numismatic Association features exhibits on many topics of objects that have been donated or loaned by their members for the enjoyment of others.

on to them all their life. However, eventually even those collections have to be sold, and when it is time to liquidate, care should be given to being sure that full value is realized for the material.

Not all coins enjoy the same degree of interest by even the most willing buyers. In order to maximize the price realized in a sale, it is necessary to locate buyers who really want to buy specific kinds of coins. A dealer or collector who specializes in paper money will probably not have much interest in coins or tokens. Ancient or foreign coins will not appeal to someone who deals only in United States coins. When looking for a willing buyer, it is important to know if that person specializes in the kinds of coins you have for sale. Some dealers or advanced collectors may well purchase everything in a large accumulation, but that is unusual and likely to produce a lower price than if the group is broken up into smaller lots of homogeneous items. Test a potential buyer by asking about his or her knowledge and interest in the various kinds of coins that you intend to sell.

Use a current catalog as your guide to values. The price of coins is determined by the demand from collectors, and that has a tendency to change frequently. It is not unusual for the value of rare coins to rise or fall by as much as 20 percent in a year. Using an outdated pricing catalog may give a false impression about current values. The Whitman *Handbook of United States Coins* (the *Blue Book*) is an excellent source of information about the average prices that dealers pay throughout the country.

It is also possible to use Whitman's *Guide Book of United States Coins* (the *Red Book*) to determine relative values for your coins, but you must remember that the values shown in the book are retail prices, which are higher than what a dealer would pay you. Dealers are in business to make a profit. They must buy coins at wholesale prices and sell them at retail prices in order to stay in business. Do not expect a dealer to pay full *Red Book* prices for coins that they purchase. They usually sell coins at *Red Book* prices and buy them at *Blue Book* prices.

There is no general rule of thumb about how much profit any dealer makes on coin sales. It varies with the kind of coins involved, the size of a dealer's operation, overhead, and the demand for various kinds of coins. Certain coins that do not sell well, and may have to remain in inventory for a long time, may be bought by a dealer for only a small fraction of their retail price. Other coins that are very popular and sell quickly are apt to be bought for as much as 90 percent or more of retail value. An average assortment of desirable coins can usually be sold to a dealer for about 70 percent of retail value.

These approximations show what you can expect to be paid for coins that are needed by dealers. Prices may vary depending on market conditions and the type of store or business making the purchase. The spot price of silver and gold can be found in most daily newspapers in the future section of the financial page. In a strong market dealers often pay over spot for either gold or silver, and in a weak market the price may be discounted by several points.

Comparison Buying Prices of Various Kinds of Coins	
Common-date circulated silver coins	Spot price* less 5%
Bullion gold coins	Approximate spot price
U.S. common-date gold coins	85% of retail
Sets of circulated coins	50% of retail
Classic type coins	70% of retail
Common-date circulated coins	30% of retail
Key dates and scarce coins	90% of retail
Canadian coins	75% of face value
General foreign coins	50% of retail
Tokens and medals	40% of retail

* "Spot" price refers to the daily newspaper price quoted for the value of precious metals.

When you are thinking about selling your coins, you should speak to a minimum of three dealers, or auction houses, and ask about their policies for the kinds of coins you want to sell. Chances are that you may not be able find the names of dealers in your local telephone directory. If there are none in your area, you may have to do business by mail. You can find advertisements for dealers in most of the coin publications listed in chapter 4 of this book. Check the magazine rack in your grocery store, bookstore, or newsstand for monthly numismatic magazines.

Call or write to a few of the coin dealers who seem to deal primarily in the kinds of material that you have for sale. Describe your coins briefly and ask if they are interested. They will want to know the quantity of items and their condition and will especially need to know about any scarce dates or unusual items. They may ask if you have a price in mind. A good response would be to tell them which book or catalog you have used to arrive at your estimate.

Ask the potential buyer about buying policies. How much is being paid for circulated silver coins (the so-called junk silver)? The answer may be "8 percent back of bid" or "12 times face." The first response means that the dealer is paying 8 percent less than the spot price of silver as listed that day. The second response means that the price is twelve times the face value for each denomination, i.e., $1.20 for each dime or $3 for each quarter, and so on. Either quotation will give you a good fix on what that dealer is paying. You might also want to ask about some of the other pricing discussed above.

With this information you can make a direct comparison with the prices that other dealers are paying. When you locate two or three dealers who are paying essentially the same prices, you can be fairly sure that you are being quoted reasonable values. Avoid any dealer who pays substantially less than the others, and be equally cautious of anyone who offers unusually high prices without actually seeing your coins. The high bid may be a signal that you will be given a lower quotation when it comes time to make the sale.

You will also need to ask a few other questions. Do they pay immediately for all of their purchases? Can you ship your coins to them? Will they return anything they don't want? Do you need to include return postage in case coins need to be returned?

Auctions are another option for selling a collection if the coins are valuable enough. Many professional coin auction firms require that each coin, or individual lot, must be valued at over $100, so this would not be practical for low-valued items. You can find information about firms that conduct mail-bid numismatic auctions by reading their advertisements in any of the coin periodicals mentioned elsewhere in this book. A number of auction services also have websites where coins are auctioned regularly. Anyone interested in participating in a numismatic auction should inquire of the company and obtain full instructions about their services. Buying and selling through auctions can be fun, but there are rules and regulations that are different than for normal coin sales.

When the time comes to deliver or ship your coins to a buyer, your number one concern should be to have a carefully made inventory of every item. List everything clearly by country, date, and mintmark. Describe special features and make your best estimation of condition. Also show the price at which you value each item, and your total asking price. If possible keep a photographic record of the coins. This can be as simple as a quick scan, Xerox copy, or iPhone shot of each piece. Be sure to keep a copy of your inventory, and include a copy with the coins. If you are shipping by mail, be sure to use insured or registered service. You can insure your coins for their full value and request a return receipt to be sure that the package arrived safely.

Professional coin dealers are among the most trustworthy people in any trade, but you should not tempt fate by sending uninsured packages or coins that they have not specifically requested. Using a few precautions can save you many problems later. Have a clear understanding with the person to whom you are sending your coins, and your transaction can be easy and rewarding.

UNITED
STATES O
IN GOD WE TRUST

CHAPTER 8

Collecting with a Stated Purpose

The many reasons for collecting coins extend way beyond simply enjoying saving them as a casual pastime. And it is important to establish some personal goals and guidelines before becoming too deeply involved in the hobby. There are various options to consider before making a hasty beginning that may be regretted later.

Yogi Berra was fond of saying, "You've got to be very careful if you don't know where you're going, because you might not get there." His words of wisdom are certainly true about many things in life, and especially concerning collecting and investing in coins, where mistakes can be costly.

Fortunately for beginners, as well as seasoned collectors and investors, there is a plethora of information available for guidance. Paramount among those resources is the industry's standard reference known as the *Red Book*, which contains an indispensable amount of information keyed to all aspects of U.S. coins.

The coins illustrated in this chapter form a virtual type set of all the important coins made since the beginning of the Mint in 1793; they reflect a history of money that has circulated throughout the nation since that time. The coins are shown larger than actual size for ease of identification, and then again in the appendix with each denomination at actual size.

Historical commentary on individual coins is supplied here to add to the enjoyment of collecting these treasures. Some are classic rarities worth millions of dollars and others can still be found in circulation today or purchased from the Mint. Basically, all coins are valued on rarity, condition, and collector demand. Individual valuations fluctuate and are sometimes tied to the basic bullion value of gold and silver.

Comprehensive monthly listings of current values for all dates and mint marks can be found in the *CPG Coin & Currency Market Review* at www.greysheet.com. And detailed statistical information is readably available in *A Guide Book of United States Coins* (the *Red Book*) and the *Handbook of United States Coins* (the *Blue Book*, which lists prices generally paid by dealers when buying coins).

U.S. Copper Coins

Included in this category are all the copper and bronze coins that have been issued by this country since the very beginning of regular coinage in 1793. Copper cents and half cents were the first coins ever minted by the new government (aside from special silver half dismes struck in a temporary facility in 1792), and collecting them has been a favorite pastime of hobbyists for the past 160 years. Those who specialize in them usually attempt to save one of each year and major variety. The series are remarkably complete because cents were made in nearly each year, with the exception of 1815. Most dates are relatively common and available even in high-grade condition because of the huge quantities minted each year.

The more serious collectors try to assemble sets of early cents and half cents not only for each date but also with examples of each recognizable minor die variety, or minor variation in the position of letters or design. Because of the specialized interest in these coins by die-variety collectors, the series are usually thought of as the domain of advanced collectors rather than investors, and interest in purchasing these pieces is often left to specialists.

The copper-nickel-alloy coins that were made starting in 1857 with the Flying Eagle cents and, later, the bronze Indian Head cents were issued in great numbers and have long been a favorite collecting area for beginners. Most old-time collectors will acknowledge starting their hobby by putting together a set of Indian Head cents or Lincoln cents taken from circulation. Up until around 1970 the challenge of assembling a set of Lincoln cents from circulation was still the number-one collecting activity for most beginners. This interest changed somewhat when most of the early-date coins were finally gone from circulation and collections could be completed only by the purchase of the scarcer "key" dates from dealers or other collectors.

For these reasons, and because copper coins are the most difficult of all to store and preserve in high-grade condition, copper and copper-alloy coins have never been as popular with investors as the larger and shinier silver and gold pieces. As a consequence of this, the values of these coins are very much a factor of collector demand rather than investor pressure, and in many cases, they have not gone up in price at the same rate as classic investor coins. Conversely, the demand for coppers by collectors has been relatively steady throughout the years.

HALF CENTS

The copper half cent is the lowest-denomination coin issued by the United States. Its unusual value makes it a popular favorite among collectors, especially so because it was the first coin struck at the newly formed U.S. Mint. Coinage began in 1793 and was discontinued in 1857; however, none were issued for circulation in several years throughout that time. All were coined at the Philadelphia Mint.

The various designs that were used on all half cents are similar, with a head of Liberty on the obverse and the denomination within a wreath on the reverse. For no particular reason, Liberty is shown facing right on some and left on others. In addition to the coins that were made for circulation, a limited number of Proof specimens were made to satisfy collector demand. These are especially rare and valuable with current prices in the thousands of dollars each, for both original examples and restrikes that were made at a later date.

Collector demand for the 1793 coins has made them among the most desirable in the series; unfortunately, the majority of them show excessive wear because of their long-time use throughout the years. Even a well-worn example is considered a prized collector item, and the few pieces that have somehow been preserved in near-perfect condition are valued in the $50,000 range.

Assembling an attractive type set of half cents is a popular pursuit and can easily be done on a modest budget. High-grade examples of most types can be found in each series and are generally available at prices from $100 to $200 each.

As a cautionary word to the wise, all copper coins should be handled and stored as carefully as possible to avoid damage to their fragile surfaces.

Moisture, unsafe climate conditions, fingerprints, and even droplets from sneezes can do irreparable harm. Sturdy, inert (i.e., chemically non-reactive) plastic holders are considered a harmless protection.

Liberty Cap, 1793–1797

Liberty Cap half cents show the effigy of Liberty bearing on her shoulder a pole with a so-called liberty cap (also known as a Phrygian cap) hung on the end. On coins from the first year of issue, 1793, Liberty faces left; thereafter, she faces right.

Head Facing Left

Head Facing Right

	GSID	AG-3	G-4	VG-8	F-12	VF-20	EF-40	AU-50
Head Facing Left, 1793	73819	$3,125	$4,500	$5,600	$8,750	$13,200	$20,400	$33,000
Head Facing Right, 1794–1797	72297	390	550	1,025	1,300	2,000	5,000	6,500

Draped Bust, 1800–1808

Beginning in 1800, Liberty's hair is held back with a ribbon, and the liberty cap and pole are absent. A garment is loosely draped around her bust and shoulder.

	GSID	AG-3	G-4	VG-8	F-12	VF-20	EF-40	AU-50
1800–1808	72299	$55	$100	$120	$150	$200	$425	$650

Classic Head, 1809–1836

In 1809, the designer faced Liberty toward the left once more. Instead of a hair ribbon in back, she wears a band around her head with the word LIBERTY on the side. The garment is no longer visible.

	GSID	G-4	VG-8	F-12	VF-20	EF-40	AU-50	MS-60	MS-63
1809–1836	72294	$90	$92	$95	$100	$120	$180	$290	$575

Braided Hair (or Coronet), 1840–1857

Still facing left, Liberty now wears her hair up in an elaborate bun. The hair band has been replaced by a simple coronet bearing the word LIBERTY. This is the final half cent design, lasting until the denomination was discontinued in 1858.

	GSID	VG-8	F-12	VF-20	EF-40	AU-50	MS-60	MS-63
1849–1857*	72302	$92	$95	$100	$110	$160	$230	$425

* In 1840–1848 and 1852, half cents were made only as Proofs, all of which are very rare.

Large Cents

Coinage of large cents started in 1793 and was discontinued in 1857. All were coined at the Philadelphia Mint. No large cents were issued in 1815.

I fondly remember the old large copper cents of our forefathers from my early days of collecting and learning about coins along with the history of our country. Of course, we called then *pennies* back then, and they could often be found in household "penny jars," an old purse, some long-forgotten accumulation, or perhaps even those lovingly placed on grandpa's eyes at the time of his death.

Advanced collectors at that time were able to examine quantities of the large-size coppers and select whatever types and varieties they felt might meet their goal of completeness. Articles, monographs, and books were written describing the vast array of variations in the many dies that were used to mint those coins, and it was challenging to see who could accumulate each of them. To the delight of all, the hunt was vastly helped through the efforts of Dr. William H. Sheldon and H. K. Downing in the publication of their 1949 book, *Early American Cents 1793–1814.*

The detailed information in that book was an inspiration for me to investigate this area of collecting and try to form a respectable group based on the text and pictures, which were often less than adequate. Thus, I was delighted when I learned that a revised edition was being contemplated, and that Sheldon was to be assisted by two of my other acquaintances, Dorothy Paschal and Walter Breen.

My hobby interests at that time included both numismatics and photography, and I was selected to photograph their collections and hopefully improve the images. It was then that I began to seriously appreciate the lure of aged copper coins, and how to grade them by examining Sheldon's personal collection and using his now-universal numbering scale.

The enjoyment of early large cents goes far beyond those of the classic pre-1814 issues and continues on through 1857, when the denomination was replaced with the small-size cents with a totally different design. Classic pieces like the 1793 Chain cent and the rare dates of 1799 and 1804 are still among the most desirable in the series and command prices ranging from thousands to $50,000 and beyond.

As a cautionary word to the wise, all copper coins should be handled and stored as carefully as possible to avoid damage to their fragile surfaces. Moisture, unsafe climate conditions, fingerprints, and even sneezing droplets can do irreparable harm. Sturdy plastic holders are considered a harmless protection.

Flowing Hair, 1793

The first one-cent U.S. coins are strikingly simple in their design: a bust of Liberty facing right, hair unbound, with no adornment of any kind. The word LIBERTY is above and the date is below. The first issues, struck in early 1793, have the denomination, ONE CENT, encircled by a chain, with UNITED STATES OF AMERICA (sometimes abbreviated AMERI.) surrounding. Coins struck later in the year have the denomination surrounded by a wreath.

Obverse

Chain, AMERI. Reverse

Chain, AMERICA Reverse

Wreath Reverse

	GSID	AG-3	G-4	VG-8	F-12	VF-20	EF-40	AU-50
Chain Reverse, 1793	72308	$5,750	$7,900	$11,250	$19,200	$26,400	$57,600	$78,000
Wreath Reverse, 1793	72309	2,250	3,250	4,500	6,550	10,900	22,800	27,000

Liberty Cap, 1793–1796

The unpopular Flowing Hair obverse lasted barely a year, and was supplanted by a right-facing Liberty who, as on the Liberty Cap half cents of the period, carries a liberty or Phrygian cap on a pole at her shoulder.

	GSID	AG-3	G-4	VG-8	F-12	VF-20	EF-40	AU-50
1793–1796	72312	$310	$500	$725	$1,100	$1,700	$3,750	$5,250

Draped Bust, 1796–1807

Beginning in 1796, some of Liberty's hair is tied back with a bow, and a garment is draped about the bust.

	GSID	AG-3	G-4	VG-8	F-12	VF-20	EF-40	AU-50
1796–1807	72314	$75	$100	$130	$260	$500	$1,100	$1,750

Classic Head, 1808–1814

In 1808, Liberty begins facing left. Instead of a hair ribbon in back, she wears a band around her head with the word LIBERTY on the side, and the garment is no longer visible. A similar design was adopted on the half cent the following year.

	GSID	AG-3	G-4	VG-8	F-12	VF-20	EF-40	AU-50
1808–1814	72325	$95	$145	$260	$520	$960	$1,700	$2,875

Liberty Head (or Coronet), 1816–1857

Still facing left, Liberty now wears her hair partly up in the back. Her hair band has been replaced by a simple coronet bearing the word LIBERTY. The effigy and other details were remodeled several times over the next forty years, until the large cent was discontinued in 1858. Many collectors refer to the early style, through 1839, as the Matron Head or Liberty Head, and the later styles as the Young Head or Braided Hair from 1839 onward.

	GSID	G-4	VG-8	F-12	VF-20	EF-40	AU-50	MS-60	MS-63
Matron Head, 1816–1839	72328	$25	$35	$45	$80	$150	$250	$380	$725
Braided Hair, 1839–1857	72331	26	27	34	40	60	145	210	310

Small Cents

With the cost of copper rising in the 1850s, the Mint considerably reduced the size of the one-cent coin to lower expenses.

Flying Eagle, 1856–1858

Named for the large eagle flying leftward across the obverse, these cents were coined officially at the Philadelphia Mint during 1857 and 1858 only. The pieces dated 1856 are pattern or experimental coins and are very rare.

	GSID	G-4	VG-8	F-12	VF-20	EF-40	AU-50	MS-60	MS-63
1856–1858	72334	$27	$40	$55	$85	$180	$350	$725	$1,225

Indian Head, 1859–1909

Replacing the Flying Eagle design in 1859, the so-called Indian Head cent is actually a depiction of Liberty in a native feathered headdress. Coins from the first year of production have a laurel wreath on the reverse; thereafter, they have an oak wreath.

The first Indian Head cents, coined from 1859 to 1864, were made of copper-nickel and were about twice as thick as a modern cent. In 1864 the composition was changed to bronze and the thickness reduced. In 1908 and 1909 cents were coined at the San Francisco Mint as well as in Philadelphia. All others were made at the Philadelphia Mint and have no mintmark.

Laurel Wreath Reverse

Oak Wreath Reverse

	GSID	G-4	VG-8	F-12	VF-20	EF-40	AU-50	MS-60	MS-63
Copper-Nickel, Laurel Wreath, 1859	72335	$13.50	$18.00	$24.00	$50.00	$145	$240	$425	$850
Copper-Nickel, Oak Wreath, 1860–1864	72336	11.50	152.50	16.00	32.00	60	95	180	425
Bronze, 1864–1909	72337	1.60	2.15	2.40	3.50	7	23	45	85

Lincoln, Wheat Reverse, 1909–1958

Lincoln cents were designed by Victor D. Brenner, first coined in 1909, and have been struck at the Philadelphia, Denver, and San Francisco mints ever since. The simple, well-known obverse shows a bust of the 16th president facing right. Through 1958, Lincoln cents have a pair of wheat ears on the reverse. All Wheat cents were made of bronze alloy, except for the zinc-coated steel cents struck in 1943.

The 1909-S V.D.B. is the most valuable coin in the Lincoln cent series. The designer's initials, in small letters, are on the reverse side only on some coins dated 1909. From 1918 to the present, the initials are on the truncation of the bust. The mintmark is located below the date.

	GSID	VG-8	VF-20	EF-40	AU-50	MS-60	MS-63	MS-65
1909–1958	72340	$0.18	$0.19	$0.20	$0.22	$0.25	$0.40	$2.15

Lincoln, Memorial Reverse, 1959–2008

Continuing the original obverse design, cents beginning in 1959 bear the Lincoln Memorial on the reverse. The bronze composition was changed to copper-plated zinc in 1982. The Memorial design was used through 2008.

Cents made after 1958 are generally collected only in Uncirculated condition.

	GSID	MS-60	MS-63	MS-65
1959–2008	72340	$0.20	$0.50	$2.50

Lincoln, Birth Bicentennial, 2009

In 2009, to honor the bicentennial of Lincoln's birth and the 100th anniversary of the first Lincoln cent, the Mint struck a series with four special reverse designs, each representing part of the president's life: Birth and Early Childhood, Formative Years, Professional Life, and Presidency.

These coins can be found in pocket change but are generally collected in Uncirculated condition, in which they can be purchased for less than a dollar.

Birth and Early Childhood

Formative Years

Professional Life

Presidency

Lincoln, Union Shield Reverse, 2010 to Date

After the Birth Bicentennial designs, the reverse emblem in 2010 was changed to a Union shield, "an image emblematic of President Lincoln's preservation of the United States of America as a single and united country."

These coins can be found in pocket change but are generally collected in Uncirculated condition, in which they can be purchased for less than a dollar.

U.S. Odd-Denomination Coins

Few people realize that the United States once issued two-cent and three-cent coins as part of our regular monetary system. These were intended as a convenience in making change or, in the case of the three-cent pieces, for the purchase of postage stamps. The two-cent coins were issued from 1864 through 1873, and the three-cent pieces were made first in silver and later in nickel from 1851 through 1889. There is but a single basic design for each of these three coins, but the silver pieces (called trimes) come in three distinct variations.

As a group, these odd-denomination coins hold great interest for collectors and non-collectors alike because they seem so strange to us today. They form a necessary part of any type collection and are always a topic of conversation and amazement when displayed to those not acquainted with the numismatic history of our country. Over the years price performance of these coins has seen a fairly steady upward movement because of consistent demand from collectors and investors.

The two-cent pieces, like other copper coins, are subject to the ravages of age and often show black or green spots from moisture or careless storage. They tend to lose their original red color and become faded or dull or turn to various shades of brown. Like the early cents and half cents, they appeal more to collectors than investors, and as such, seem to be undervalued in all grades of condition.

The three-cent pieces made of nickel alloy from 1865 through 1889 are another type of unusual coin that appeals more to collectors than to investors. These coins can present problems in storage and are subject to the same kinds of moisture spots and corrosion associated with copper coins. Be sure to store all copper and nickel coins as far away from moisture as possible to preserve their delicate finish. Many dealers and investors do not want to accept this responsibility and prefer to concentrate on the safer and more traditional items, such as gold and silver coins. For these reasons, the values of many of these coins are often lower than for coins in other series.

Three-cent pieces were made of silver from 1851 through 1873. The pieces dated 1851 and made at the New Orleans Mint are unique in that they are the only branch-mint coins in the series, and the only branch-mint coins made for any minor denomination prior to the cents of 1908. All silver three-cent coins are either scarce or rare as coinage was limited to only a few hundred thousand pieces each year. Most of the pieces coined after 1862 were melted for their silver content, and the series was generally replaced by the larger pieces that were struck in nickel alloy. All of the Proof coins in this series are very rare, with fewer than one thousand having been made for each date.

Silver three-cent coins in every grade of condition are very popular with collectors. They are all difficult to locate and in constant demand. They were made with three distinct variations of design, so collectors generally attempt to acquire at least one of each kind for their sets. Investors are only somewhat interested in these coins, for a couple of reasons. First, these coins are small. In fact, they are the lightest in weight of all United States coins, and barely larger than the gold dollars. Beyond that, they are not particularly attractive and are usually available only in the lower grades of condition—weakly struck or badly tarnished. In light of their scarcity, in high grade condition, they are probably some of the most undervalued coins in the United States series.

Two-Cent Pieces

These were the first U.S. coins to use the motto IN GOD WE TRUST.

Union Shield, 1864–1873

Two-cent pieces were coined only at the Philadelphia Mint. This unusual denomination was introduced in 1864 to ease the coin shortage caused by the Civil War. Only Proof coins were made in 1873, which was the last year of issue.

	GSID	G-4	VG-8	F-12	VF-20	EF-40	AU-50	MS-60	MS-63
1864–1873	72347	$20	$22	$24	$32	$55	$85	$130	$220

Silver Three-Cent Pieces

Silver three-cent pieces, or trimes, were issued from 1851 to 1873. They were struck at the Philadelphia Mint each year during this period and at the New Orleans Mint in 1851. Only Proof specimens were coined from 1863 to 1873, and these are all rare.

Trime, 1851–1873

The obverse bears a six-pointed star with a shield in the center, while the reverse depicts the denomination as a III encircled by an ornate letter C. On Type 1 trimes, there is no border around the rim of the star. Type 2 trimes have a double border around the star, while Type 3 trimes have a single border.

	GSID	G-4	VG-8	F-12	VF-20	EF-40	AU-50	MS-60	MS-63
Type 1, 1851–1853	73773	$45	$55	$65	$80	$115	$170	$230	$310
Type 2, 1854–1858	73774	55	60	75	90	160	230	425	900
Type 3, 1859–1873	73775	55	60	70	75	125	180	290	450

Nickel Three-Cent Pieces

Nickel three-cent pieces were issued as substitutes for the silver three-cent coins, which were at that time being melted and exported for their high silver content. Coinage commenced in 1865 and was discontinued in 1889. They were coined only at the Philadelphia Mint.

Liberty Head, 1865–1889

On the obverse, a left-facing effigy of Liberty wears her hair partly up in the back and topped with a coronet; on the reverse, the denomination is rendered as a large III encircled in a wreath.

	GSID	G-4	VG-8	F-12	VF-20	EF-40	AU-50	MS-60	MS-63
1865–1889	72350	$16.00	$17.50	$19	$26	$45	$70	$145	$220

U.S. Nickel Coins

The U.S. five-cent coins have long been known as "nickels" despite the fact that they are actually made of an alloy of 75 percent copper and 25 percent nickel. The old Shield design coins were pretty much gone from circulation long before the general interest in collecting by date and mintmark started people saving full sets of nickels. In the early days collectors usually concentrated only on acquiring a Proof specimen of each date in both the Shield and Liberty Head series.

In the 1930s collectors began saving one coin of each date and mintmark taken out of circulation in order to fill their coin boards. It was easy to find full sets of the old Liberty Head coins, as well as the then-current Buffalo nickels. A few ambitious collectors even attempted to fill their sets with Uncirculated specimens, but they quickly learned just how scarce new coins were even at that time.

The fortunate people who persevered in assembling sets of Uncirculated coins were responsible for preserving what few choice examples still exist today. Buffalo nickels were in use throughout the Great Depression years, and very few were made in some years, with even fewer being saved in new condition because even five cents was a considerable amount of money in those troubled times. Apart from these considerations, the mints attempted to save money by using the Buffalo nickel dies as long as possible, and many of the coins that they made show the effects of worn or defective dies that left the coins looking anything but beautiful. In some cases, branch-mint nickels of that period were so weakly struck that it is impossible to distinguish which mintmark was used on the pieces even when they are in new condition.

The Jefferson nickels, which were first made in 1938, replaced all of the older types, and they soon became of interest to beginning collectors, although only to a limited degree because they are common in every grade of condition. The unusual 1950-D nickel is an exception to the rule in that collectors saved large quantities of this low-mintage issue as soon as the coins were released for circulation. As a result of this speculation, Uncirculated coins are nearly as common as circulated pieces, and are much easier to locate. Assembling circulated sets of Jefferson nickels is hardly a major challenge for anyone, and investors have little interest in such coins. Proof coins and some of the scarcer dates in very high-grade Uncirculated condition have a good potential for price appreciation because they are generally undervalued.

NICKEL FIVE-CENT PIECES

Shield, 1866–1883

Shield nickels, so called for the elaborate shield on the obverse, were coined only at the Philadelphia Mint, from 1866 to 1883 inclusive. The reverse variety with rays between the stars was used only in 1866 and part of 1867.

With Rays between Stars

Without Rays

	GSID	G-4	VG-8	F-12	VF-20	EF-40	AU-50	MS-60	MS-63
With Rays, 1866–1867	72351	$32	$45	$70	$110	$170	$220	$400	$575
Without Rays, 1867–1883	72352	31	34	38	45	85	115	160	250

Liberty Head, 1883–1913

The obverse depicts the head of Liberty facing left with her hair in a bun beneath a coronet. The denomination on the reverse is a large V inside a wreath. The first of these nickels struck in 1883 did not have the word CENTS anywhere on the coin, and some fraudulently plated in gold and passed off as $5 coins. The design was changed late in that year, and the missing word was added to the reverse side. Pieces were coined each year from 1883 to 1912 at the Philadelphia Mint and also in Denver and San Francisco during 1912. The extremely rare Liberty Head nickels dated 1913 are fascinating but effectively uncollectible, as only five are known to exist.

Without CENTS

With CENTS

	GSID	G-4	VG-8	F-12	VF-20	EF-40	AU-50	MS-60	MS-63
Without CENTS, 1883	72815	$6.75	$8.00	$9.50	$11.00	$15	$20	$55	$95
With CENTS, 1883–1913	72359	1.60	2.25	4.00	9.50	32	55	90	150

Indian Head or Buffalo, 1913–1938

Coined from 1913 to 1938, Indian Head or Buffalo nickels were struck at the Philadelphia, Denver, and San Francisco mints. None were issued in 1922, 1932, or 1933. Two varieties were made in 1913. The first, or Type 1, has the buffalo standing on a mound that reaches the bottom edge of the coin, with FIVE CENTS in raised type on the mound itself. This exposed the words to excessive wear, so the design was changed later that year. The area below the mound was recessed so that FIVE CENTS would be more protected, creating what is now called Type 2.

Type 1, FIVE CENTS on Raised Ground

Type 2, FIVE CENTS in Recess

	GSID	G-4	VG-8	F-12	VF-20	EF-40	AU-50	MS-60	MS-63
Type 1, 1913	72360	$9.50	$12.25	$13.50	$16.00	$23.00	$26.00	$38	$75
Type 2, 1913–1938	72361	0.70	0.90	1.15	1.50	2.60	7.50	23	27

Jefferson, Original Portrait and Monticello Reverse, 1938–2003

Struck from 1938 to the present, Jefferson nickels are produced at the Philadelphia, Denver, and San Francisco mints. The obverse portrait through 2005 shows Jefferson facing to the left, while the original reverse is a rendering of his famous home, Monticello. Though normally coined in a nickel alloy consisting of 75 parts copper and 25 parts nickel, during the war years of 1942 to 1945 the metal was changed to 56 percent copper, 35 percent silver, and 9 percent manganese. On those coins the mintmark was made larger and placed above the dome of Monticello. All other coins in this series have the mintmark on the reverse, at the right side of the building before 1968, and near the date thereafter.

Wartime Silver Alloy

	GSID	VF-20	EF-40	AU-50	MS-60	MS-63	MS-65	MS-66	MS-63
Nickel Alloy, 1938–2003	374526	$0.20	$0.20	$0.20	$0.21	$0.40	$1.50	$2.60	$725
Wartime Silver Alloy, 1942–1945	85088	2.10	2.25	2.50	4.00	8.00	16.00	32.00	310

Jefferson, Westward Journey, 2004–2005

New designs for the Jefferson nickel were used to commemorate the bicentennial of the Louisiana Purchase and the journey of Meriwether Lewis and William Clark to explore that vast territory. The reverse of 2004 depicts the Peace Medal design and a keelboat. Those of 2005 show a revised Jefferson head on the obverse, with a bison and an ocean view on the reverse. All of these are commonly found in circulation and have numismatic value only when in Uncirculated condition.

2004 Obverse

Peace Medal

Keelboat

2005 Obverse

American Bison

Ocean in View

Jefferson, Modified Portrait, Monticello Reverse Resumed, 2006 to Date

In 2006 the Mint returned to the Monticello reverse, with a new portrait of Thomas Jefferson. These coins are common in circulation and their regular issues are worth face value.

U.S. Silver Half Dimes Through Quarters

United States silver coins are avidly saved by nearly all collectors and investors. For collectors they form the basis of their type sets, and date and mint runs of coins ranging from the very first issues of 1794 through the pieces still made today that only imitate the old specie. Silver is no longer used in our national coins, and the old familiar denominations are now made of substitute metal. Even so, all modern coins from dimes to dollars are included in the same category by collectors, although they are now made of base metals. The various designs, changes, and innovations seen in our country's money over the years provides a numismatic legacy enjoyed by more than five million collectors who take pleasure in the hobby of saving and studying these coins.

The silver half dimes that were coined from the inception of the Mint in 1792 through 1873 are probably the least attractive of our low-value coins because of their small size. They have never held a popular place with collectors and are equally overlooked by investors. In recent years prices have remained relatively unchanged in all grades of condition because of the lack of demand. Considering the limited numbers made each year, these seem relatively inexpensive, and can be expected to increase in value and interest in the future.

Early-date dimes have also maintained steady prices over the past several years. The greatest buyer activity in this series seems to come from investors who are interested in acquiring Liberty Seated and Barber dimes in Proof or Uncirculated specimens in MS-65, or the highest grade possible. The newer Mercury dimes are still too new to demand much attention from investors, but it is here that the more serious collectors can find some very interesting challenges. Common-date Mercury dimes, those made near the end of the series, are still quite plentiful in all grades of condition. Those made from 1916 to 1938 are easily available in grades below Extremely Fine, except for some of the scarce dates. The key to the series is 1916-D, which is practically unobtainable even when well worn. There is no explaining why the twenty-cent coin is not valued substantially higher than it is. All dates are rare, and every collector should have at least one example of this most unusual denomination. Only a scant 1.4 million pieces were made of all dates and mints, and those that were not melted were heavily circulated. Here is a desirable coin that is nearly unobtainable in high-grade condition, and yet is still selling for low prices, and with little interest from speculators, collectors, or investors. Attractive specimens in any grade will probably always be in demand and difficult to obtain at bargain prices.

Collecting quarters can be a real challenge. This is a long series with many variables. Caution is advised for anyone starting to save these coins by date and mint. Some are very rare, some are very common, and prices can range from two or three dollars for recent issues to more than $50,000 for a decent specimen of the first year of issue. It will not be possible to obtain Uncirculated specimens of every date, as some are just not available. The early dates before 1831 in particular are difficult to find, even in worn condition.

The Liberty Seated quarters have never caught on as a series. This is probably because there are so many different dates and mints to contend with. Most collectors are content to have only a basic type set of the early quarters, and to concentrate on trying to obtain pieces that grade Very Fine or better. Investors seem to be attracted to choice Proof or Uncirculated pieces and are often willing to pay many times more than the prices for lower-grade coins. The same can be said for Barber quarters, although the challenge of putting together a fairly complete set of dates is not quite as daunting as with the earlier coins. Interest in both of these earlier coinage series is slowly but steadily on the rise, with collectors able to join the Liberty Seated Collectors Club (www.lscc.org) and the Barber Coin Collectors Society (www.barbercoins.org), both of which publish attractive and entertaining journals.

Standing Liberty quarters were minted from 1916 through 1930. They are one of the most attractive of all modern coins and a favorite among collectors. Dealers and investors often tend to avoid these pieces because they are among the most difficult of all coins to grade accurately. The independent third-party grading services do a good job of setting grades on these pieces and can be relied upon to help the untrained in buying them. Caution is advised for anyone buying Uncirculated Standing Liberty quarters that have not been professionally graded.

Sets of circulated quarters, both Standing Liberty and Washington pieces, are fun to collect. There are some tough dates in the Standing series, but most of the more common pieces can be obtained at modest prices. The Washington coins are common and plentiful in all grades up to Brilliant Uncirculated. Hoards of old silver coins often contain at least one of each date and mint for the entire series, with the possible exception of the 1932-D and S.

Half Dimes

All half dimes made prior to 1829 are very scarce. The 1802 is one of the major rarities in the U.S. series. Those made from 1800 to 1805 have a heraldic eagle on the reverse. All were coined at Philadelphia; the New Orleans Mint produced half dimes starting in 1838, and San Francisco starting in 1863.

Half Disme, 1792

These rare coins depict Liberty on the obverse and a small eagle, wings spread, on the reverse.

	GSID	AG-3	G-4	VG-8	F-12	VF-20	EF-40	AU-50	MS-60	MS-63
1792	3715	$44,400	$52,800	$66,000	$84,000	$103,200	$144,000	$168,000	$222,000	$360,000

Flowing Hair, 1794–1795

On the obverse, Liberty faces right with her hair loose and flowing. A perching eagle with its wings spread is depicted on the reverse.

	GSID	AG-3	G-4	VG-8	F-12	VF-20	EF-40	AU-50	MS-60	MS-63
1794–1795	72449	$1,150	$1,550	$2,000	$2,700	$3,500	$6,000	$7,000	$10,500	$13,450

Draped Bust, 1796–1805

Liberty's hair is partly held back with a ribbon. On the reverse of coins dated 1796 and 1797, a slender eagle perches somewhat toward the left with its wings spread. Thereafter, a larger, more stylized "Heraldic" eagle with a shield on its breast faces slightly to the right.

Small Eagle Reverse

Heraldic Eagle Reverse

	GSID	AG-3	G-4	VG-8	F-12	VF-20	EF-40	AU-50	MS-60	MS-63
Small Eagle, 1796–1797	72450	$1,150	$1,625	$2,000	$3,450	$4,800	$5,750	$8,750	$16,800	$22,800
Heraldic Eagle, 1800–1805	72451	1,150	1,700	1,950	2,375	3,250	5,600	7,750	12,300	18,600

Capped Bust, 1829–1837

The last of the bust-type half dimes were coined from 1829 to 1837. Liberty, facing left, wears a loose cap with LIBERTY on the band, and fabric is draped about her shoulders. The reverse is a heraldic eagle with shield.

	GSID	G-4	VG-8	F-12	VF-20	EF-40	AU-50	MS-60	MS-63
1829–1837	72452	$75	$95	$115	$145	$210	$290	$550	$1,000

Liberty Seated, 1837–1873

The major device on this type is the figure of Liberty seated on a boulder, holding a pole with a liberty cap on the end in her left hand, and with her right hand lowered toward a shield with the word LIBERTY leaning against the boulder next to her. The reverses vary by denomination; Liberty Seated half dime and dime reverses have the denomination within a wreath. The half dimes were struck in three major types:

- **No Stars on Obverse** (with a plain field behind Liberty, struck in 1837 and 1838);
- **Stars on Obverse** (with a border of stars around Liberty, 1838–1859); and
- **Legend on Obverse** (with UNITED STATES OF AMERICA, formerly on the reverse, replacing the stars around Liberty, 1860–1873).

The beginning collector who develops an enthusiasm for the series may also be interested in the following major variations, which many collectors consider to be types in themselves:

- **Stars on Obverse, No Drapery** (i.e., no fabric below Liberty's left elbow, a feature found only on coins struck from 1838 partway into 1840)

- **Stars on Obverse, With Drapery, Arrows at Date** (with two small arrows alerting the public to a newly changed coin weight, struck 1853–1855; the arrows were discontinued after the public had time to become aware of the new weight and silver content)

Liberty Seated half dimes were struck at the Philadelphia and New Orleans mints, with additional production commencing in San Francisco in 1856 and Carson City in 1871.

No Stars on Obverse

No Drapery from Elbow (1837–1840)

Drapery from Elbow (1840 onward)

Arrows at Date

Stars on Obverse

Legend Obverse

	GSID	G-4	VG-8	F-12	VF-20	EF-40	AU-50	MS-60	MS-63
No Stars on Obverse, 1837–1838	72444	$50	$75	$115	$180	$300	$500	$775	$1,225
Stars on Obverse, 1838–1859									
No Drapery, 1838–1840	72445	38	45	50	75	120	210	360	600
Drapery, No Arrows, 1840–1853, 1856–1859	72446	32	36	45	50	80	145	200	310
Drapery, Arrows, 1853–1855	72447	32	36	45	50	80	145	210	340
Legend on Obverse, 1860–1873	72448	30	35	38	40	55	95	200	310

Dimes

Dimes, initially struck in 1796, were among the first silver coins minted by the United States. Early dimes are similar to the half dimes in many respects.

Draped Bust, 1796–1807

Liberty is shown facing right with her hair partly held back with a ribbon and a garment draped about her shoulders. The reverse design for the first two years of production is a slender eagle, wings spread, facing slightly left and encircled in a wreath, as shown here. Beginning in 1798, a heraldic eagle faces the viewer, wings spread, a shield on its breast (see the illustrations for the Draped Bust, Heraldic Eagle half dime). All were struck at the Philadelphia Mint.

Small Eagle Reverse

	GSID	AG-3	G-4	VG-8	F-12	VF-20	EF-40	AU-50	MS-60	MS-63
Small Eagle Reverse, 1796–1797	72453	$2,625	$3,500	$4,375	$4,875	$5,500	$9,000	$11,750	$20,400	$43,200
Heraldic Eagle Reverse, 1798–1807	72454	575	700	1,025	1,225	1,750	3,125	4,000	6,250	9,000

Capped Bust, 1809–1837

Liberty, facing left, wears a loose cap with LIBERTY on the band, and fabric is draped about her shoulders. The reverse is an eagle with shield. Through 1828, the diameter is about 19 millimeters, and from 1828 onward, 18.5 millimeters, although examples can vary. The two sizes go by different names, typically Large versus Small Planchet, Large versus Small Dentils, or Wide Border versus Modified Design. All were struck at the Philadelphia Mint.

	GSID	AG-3	G-4	VG-8	F-12	VF-20	EF-40	AU-50	MS-60	MS-63
Large Planchet, 1809–1828	72455	$60	$85	$125	$180	$260	$600	$750	$1,375	$2,625
Small Planchet, 1828–1837	72456		40	60	85	130	290	500	875	1,800

Liberty Seated, 1837–1891

Liberty Seated half dimes and dimes have the denomination within a wreath on the reverse. The dimes were struck in three major types:

- **No Stars on Obverse** (with a plain field behind Liberty, struck in 1837 and 1838);
- **Stars on Obverse** (with a border of stars around Liberty, 1838–1860); and
- **Legend on Obverse** (with UNITED STATES OF AMERICA, formerly on the reverse, replacing the stars around Liberty, 1860–1891; the space freed up on the reverse is given to an updated wreath style).

The beginning collector who develops an enthusiasm for the series may also be interested in the following major variations:

- **Stars on Obverse, No Drapery** (i.e., no fabric below Liberty's left elbow, a feature found only on coins struck from 1838 partway into 1840)
- **Stars on Obverse, With Drapery, Arrows at Date** (with two small arrows alerting the public to a newly changed coin weight, struck 1853–1855; the arrows were discontinued after the public had time to become aware of the new weight and silver content)
- **Legend on Obverse, Arrows at Date** (similar to the preceding, struck 1873–1874 and discontinued thereafter)

Liberty Seated dimes were struck at the Philadelphia and New Orleans mints, with additional production commencing in San Francisco in 1856 and Carson City in 1871.

See the Liberty Seated half dimes for additional comments and illustrations.

No Stars on Obverse

Stars on Obverse

Legend on Obverse

	GSID	G-4	VG-8	F-12	VF-20	EF-40	AU-50	MS-60	MS-63
No Stars on Obverse, 1837–1838	72457	$75	$105	$170	$260	$575	$850	$1,300	$2,200
Stars on Obverse, 1838–1860									
No Drapery, 1838–1840	72458	20	27	38	95	230	330	600	1,000
Drapery, No Arrows, 1841–1853, 1856–1860	72459	16	18	19	32	80	190	340	550
Drapery, Arrows, 1853–1855	72460	19	20	22	36	90	180	370	675
Legend on Obverse, 1860–1891									
No Arrows, 1860–1873, 1875–1891	72461	15	16	19	24	30	80	170	290
Arrows, 1873–1874	72462	19	23	30	65	170	340	500	850

Barber, 1892–1916

On Charles Barber's right-facing bust of Liberty, both a laurel wreath and a small brow-piece with the word LIBERTY are placed over the cap. The reverse simply bears the denomination within a wreath. Barber dimes were struck at Philadelphia, New Orleans, San Francisco, and Denver.

	GSID	G-4	VG-8	F-12	VF-20	EF-40	AU-50	MS-60	MS-63
1892–1916	72463	$6.00	$6.50	$7.25	$13.50	$45	$75	$145	$200

Mercury (or Winged Liberty), 1916–1945

Despite the coin's popular name, the obverse design is actually a left-facing head of Liberty wearing a Phrygian (liberty) cap with small wings, symbolizing freedom of thought. On the reverse are a fasces—a bundle of rods with an axe at the top, symbolizing strength and authority—and an olive branch. Coins were struck at Philadelphia, Denver, and San Francisco.

	GSID	G-4	VG-8	F-12	VF-20	EF-40	AU-50	MS-60	MS-63	MS-65
1916–1945	72464	$3.50	$3.50	$3.60	$4.25	$5.00	$5.25	$9.50	$13.50	$30

Roosevelt, 1946 to Date

The head of Franklin D. Roosevelt faces left on the obverse, while the reverse features a torch flanked by olive and oak branches.

From 1946 to 1964, dimes were struck in the traditional silver alloy and had a mintmark on the reverse. Dimes struck for circulation from 1965 onward are made with an inner core of copper bonded to outer layers of copper-nickel. Special numismatic versions are made in silver for collector sets. Current dates are worth only face value if circulated. Roosevelt dimes are struck at Philadelphia, Denver, and San Francisco, with a couple of special strikes in 2015 and 2016 at West Point.

	GSID	EF-40	AU-50	MS-60	MS-63	MS-65
Silver, 1946–1964	76246	$3.50	$3.50	$3.50	$3.75	$9.50

Twenty-Cent Pieces

The twenty-cent piece was a short-lived coinage experiment. It was discontinued after only four years because of its similarity to the quarter dollar. Coins were struck at Philadelphia, Carson City, and San Francisco.

Liberty Seated, 1875–1878

The obverse of the twenty-cent piece features a seated figure of Liberty holding a pole with a liberty cap on the end. The reverse bears an eagle with its wings spread and its talons holding an olive branch and arrows.

The 1876-CC piece is a great rarity, because only about 10 are in existence. The 1877 and 1878 coins were struck only in Proof.

	GSID	G-4	VG-8	F-12	VF-20	EF-40	AU-50	MS-60	MS-63
1875–1878	72420	$130	$150	$200	$230	$280	$390	$875	$1,250

QUARTER DOLLARS

Quarter dollars were first coined in 1796. Early designs follow the pattern of the half dimes and dimes of that period.

Draped Bust, 1796, 1804–1807

Liberty faces to the right, her hair tied back and a garment draped about her shoulders. The reverse of 1796 has a slender eagle with its wings spread (see the illustrations for the Draped Bust, Small Eagle half dime). The reverse of 1804–1807 depicts a heraldic eagle with a shield on its breast and clouds and stars above. All were produced in Philadelphia.

Heraldic Eagle Reverse

	GSID	AG-3	G-4	VG-8	F-12	VF-20	EF-40	AU-50	MS-60	MS-63
Small Eagle Reverse, 1796	74207	$10,100	$12,600	$21,600	$31,200	$40,800	$62,400	$67,200	$108,000	$198,000
Heraldic Eagle Reverse, 1804–1807	72424	220	400	550	800	1,500	3,125	5,000	11,250	15,600

Capped Bust, 1815–1838

Liberty, facing left, wears a loose cap with LIBERTY on the band. Her hair is down, and fabric is draped about her shoulders. The reverse is an eagle with shield. Through 1828, the diameter is about 27 millimeters ("Large Diameter"); after a hiatus in production from 1829 to 1830, the quarter returned in 1831 with a diameter of 24.3 millimeters ("Reduced Diameter"). All were produced in Philadelphia.

	GSID	AG-3	G-4	VG-8	F-12	VF-20	EF-40	AU-50	MS-60	MS-63
Large Diameter, 1815–1828	72425	$100	$150	$210	$340	$525	$1,300	$2,050	$3,875	$6,250
Reduced Diameter, 1831–1838	72426	55	110	130	145	180	400	725	2,025	3,750

Liberty Seated, 1838–1891

Liberty Seated quarters, half dollars, and silver dollars have on their reverse an eagle with wings spread and a shield on its breast. The quarters were produced in two major types:

- **No Motto above Eagle** (with a plain field above the eagle's head on the reverse, struck 1838–1865), and
- **Motto above Eagle** (with a banner reading IN GOD WE TRUST above the eagle, 1866–1891).

The beginning collector who develops an enthusiasm for the series may also be interested in the following major variations:

- **No Motto above Eagle, No Drapery** (i.e., no fabric below Liberty's left elbow, a feature found only on coins struck from 1838 partway into 1840)

- **No Motto above Eagle, Arrows at Date, Rays** (with two small arrows alerting the public to a newly changed coin weight, plus decorative rays added around the eagle; struck only in 1853, as the rays were removed the following year)
- **No Motto, Arrows at Date, No Rays** (a continuation of the above once the rays were removed; struck in 1854 and 1855, then discontinued after the public had time to become aware of the new weight and silver content)
- **Motto above Eagle, Arrows at Date** (similar to the preceding, struck in 1873 and 1874 and discontinued thereafter)

Liberty Seated quarters were struck at the Philadelphia and New Orleans mints, with additional production commencing in San Francisco in 1855 and Carson City in 1870.

See the Liberty Seated half dimes for additional comments and illustrations.

No Motto above Eagle, Arrows at Date, Rays on Reverse

Motto above Eagle, No Arrows at Date

	GSID	G-4	VG-8	F-12	VF-20	EF-40	AU-50	MS-60	MS-63
No Motto above Eagle, 1838–1865									
No Drapery, 1838–1840	72427	$50	$65	$125	$250	$525	$1,050	$1,750	$4,500
Drapery, No Arrows, No Rays, 1840–1853, 1856–1865	72427	38	55	100	280	575	1,150	1,875	5,000
Arrows and Rays, 1853	72434	35	45	55	95	220	425	1,150	1,725
Arrows, No Rays, 1854–1855	72435	30	34	40	45	115	260	725	1,200
Motto above Eagle, 1866–1891									
No Arrows, 1866–1873, 1875–1891	72436	30	32	35	45	75	160	290	550
Arrows, 1873–1874	72437	30	34	45	95	210	500	900	1,500

Barber, 1892–1916

On Charles Barber's right-facing bust of Liberty, both a laurel wreath and a small brow-piece with the word LIBERTY are placed over the cap. The reverse of the quarter depicts a heraldic eagle. Coins were struck in Philadelphia, New Orleans, San Francisco, and Denver.

	GSID	G-4	VG-8	F-12	VF-20	EF-40	AU-50	MS-60	MS-63
1892–1916	72438	$12.50	$13.50	$19	$30	$60	$135	$260	$350

Standing Liberty, 1916–1930

On the obverse, a shield-bearing Liberty is shown as if stepping through a gate or doorway; on the reverse an eagle flies from left to right. On coins dated 1916 and some dated 1917, there are no stars below the eagle (Type 1). From 1917 onward, three stars were added below the eagle (Type 2). Standing Liberty quarters were struck at the Philadelphia, Denver, and San Francisco mints. None were issued in 1922. On those coined after 1924, the date is slightly recessed to prevent wear.

Type 1, No Stars Below Eagle

Type 2, Stars Below Eagle

	GSID	G-4	VG-8	F-12	VF-20	EF-40	AU-50	MS-60	MS-63
Type 1, 1916–1917	72439	$24.00	$50.00	$70	$100	$150	$180	$260	$380
Type 2, 1917–1930	72441	9.50	10.50	12	16	40	95	190	280

Washington, 1932 to Date

Washington quarters were struck for circulation from 1932 to 1964 in 90 percent pure silver; thereafter, they have a copper core bonded to an outer layer of copper-nickel. The Mint also produces silver pieces for collectors. Special circulating series to date include the following:

- Bicentennial quarters (1975 and 1976)—dated 1776–1976
- 50 State Quarters series (1999–2009)—five special reverse designs per year honoring each of the 50 states, the District of Columbia, and the five U.S. territories
- America the Beautiful series (2010–2020)—five special reverse designs per year honoring a natural or historic site in each of the states, the District of Columbia, and the U.S. territories
- Washington Crossing the Delaware (2021)—a one-year reverse design depicting the famous historical scene
- American Women series (2022–2025)—five special reverses per year honoring prominent American women and the ratification of the 19th Amendment, granting women the right to vote; plus a special Washington obverse portrait designed in 1932 by Laura Gardin Fraser

Washington quarters are struck at Philadelphia, Denver, and San Francisco. Those made of silver at San Francisco with the S mintmark command a premium. Since 2012 the San Francisco Mint has also produced a relatively small number of each design in copper-nickel with the S mintmark; these are offered for sale to collectors in rolls and bags.

Regular issues are commonly found in circulation and are mostly collected only in Uncirculated condition.

Washington, Eagle Reverse

Examples of State, D.C., and U.S. Territories Quarters

Examples of America the Beautiful ("National Park") Quarters

Crossing the Delaware Quarter

Laura Gardin Fraser Obverse

American Women Quarters

	GSID	VG-8	F-12	VF-20	EF-40	AU-50	MS-60	MS-63	MS-65
Silver, 1932–1964	72443	$8.50	$8.50	$8.50	$8.50	$8.50	$9.00	$9.25	$16

U.S. Silver Half Dollars, Silver Dollars, and Modern Dollars

Before the middle of the 20th century, the United States' economy and strength of money was based largely upon silver and gold resources in the form of actual coins that were stored as reserves or as backing for our paper money.

Half Dollars

Before 1840, when there were no large quantities of silver dollars, it was the silver half dollar that was stored by the thousands to satisfy reserve requirements. A fortunate consequence of this is the legacy we now enjoy in the form of a supply of early-date half dollars in high-grade condition. True, many of them were melted for their bullion content over the years, but many others were preserved.

There was, however, a price to be paid for this legacy. The coins that were held in storage by banks had to be counted periodically, and during this procedure they were slid across the surface of a counting table and rather carelessly handled in the accounting process. Very few such coins escaped the inevitable rubs and scratches that resulted from this rough treatment, and although there are still many technically Uncirculated coins from this era, most of them show signs of abrasions from the counting process. These are generally accepted as being in MS-60, or in some cases a slightly higher grade of condition, but a true MS-65 coin must not exhibit any such signs of friction even on the highest points of the design.

The Liberty Seated half dollars made between 1839 and 1891 are probably more popular with investors than collectors. This may have something to do with their size and luster. Investors seem attracted to large, shiny coins, while collectors tend to appreciate all coins equally, or perhaps recognize their historical and artistic merits. Collectors also often find the long run of dates and mintmarks in this series beyond their financial means and avoid saving anything more than a few type coins from each design or major variation. Interest is increasing, though, with the formation of active hobby groups such as the Liberty Seated Collectors Club (www.lscc.org).

Silver Barber half dollars continue to captivate many segments of the coin market, and they offer some unusual opportunities for those who would like to speculate in these attractive pieces. Collectors are usually faced with having to settle for either Extremely Fine or poorer pieces or move up to the Uncirculated range to find specimens for their type or date sets. For some unexplained reason very few of these pieces have survived in About Uncirculated grade. Those that just barely make it into the MS-60 range are often spotted, badly toned, or generally unattractive.

No one can ignore the grace and beauty of Adolph Weinman's Liberty Walking half dollar design. Few collectors would deny that these coins are among the most difficult to properly grade and evaluate. The reason is somewhat similar to the problems encountered with the early Bust halves, for these coins were also subjected to rubbing on the high points of the design while in storage. The difference here is that the Walkers were stored in bank-wrapped rolls, and the rub marks are most prominent on Liberty's breast. The problem is made even worse by the weak impressions given to the coins made during World War II, when dies were used well beyond their capacity and quality control became a wartime casualty.

For this reason, coins in Extremely Fine condition are sometimes almost as attractive as Uncirculated pieces. Early-date Walkers, those made from 1916 through 1933, are quite scarce in high-grade Uncirculated condition and command high prices. Most collectors and investors are content to assemble high-grade "short" sets of these coins made from 1934 (or later) through 1947.

None of the recent issues of United States coins have proven themselves to be particularly good investments up to this time. That is not to say that they will not do well in the future, but for the most part any of the coins made since 1950 are still too common to have much of a following or price appreciation. Collectors who had seen the value of Uncirculated coins rise at a rather steady rate over the years were quick to save rolls and bags of just about every issue made since the end of World War II. These pieces are still available in sufficient quantities to satisfy most market demands for many years to come. Anyone willing to speculate in rolls of today's common coins may well pick a winner, but it is a gamble that should not be undertaken without a thorough study of available supplies of these coins.

Flowing Hair, 1794–1795

Struck only at the Philadelphia Mint, the Flowing Hair type features a plain bust of Liberty facing right, her hair unbound. The reverse depicts a slender eagle with wings spread. Edges are lettered FIFTY CENTS OR HALF A DOLLAR.

	GSID	AG-3	G-4	VG-8	F-12	VF-20	EF-40	AU-50
1794–1795	72408	$1,000	$1,475	$2,000	$2,700	$4,000	$6,900	$14,400

Draped Bust, 1796–1807

Liberty's hair is now pulled partly back with a ribbon, and a garment is draped about her shoulders. The reverse features a small eagle with wings spread (see the illustrations under the Draped Bust, Small Eagle half dime) through 1797. After a brief hiatus in production, the design resumed with a Heraldic Eagle reverse. Edges are lettered FIFTY CENTS OR HALF A DOLLAR.

Heraldic Eagle Reverse

	GSID	G-4	VG-8	F-12	VF-20	EF-40	AU-50	MS-60	MS-63
Small Eagle Reverse, 1796–1797	72409	$33,600	$40,800	$46,800	$57,600	$103,200	$150,000	$300,000	$198,000
Heraldic Eagle Reverse, 1801–1807	72410	275	375	575	850	1,650	2,250	7,500	15,600

Capped Bust, 1807–1839

Capped Bust half dollars of 1807 to 1836 have the edge lettered FIFTY CENTS OR HALF A DOLLAR. Some of 1836 and all those of 1837 to 1839 have a reeded edge. Liberty faces left on the obverse, her hair down; she wears a loose cap with LIBERTY on the band and a garment draped around her shoulders. The reverse eagle is perched with wings spread, a shield on its breast.

	GSID	G-4	VG-8	F-12	VF-20	EF-40	AU-50	MS-60	MS-63
Lettered Edge, 1807–1836	72411	$70	$85	$95	$115	$210	$330	$1,000	$1,700
Reeded Edge, 1836–1839	72412	75	90	120	160	290	550	1,250	3,000

Liberty Seated, 1839–1891

Liberty Seated quarters, half dollars, and silver dollars have on their reverse an eagle with wings spread and a shield on its breast. The half dollars were produced in two major types:

- **No Motto above Eagle** (with a plain field above the eagle's head on the reverse, struck 1839–1866), and
- **Motto above Eagle** (with a banner reading IN GOD WE TRUST above the eagle, 1866–1873).

The beginning collector who develops an enthusiasm for the series may also be interested in the following major variations:

- **No Motto above Eagle, No Drapery** (i.e., no fabric below Liberty's left elbow, a feature found only on some coins struck in 1839)
- **No Motto above Eagle, Arrows at Date, Rays** (with two small arrows alerting the public to a newly changed coin weight, plus decorative rays added around the eagle; struck only in 1853, as the rays were removed the following year)
- **No Motto, Arrows at Date, No Rays** (a continuation of the above once the rays were removed; struck in 1854 and 1855, then discontinued after the public had time to become aware of the new weight and silver content)
- **Motto above Eagle, Arrows at Date** (similar to the preceding, struck in 1873 and 1874 and discontinued thereafter)

Liberty Seated half dollars were struck at the Philadelphia and New Orleans mints, with additional production commencing in San Francisco in 1855 and Carson City in 1870.

See the Liberty Seated half dimes for additional comments and illustrations.

No Motto above Eagle, Arrows at Date, Rays on Reverse

Motto above Eagle, No Arrows at Date

	GSID	G-4	VG-8	F-12	VF-20	EF-40	AU-50	MS-60	MS-63
No Motto Above Eagle, 1839–1866									
No Drapery, 1839	74466	$400	$475	$625	$1,000	$2,250	$3,500	$10,000	$27,500
No Arrows, No Rays, 1839–1853, 1856–1866	72415	55	65	75	95	160	310	575	1,225
Arrows and Rays, 1853	72416	70	90	130	160	340	625	1,500	3,750
Arrows, No Rays, 1854–1855	72417	55	65	80	100	180	280	575	1,250
Motto Above Eagle, 1866–1891									
No Arrows, 1866–1873, 1875–1891	72418	55	65	75	95	130	220	450	825
Arrows, 1873–1874	72419	55	65	85	110	260	450	975	2,000

Barber, 1892–1915

On Charles Barber's right-facing bust of Liberty, both a laurel wreath and a small brow-piece with the word LIBERTY are placed over the cap. The reverse of the quarter depicts a heraldic eagle. Coins were struck in Philadelphia, New Orleans, San Francisco, and Denver.

	GSID	G-4	VG-8	F-12	VF-20	EF-40	AU-50	MS-60	MS-63
1892–1915	72413	$20	$24	$60	$160	$260	$350	$625	$950

Liberty Walking, 1916–1947

On the obverse, the figure of Liberty strides to the left in front of a rising sun, her star-spangled garment billowing around her. The eagle on the reverse stands with its wings held open and to the back. All were struck at the Philadelphia, Denver, and San Francisco mints. Those made in 1916 and some of the 1917 issue have the mintmark on the obverse, below the motto; all others have it on the reverse side near the left border.

	GSID	G-4	VG-8	F-12	VF-20	EF-40	AU-50	MS-60	MS-63
1916–1947	72414	$18	$18	$18	$19	$20	$22	$38	$60

Franklin, 1948–1963

With its right-facing bust of Benjamin Franklin on the obverse and the Liberty Bell on the reverse, the Franklin half dollar was coined from 1948 until 1963. All are made of 90 percent silver, and the value of circulated examples is based on bullion prices.

	GSID	VF-20	EF-40	AU-50	MS-60	MS-63	MS-65
1948–1963	76527	$18.50	$18.50	$19	$20	$23	$32

Kennedy, 1964 to Date

On the obverse, a portrait of the late president faces left, while the reverse depicts an adaptation of the Great Seal of the United States. The 1964 issue was struck in 90 percent silver. From 1965 through 1970, the coins are of 40 percent silver composition; regular issues thereafter have a copper core bonded to outer layers of copper-nickel. A special Bicentennial design, dated 1776–1976, was used during 1975 and 1976. Although half dollars have been minted each year, none have been officially released for circulation since 2001 (although there have been rumors that some were struck for circulation in the early 2020s).

Bicentennial

	GSID	AU-50	MS-60	MS-63	MS-65
Silver, 1964	24983	$18.00	$18.50	$19.00	$27
Silver Clad, 1965–1970	24984	6.00	6.50	7.00	27
Clad, 1971–Date	24985	0.90	1.10	1.50	8

Silver Dollars

The very first U.S. silver dollars, those made from 1794 through 1803, are now so rare in high-grade condition that only a very few ever appear on the market each year, and when they do, they bring extremely high prices in competitive bidding. In Uncirculated condition the most common of the early dates sell for $30,000. For the average collector, coins in Very Good or Fine condition can become a good investment because of their historical value, scarcity, and beauty. The extremely rare dollar dated 1804 is an exception among U.S. coins, and while it is considered to be the most valuable, it was never made to be a regular circulating coin. The original 1804 dollars were made in 1834 as presentation pieces to be given to foreign dignitaries: the King of Siam got one of them, and the Imam of Muscat received another.

Many of the original 1804 dollars are now in museums. Recently a specimen that was sold at public auction brought the amazing price of more than $7.68 million. It is estimated that no more than eight of the coins were originally made for presentation sets, but because of demand by collectors, the Mint made another seven or more pieces sometime around 1859. The later version can be identified by its slightly different reverse. Examples of that variety have sold for a bit less than the originals.

The silver dollar designed by George T. Morgan and made from 1878 through 1921 is easily one of the most common Uncirculated numismatic survivors of the 1800s and early 1900s. Despite the untold numbers of bags of these coins that still exist today, they have become the very basis of most coin investments and collections. They have been heavily promoted in every grade of condition. During the lifetime of these coins, they were stored in enormous quantities as backing for our nation's currency. When such backing was no longer required by law, and when the value of silver bullion began to rise in 1964, millions of these coins were sold by the Treasury and ended up in the hands of speculators and dealers.

For some reason, Peace dollars have never been as popular with collectors as the Morgan design. Perhaps it is the historical mystique of the older coins of the Old West that makes the Morgans a favorite, or perhaps it is a resistance to what some may see as a less-attractive design, and to the fact that the Peace dollars are usually lacking in luster and details. Whatever the answer, the Peace dollars seem to have only limited appeal to collectors as a date series.

Flowing Hair, 1794–1795

The first U.S. silver dollars, dated 1794 and 1795, show a head of Liberty on the obverse, facing right with her hair flowing behind. The reverse has a rather spindly eagle with its wings spread, encircled in a wreath.

	GSID	AG-3	G-4	VG-8	F-12	VF-20	EF-40	AU-50	MS-60
1794–1795	72398	$2,300	$3,000	$4,000	$5,750	$7,800	$13,800	$21,600	$62,400

Draped Bust, 1795–1804

The Flowing Hair obverse design was soon changed to a larger bust type, with Liberty's hair partly pulled back with a ribbon and fabric draped around the bust. The eagle was slightly more robust, but still small, and in 1798 a heraldic eagle replaced it on the reverse. All of the early dollars were made at the Philadelphia Mint, and they all have a lettered edge. The 1804 dollar is one of the most valuable United States coins.

Small Eagle Reverse

	GSID	AG-3	G-4	VG-8	F-12	VF-20	EF-40	AU-50	MS-60
Small Eagle, 1795–1798	72399	$1,875	$2,500	$3,000	$4,050	$5,000	$8,250	$12,600	$50,400
Heraldic Eagle, 1798–1804	72400	1,100	1,250	1,550	2,125	2,750	4,050	6,500	22,200

Liberty Seated, 1840–1873

Liberty Seated silver dollars are a simpler type than their counterparts among the half dimes, dimes, quarters, and half dollars. As on the quarters and half dollars, their reverse depicts an eagle with wings spread and a shield on its breast. The silver dollars were produced in two major types:

- **No Motto above Eagle** (with a plain field above the eagle's head on the reverse, struck 1840–1865), and
- **Motto above Eagle** (with a banner reading IN GOD WE TRUST above the eagle, 1866–1873).

Liberty Seated silver dollars were struck at the Philadelphia and New Orleans mints, with additional production commencing in San Francisco in 1859 and Carson City in 1870.

See the Liberty Seated half dimes for additional comments and illustrations.

No Motto above Eagle

Motto above Eagle

	GSID	VG-8	F-12	VF-20	EF-40	AU-50	MS-60	MS-63
No Motto, 1840–1865	72401	$425	$500	$575	$850	$1,100	$2,000	$4,250
With Motto, 1866–1873	72402	400	450	500	725	925	2,125	4,250

Trade Dollars, 1873–1885

Special "trade" dollars were coined for use in Asia, where merchants were accustomed to using a dollar-sized Mexican 8-real coin that was slightly heavier than the U.S. silver dollar. The design reflects the trade dollar's purpose: on the obverse, a figure of Liberty seated, facing the sea, on bound bundles of merchandise with a sheaf of wheat behind her; and on the reverse, a spread-winged eagle with the coin's silver fineness and the words TRADE DOLLAR below. These pieces were struck at the Philadelphia, San Francisco, and Carson City mints from 1873 to 1878. From 1879 to 1885, only a limited number of Proofs were made.

	GSID	VG-8	F-12	VF-20	EF-40	AU-50	MS-60	MS-63
1873–1885	72403	$220	$260	$350	$450	$500	$1,100	$1,500

Morgan, 1878–1821

George T. Morgan's obverse features a head of Liberty facing left, a small liberty cap perched on her curling hair along with an agricultural wreath and a band reading LIBERTY. The reverse bears a facing eagle with spread wings. Morgan dollars were coined at the five U.S. mints in Philadelphia, Denver, San Francisco, New Orleans, and Carson City, and were made each year from 1878 to 1904 and then again in 1921. Varieties of the 1878 coins show either seven or eight tail feathers on the eagle.

See "1921 Silver Dollar Anniversary" in the Modern Dollars section for current coins in the Morgan design.

	GSID	VF-20	EF-40	AU-50	MS-60	MS-63	MS-65
1878–1904	72404	$50	$50	$55	$70	$85	$200
1921	71697	40	42	45	45	50	160

Peace, 1921–1935

The standard coin of our country, the silver dollar (including the Peace dollar), has for some reason never been a very popular *circulating* coin. Through the years most silver dollars were stored in banks or by the government in Treasury vaults. Replacing the Morgan dollar in 1921, the Peace dollar bears a head of Liberty facing left, her hair pulled up in a loose bun, and a diadem of rays projecting from her head. The reverse has an eagle with folded wings facing the rays of a rising sun. Coins were struck in Philadelphia, Denver, and San Francisco.

See "1921 Silver Dollar Anniversary" in the Modern Dollars section for current coins in the Peace design.

	GSID	VF-20	EF-40	AU-50	MS-60	MS-63	MS-64	MS-65	MS-66
1921–1935	72407	$35	$38	$42	$45	$70	$85	$130	$550

Modern Dollars

The last Peace dollars were struck in 1935, and the denomination wasn't struck again until 1971, when it was produced in a copper-nickel alloy instead of 90 percent silver. The first of these, the Eisenhower dollars, were produced in the same size as older Peace and Morgan dollars. Then the Mint introduced several series of smaller dollar coins starting in 1979.

Eisenhower, 1971–1978

Coined for circulation from 1971 through 1978 at Philadelphia, Denver, and San Francisco, these pieces were made to honor President Dwight D. Eisenhower and the first landing of man on the Moon. The design on the reverse is an adaptation of the official *Apollo 11* insignia. Bicentennial pieces, dated 1776–1976, depict the Liberty Bell in front of the Moon on the reverse. Collectors' coins were struck in 40 percent silver composition, and circulation issues in copper-nickel.

Bicentennial

	GSID	EF-40	MS-63	MS-65	MS-66
1971–1978	7914	$3	$8	$24	$35

Susan B. Anthony, 1979–1999

Starting in 1979 the size of the U.S. dollar coin was reduced from 38.1 mm to 26.5 mm. The Susan B. Anthony dollar is round, but the perimeter has a multi-sided border to distinguish it from other coins. The reverse uses the same design as the regular Eisenhower dollar. Coins were struck in Philadelphia, Denver, and San Francisco, with the Philadelphia coins bearing a P mintmark for the first time. Coins dated 1981 were issued only in official government Mint Sets.

	GSID	EF-40	MS-63	MS-66
1971–1978	7977	$3	$8	$35

Sacagawea, 2000–2008

In 2000 the design of the dollar coin was again changed, as was the composition and color. The obverse design, selected in a competition, honors the young Native American Shoshone woman who acted as a guide for Lewis and Clark during their journey westward to the Pacific. The reverse shows an eagle in flight, viewed slightly from below. The edge of this coin is plain; the composition is copper with a golden outer layer of manganese brass.

	GSID	MS-65	MS-66	MS-67
2000–2008	82168	$3.25	$4.00	$5.50

Presidential, 2007–2016

Former U.S. presidents were honored on the obverses of this series of dollar coins, which have the same gold composition as the Sacagawea dollars. The reverse holds a modern view of the Statue of Liberty. They were issued for general circulation from 2007 through 2011, and only for numismatic sales by the Mint thereafter. They are seldom found in pocket change. The date. mintmark, and mottoes are incused into the plain edge.

Common Reverse

Date, Mintmark, and Mottoes Incused on Edge

	GSID	MS-65	MS-66	MS-67
2007–2016, 2020	82242	$3.50	$8	$19

Native American, 2009 to Date

The Sacagawea dollar gave way in 2009 to a broader series with the Sacagawea obverse and annually changing reverse designs honoring Native Americans. Since 2012 these coins have not been released for general circulation but are sold in sets, rolls, and bags to collectors; they are seldom found in change.

Common Obverse

	GSID	MS-65	MS-66	MS-67
2009 to Date	82169	$3.25	$3.50	$5.50

American Innovation, 2018 to Date

The newest golden dollar series honors four different states each year. The common obverse bears the Statue of Liberty on a plain field, with a special privy mark for each year. The reverse designs highlight the respective states' major contributions to science and culture, except for the single issue from the first year, which honors American innovation in general. They are not released for general circulation but are sold in sets, rolls, and bags to collectors.

Common Obverse

	GSID	Uncertified
2018 to Date	82115	$6

Note: Uncertified values are for coins in their original, unopened government packaging.

1921 Silver Dollar Anniversary, 2021 to Date

Under the 1921 Silver Dollar Coin Anniversary Act, signed into law in 2021, the Mint produces special silver dollars to honor the 100th anniversary of the year when the Morgan series concluded and the Peace series commenced. Unlike the original Morgan and Peace coins, they are 99.9 percent silver, and the designs are updated renderings using modern technology. they are struck at Philadelphia, Denver, and San Francisco, and some of the first-year coins have special privy marks.

	GSID	Uncertified	MS-69	MS-70
Morgan, 2021 to Date	85115	$100	$100	$145
Peace, 2021 to Date	85117	100	100	145

Note: Uncertified values are for coins in their original, unopened government packaging.

U.S. Gold Coins

United States gold coins are the glamor stock of numismatic investments and favorites of collectors as well. All gold coins are costly because of their precious-metal content and their long history of universal demand. The value placed on common gold coins is directly related to the price of raw gold, and so fluctuates with the spot price of that metal. Thus, the currently issued American Eagle gold bullion coins and fractional denominations are constantly changing in value depending on the worldwide demand for gold.

The older gold coins that were issued in this country, from their beginning in 1795 until the recall in 1933, are now quite scarce and command a premium over their gold content. In the case of some of the low-grade pieces, and even the plentiful $20 double eagles in grades up to MS-62, the numismatic values placed on these coins is tied to the bullion price of gold, with only a slight additional premium for the collector value. Such coins are called "semi-numismatic" pieces and are considered by many to be a good investment because of their chances of increasing in value based on the two influences of demand. Collectors always enjoy them, and in any situation where gold bullion shows a significant price rise, these semi-numismatic coins perform well as a hedge against inflation.

The smallest of our gold coins is the diminutive gold dollar issued from 1849 through 1889. Barely larger than a fingernail, these coins were never popular in circulation because they could be lost or misplaced so easily. Production was never large, and many have been destroyed over the years through melting or damaged through use in jewelry. The few remaining gold dollar coins are all scarce in any grade of condition.

Collectors have paid premium prices for gold dollars from very early times because they have always been considered scarce and desirable. Today they are acknowledged as being extremely difficult to find in high grade, and they bring commensurate prices. The last issue of Indian Head type coins is seemingly the most common, even though the average yearly mintage was less than 10,000 pieces. Today all pieces in this series are known to be scarce and valuable.

Quarter eagles, or $2.50 gold pieces, were made from 1796 to 1929 and form an important part of our coinage history. They were a popular form of currency that served the system well and provided a necessary and convenient denomination. Many of the existing coins have survived only in well-worn condition, and high-quality Uncirculated pieces are truly scarce, if not rare, for most dates. This is especially true of the early pieces made before 1840. As a group, all of the old quarter eagles made from 1796 through 1834 are rare and seldom available to collectors.

The Liberty Head $2.50 gold pieces made from 1840 through 1907 form the bulk of this series and can still be purchased at reasonable prices in ordinary condition. Prices for these pieces are not tied to bullion value and, like the gold dollars and three-dollar coins, they are all worth a premium well over their gold content. Supplies of these coins are always limited, with no large holdings known to exist either here or in foreign banks.

The same is true of the later Indian Head quarter eagle coins, which are even more popular with collectors than the Liberty Head types.

United States $3 gold coins were issued from 1854 through 1889. No one knows exactly why this unusual denomination was chosen, but popular belief is that it was made as a convenience for purchasing 100 three-cent trimes or 100 three-cent postage stamps. (This is an unlikely argument for creating a denomination that was so close to the long-established and very successful $2.50 quarter eagle.) Three-dollar gold coins seem to have been popular in circulation in their day, because many have survived in heavily worn condition. The design used on this unusual coin is identical to that of the gold dollar of the period. Quantities made each year seldom exceeded 50,000, and today all $3 dollar coins are difficult to find and command high premiums.

Low-grade gold coins in the denominations of $5, $10, and $20 are relatively common and tend to be tied in value to the price of gold bullion. They do, of course, command a numismatic premium, but the values of these pieces rise and fall according to the overall demand for gold in any form. As semi-numismatic pieces they appeal to both collectors and bullion buyers who see them as a hedge against inflation. When prices of other goods rise because of inflation factors or troubled times, the value of gold traditionally rises. The numismatic value of low-grade obsolete U.S. gold coins also appreciates in such times, and these pieces have a double chance of becoming more valuable.

These factors do not apply to gold coins in Uncirculated grades because their rarity, demand, and collector value make them worth far more than the bullion price. They do not apply to the early-date pieces made before 1839, either, since nearly all are extremely rare. As a group, the early-date $5 and $10 coins are considered to be some of the most desirable and scarcest of all American series. Current values reflect their years of popularity.

Liberty Head $5 gold pieces made from 1839 through 1866 are scarce in high-grade condition. Even so, the demand for them is rather limited, as neither collectors nor investors make much of the minor distinction between the early dates and those made later with the addition of the motto IN GOD WE TRUST. The popular Indian Head design that was made from 1908 to 1929 is valued higher than the older pieces because of constant demand and collector pressure.

The early-date U.S. eagles, or $10 gold coins, are similar to the $5 pieces in that they are classic rarities held in high esteem by collectors and investors alike. All of the dates and types made prior to 1839 have gone up in value at a steady rate for years. These rather expensive coins are considered the ultimate course for any numismatic feast, and will no doubt continue to be in strong demand by all who can afford them for as long as there are collectors and museums.

Liberty Head eagles made from 1866 to 1907 are relatively common in circulated grades and are often available at prices only slightly over their gold content. The Indian Head type, however, is quite a different story. The design is considered one of the classics in the U.S. series, and Indian $10 coins are in constant demand. Prices for these coins are always somewhat higher than for the older Liberty Head pieces, and there are many extremely rare dates and mints in this series.

The American double eagle was known around the world as a symbol of our country's strength and financial stability. Today these coins are treasured by collectors and are a popular favorite of all investors. Collectors who can afford to save these coins by date and mint find them a rewarding challenge and have learned that many dates are far rarer than catalog prices would indicate. Some do not exist in Uncirculated condition. Vast hoards of these coins were held in Europe after the gold-withdrawal order of 1933, and they continue to appear on the market in sufficient quantities to maintain relatively stable prices for the common dates.

When President Theodore Roosevelt asked the artist Augustus Saint-Gaudens to design a coin that would rival those of all other countries, he could only have hoped that the result would be as spectacular as it turned out to be. The first of these coins, made in 1907, were produced in a special high relief and looked more like a medal than a coin. A scant 11,250 were made, and far fewer still remain today in collections and museums. The high-relief double eagle is acknowledged worldwide to be one of the most beautiful coins of all time, and there is little question that it is highly sought by all collectors who can afford them.

The normal Saint-Gaudens double eagles made from 1907 to 1933 are relatively common even in high-grade Uncirculated condition. There are some notable exceptions, and the issue of 1933 is one of the great U.S. rarities. Unfortunately, collectors are not allowed to own specimens of the 1933 issue without special permission because no coins of that date were placed in circulation. According to Mint officials, the few pieces that survived must have somehow been taken from the Mint or switched for other coins. Over the years all but one of the 1933 double eagles that have surfaced have been confiscated by the government. Two examples have been permanently preserved in the Smithsonian Institution so that the issue will never be lost to numismatists.

Gold Dollars

Gold dollars were coined each year from 1849 to 1889 and at several mints.

Liberty Head, 1849–1854

The type issued from 1849 to 1854 has the head of Liberty facing left, with a coronet bearing the word LIBERTY in her hair. The reverse has the denomination within a wreath.

Open Wreath Reverse

Closed Wreath Reverse

	GSID	VF-20	EF-40	AU-50	AU-58	MS-60	MS-63
1849–1854	72365	$310	$350	$370	$380	$425	$600

Indian Princess Head, 1854–1889

Gold dollars issued from 1854 to 1856 have a much smaller head of Liberty wearing a feathered headdress. The reverse is similar to the that of the previous type. From 1856 to 1889 the obverse featured a larger effigy on the obverse.

	GSID	VF-20	EF-40	AU-50	AU-58	MS-60	MS-63
Small Head, 1854–1856	72366	$525	$625	$625	$775	$1,425	$4,400
Large Head, 1856–1889	72367	375	400	425	450	575	850

QUARTER EAGLES

The quarter eagle, or $2.50 gold piece, was issued from 1796 to 1929. Several different types were made. Many dates, especially those before 1834, are very scarce.

Capped Bust to Right, 1796–1807

A right-facing bust of Liberty, her hair flowing loose and a garment draped about her shoulders, wears a large conical cap reminiscent of a turban. A heraldic eagle is on the reverse. The first year of issue, the coin was produced in two obverse types: one with only the bust, LIBERTY, and the date, and the other with an added border of stars. The latter was used for the remainder of the series.

	GSID	VF-20	EF-40	AU-50	AU-58	MS-60	MS-63
No Stars Obverse, 1796	72371	$96,000	$144,000	$180,000	$270,000	$384,000	$1,200,000
Stars Obverse, 1796–1807	72372	9,000	12,250	14,400	26,400	31,200	75,600

Draped Bust to Left, 1808

A bust of Liberty in a loose garment and a soft cap with LIBERTY on the band faces left. The reverse shows an eagle with its wings spread and a shield on its breast, and a ribbon above its head with the words E PLURIBUS UNUM.

	GSID	VF-20	EF-40	AU-50	AU-58	MS-60	MS-63
1808	74467	$64,800	$132,000	$162,000	$240,000	$300,000	$600,000

Capped Head to Left, 1821–1834

The obverse is similar to that of the previous type, except that the bust is truncated, with no drapery. The reverse shows an eagle with its wings spread and a shield on its breast, and a ribbon above its head with the words E PLURIBUS UNUM. Coins of 1821–1827 have a diameter of about 18.5 millimeters; from 1829 onward, it is reduced very slightly, to 18.2 millimeters. The two types are called Large Size and Small Size, respectively.

	GSID	VF-20	EF-40	AU-50	AU-58	MS-60	MS-63
Large Size, 1821–1827	72373	$9,400	$12,600	$14,650	$24,000	$30,000	$70,200
Small Size, 1829–1834	72374	7,750	11,250	14,400	21,000	24,000	39,600

Classic Head, No Motto on Reverse, 1834–1839

A left-facing bust of Liberty with elaborate curls wears a broad ribbon with the word LIBERTY about her head. The reverse remains a spread-winged eagle with a shield on its breast, but the ribbon with motto has been removed from above its head.

	GSID	VF-20	EF-40	AU-50	AU-58	MS-60	MS-63
1834–1839	72375	$775	$1,025	$1,300	$2,250	$3,250	$8,500

Liberty Head, 1840–1907

A more reserved bust of Liberty than on the previous type faces left, and the broad ribbon around her head has been reduced to something more like a coronet. The reverse motifs are the same: an eagle with its wings spread and a shield on its breast.

	GSID	VF-20	EF-40	AU-50	AU-58	MS-60	MS-63
1840–1907	72368	$475	$500	$525	$525	$525	$600

Indian Head, 1908–1929

The obverse design of 1908, a profile portrait of a Native American man in a feathered headdress, is incused into the coin rather than in relief above the surface (the norm for most coins before and since). The incused reverse design is a large eagle, perched with its wings closed against its body.

	GSID	VF-20	EF-40	AU-50	MS-60	MS-63	MS-64
1908–1929	72369	$475	$500	$500	$525	$675	$850

THREE-DOLLAR GOLD PIECES

This unusual denomination was coined from 1854 to 1889. The dates 1873, 1875, and 1876 were struck in Proof only.

Indian Princess Head, 1854–1889

The obverse features a bust of Liberty facing left with a feathered headdress; the reverse shows the denomination enclosed in a wreath. The 1854-D is scarce, and the 1870-S is one of the rarest of all U.S. coins.

	GSID	VF-20	EF-40	AU-50	MS-60	MS-63
1854–1889	72370	$1,125	$1,350	$1,600	$2,650	$4,050

HALF EAGLES

The half eagle, or $5 gold piece, was first coined in 1795. Minted until 1929, this was the only denomination made at all seven U.S. mints.

Capped Bust to Right, 1795–1807

A right-facing bust of Liberty, her hair flowing loose and a garment draped about her shoulders, wears a large conical cap reminiscent of a turban. Two reverses were produced concurrently from 1795 to 1798: on one, a small eagle holds a wreath in its beak; on the other, a heraldic eagle is featured. The latter is the only style used from 1799 through 1807.

Small Eagle Reverse

Heraldic Eagle Reverse

	GSID	F-12	VF-20	EF-40	AU-50	AU-58	MS-60	MS-63
Small Eagle, 1795–1798	72376	$27,600	$31,200	$43,200	$51,600	$74,400	$100,800	$210,000
Heraldic Eagle, 1795–1807	72377	4,500	5,500	7,750	10,250	12,600	13,200	26,400

Draped Bust to Left, 1807–1812

A left-facing bust of Liberty wears a loose garment about the shoulders and a soft cap with LIBERTY on the band. The reverse shows an eagle with its wings spread and a shield on its breast, and a ribbon above its head with the words E PLURIBUS UNUM.

	GSID	F-12	VF-20	EF-40	AU-50	AU-58	MS-60	MS-63
1807–1812	72378	$4,250	$5,250	$7,750	$9,750	$12,000	$12,600	$19,800

Capped Head to Left, 1813–1834

The obverse is similar to that of the previous type, except that the bust is truncated, with no drapery. The reverse shows an eagle with its wings spread and a shield on its breast; a ribbon with the words E PLURIBUS UNUM ripples above its head. Coins of 1813–1828 (and some of 1829) are about 25 millimeters in diameter; from 1829 onward, coins were produced at 23.8 millimeters. The two types are called Large Size and Small Size, respectively.

	GSID	F-12	VF-20	EF-40	AU-50	AU-58	MS-60	MS-63
Large Size, 1813–1829	72379	$4,700	$5,950	$9,050	$10,400	$12,600	$13,200	$25,800
Small Size, 1829–1834	72380	21,600	33,600	54,000	66,000	76,800	81,600	132,000

Classic Head, No Motto, 1834–1838

A left-facing bust of Liberty with elaborate curls wears a broad ribbon with the word LIBERTY around her head. The reverse remains a spread-winged eagle with a shield on its breast, but there is no longer a ribbon with motto above its head.

	GSID	VF-20	EF-40	AU-50	AU-58	MS-60	MS-63
1834–1839	72381	$900	$1,200	$1,400	$2,250	$3,550	$10,500

Liberty Head, 1839–1908

A more reserved bust of Liberty than on the previous type faces left, and the broad ribbon around her head has been reduced to something more like a coronet. The reverse motifs are the same: an eagle with its wings spread and a shield on its breast. The type of 1839–1866 has no motto above the eagle, but from 1866 to 1908 the motto on a ribbon, as shown on the earlier bust designs, was restored.

No Motto above Eagle

Motto above Eagle

	GSID	VF-20	EF-40	AU-50	AU-58	MS-60	MS-63
No Motto above Eagle, 1839–1866	72382	$775	$900	$950	$1,300	$1,500	$5,250
Motto above Eagle, 1866–1908	72383	725	725	725	725	750	825

Indian Head, 1908–1929

The obverse design, a profile portrait of a Native American man in a feathered headdress, is incused into the coin rather than in relief above the surface. The incused reverse design is a large eagle, perched with its wings closed against its body.

	GSID	VF-20	EF-40	AU-50	AU-58	MS-60	MS-63
1908–1929	72384	$750	$775	$800	$800	$800	$1,100

EAGLES

The American $10 gold coin is called an eagle. Coins of this denomination were first made in 1795 and continued to be produced through 1933. Early dates are all scarce, but later issues, especially those in circulated grades, are still available in rather large quantities. The early types are similar to the quarter and half eagles.

Capped Bust to Right, 1795–1804

A right-facing bust of Liberty, her hair flowing loose and a garment draped about her shoulders, wears a large conical cap reminiscent of a turban. Two reverse designs were produced. On the first, struck 1795–1797, a small eagle holds a wreath in its beak; the second, used from 1797 through 1804, features a heraldic eagle.

Small Eagle Reverse

Heraldic Eagle Reverse

	GSID	F-12	VF-20	EF-40	AU-50	AU-58	MS-60	MS-63
Small Eagle, 1795–1797	72385	$32,400	$39,600	$64,800	$79,200	$132,000	$139,200	$388,800
Heraldic Eagle, 1797–1804	72386	11,250	12,250	16,200	19,200	27,000	30,000	60,000

Liberty Head, 1838–1907

On the obverse, Liberty faces left, her hair pulled up and a coronet reading LIBERTY on her head. The reverse depicts an eagle with its wings spread and a shield on its breast. Above the eagle's head, from 1838 through 1865, there is no motto; from 1867 to 1907, a ribbon above its head reads IN GOD WE TRUST. Both types were struck in 1866.

No Motto above Eagle

Motto above Eagle

	GSID	VF-20	EF-40	AU-50	AU-58	MS-60	MS-63
No Motto above Eagle, 1838–1866	72388	$1,475	$1,525	$1,600	$2,125	$3,750	$19,200
Motto above Eagle, 1866–1907	72389	1,425	1,425	1,425	1,425	1,425	1,725

Indian Head, 1907–1933

The Indian Head motif on the obverse of the $10 coin is quite different from that on the smaller gold denominations of the era: the design is in relief rather than incused, and it features a left-facing head of Liberty with an elaborate feathered war bonnet. The reverse design is similar to that of the other Indian Head denominations—an eagle perched to the left with its wings folded against its body—but again, the elements are in relief rather than incused. The earliest coins have an empty field to the left of the eagle, but starting in 1908, the motto IN GOD WE TRUST is seen in that location. Coins of 1933 are very rare.

No Motto on Reverse

Motto on Reverse

	GSID	VF-20	EF-40	AU-50	AU-58	MS-60	MS-63
No Motto, 1907–1908	72391	$1,450	$1,475	$1,500	$1,500	$1,550	$2,550
With Motto, 1908–1933	72392	1,425	1,450	1,450	1,450	1,475	1,800

Double Eagles

The double eagle is the largest-denomination coin made for general circulation in the United States. Production started in 1849 (a pattern coin) and continued until 1933. There are several rare dates in this series, including the last year of coinage, which was never officially released for circulation. The Saint-Gaudens type is especially treasured by many for its artistic beauty.

Liberty Head, 1850–1907

A simple head of Liberty faces left, wearing a coronet bearing the word LIBERTY. The reverse shows a heraldic eagle. The coin is seen in three major types:

- No Motto above Eagle (1849–1866);
- Motto above Eagle, Value TWENTY D. (1866–1876); and
- Motto above Eagle, Value TWENTY DOLLARS (1877–1907).

No Motto above Eagle

Motto; Value TWENTY D.

Motto; Value TWENTY DOLLARS

	GSID	VF-20	EF-40	AU-50	AU-58	MS-60	MS-63
No Motto above Eagle, 1849–1866	72393	$2,850	$2,975	$3,100	$3,325	$3,875	$7,250
Motto above Eagle, 1866–1907							
Value TWENTY D., 1866–1876	72394	2,800	2,825	2,850	2,975	2,975	6,500
Value TWENTY DOLLARS, 1877–1907	73520	2,800	2,800	2,800	2,800	2,800	2,900

Saint-Gaudens, 1907–1933

On the obverse, Liberty strides over a peak toward the viewer with raised arms, a torch in her right hand and a laurel branch in her left. The sun's rays are in the background, with the U.S. Capitol below and behind Liberty on the left. On the reverse, an eagle in profile flies leftward above a rising sun.

The first year of production, 1907, the coin was briefly issued with a high-relief design and the date in roman numerals (MCMVII). When the relief proved unworkable for mass production, it was lowered, and the date was changed to 1907 (and it remained in arabic numerals for the remainder of the series). No motto was present in 1907 and part of 1908, but later in 1908 IN GOD WE TRUST was added at the curve of the sun on the reverse.

High Relief, Roman-Numeral Date

Normal Relief, Arabic-Numeral Date

No Motto on Reverse

Motto on Reverse

	GSID	VF-20	EF-40	AU-50	AU-58	MS-60	MS-63
High Relief, Roman-Numeral Date (MCMVII), 1907	72395	$9,750	$11,000	$12,000	$13,800	$15,350	$26,400
Normal Relief, Arabic-Numeral Date, 1907–1933							
No Motto, 1907–1908	72396	2,800	2,800	2,800	2,800	2,800	2,900
With Motto, 1908–1933	72397	2,800	2,800	2,800	2,800	2,800	2,900

UNITED STATES OF AMERICA
IN GOD WE TRUST
HALF DOLLAR

Chapter 9

COMMEMORATIVE, BULLION, AND SPECIAL COINS

Commemorative coins have been popular since the days of the ancient Greeks and Romans. In the beginning they served to record and honor important events, and in the absence of newspapers they proved highly useful in passing along news of the day. Many modern nations have issued commemorative coins and such pieces are highly esteemed by collectors. Yet no nation has surpassed our own country when it comes to commemorative coins, and in this we have reason to be proud.

This ancient Roman bronze coin proclaims the prowess of Emperor Nero by depicting him dressed as Apollo playing the lyre. Folklore holds that he played while Rome was burning.

In the United States conventional commemorative coins are not made for general use in circulation. They are made in limited quantities, and are usually only seen or bought by collectors. On those few occasions when commemorative coins were made for general use, they have been extremely popular. The Washington quarter of 1932 and the Lincoln cent of 1909 were both originally intended to be commemorative coins but were continued on as a regular issue because of public demand. In 1976 special designs were issued on the quarter, half dollar, and dollar coins to celebrate the bicentennial of the birth of the nation. The 50 State quarters of 1999 through 2008, and later issues honoring national sites and presidents, are circulating commemoratives that have become extremely popular with collectors and the general public.

The unique position occupied by commemoratives in United States coinage is due largely to the fact that most commemorative coins have real historical significance. The progress and advancement of people in the New World are presented in an interesting and instructive manner on our commemorative issues. The long record of achievements that is so artistically presented on our gold and silver memorial issues appeals strongly to the collectors who favor the artistic side of numismatics. It is the historical features of the commemorative themes that create interest among many people who would otherwise have little interest in coins.

National Park Service Ranger Rivka Zuares shows the obverse design of the 2016 National Park Service 100th Anniversary commemorative $5 gold coin, during an unveiling ceremony on November 19, 2015.

New commemorative issues are recommended for coinage by two committees of Congress—the Committee on Banking, Housing and Urban Affairs, of the Senate, and the Financial Services Committee, of the House of Representatives. The Citizens Coinage Advisory Committee (www.CCAC.gov)

provides additional consideration for the appropriateness of themes and designs, and advises the secretary of the Treasury with formal recommendations, as does the U.S. Commission of Fine Arts (www.CFA.gov). Congress is guided to a great extent by the reports of these committees when passing upon bills authorizing commemorative coins.

These special coins are usually issued either to commemorate events or to help pay for monuments or celebrations that commemorate historical persons, places, or things. In most instances, commemorative coins are offered for sale by the United States Mint and the commission in charge of the event being commemorated. They are always sold at a price above the face value of the piece. All are of the standard weight and fineness of traditional gold and silver coins, and all are legal tender at the stated face value.

Commemorative coins are popularly collected either by major types or in sets with mintmark varieties. In many years no special commemorative coins were issued, and in others there have been as many as a dozen. Recent commemorative coin programs have been limited to no more than two per year, although each program may consist of multiple coins.

Those coins made prior to 1982 are considered the Classic Series, and high-quality brilliant Uncirculated pieces are worth much more than the usual low-grade circulated coins that are often dull, cleaned, or blemished by contact marks.

Very few sets of the Panama-Pacific commemorative coins were packaged and sold in special copper and glass frames when the coins were released in 1915 at the International Exposition celebrating the completion of the Panama Canal. The current value of such a set in choice condition would be in excess of $500,000.

Proof coins in the early series are extremely rare. Starting in 1982 the government began making both Uncirculated and Proof coins for each design and these coins are all issued in protective holders and cases.

Few people would ever guess, or even believe, that this country once issued an official half dollar bearing the portrait of P.T. Barnum, the famous showman credited with saying "There's a sucker born every minute." He probably never actually said that, and he had nothing to do with the coins that were made in 1936, long after his death. Still, it was an exceptional honor, and the fact that the fifty-cent coins were sold to the public for $2 each would have made him smile about bilking the public one more time.

The Bridgeport commemorative half dollar of 1936 has a portrait of the great showman P.T. Barnum.

Barnum did not have the last laugh in this matter. People who were fortunate enough to buy one of the original coins in 1936, and who saved it in perfect condition, find that their treasure is worth more than $100 today. Only 25,000 of the pieces were made, and at the time they were not very popular even with the few people who heard about them.

The Bridgeport commemorative half dollar with P.T. Barnum's portrait is but one of the many different designs that have been used on special coins made for collectors since 1892. Commemorative coins have been issued to

In 2016 American writer and humorist Mark Twain was honored on a silver dollar and a $5 gold coin.

celebrate the founding of cities, mark expositions, honor famous citizens and presidents, and, in recent years, promote the Olympics. These coins are not placed in circulation and are usually distributed at prices well over face value with the surcharge going to fund the event being celebrated.

Only in recent years has the general public become interested in commemorative coins. They have long been popular with coin collectors, who enjoy the artistry and history associated with them as well as the profits they have made from owning these scarce pieces. Very few ever reach circulation because they were all originally sold above face value and because they are all so scarce. Most early issues were of the half dollar denomination, and they were usually made in quantities of fewer than 20,000 pieces. This is miniscule when compared to the regular half dollar pieces, which are made by the millions each year.

The modern series of commemorative issues, made from 1982 to the present, have never been as popular with collectors as the Classic pieces. They have been produced in far greater quantities, with far more designs and at issue prices that exceed anything in the past. It is often possible to buy modern commemorative coins from coin dealers at prices that are lower than the original cost when sold by the Mint. The initial surcharge on each of these coins, which went to the sponsoring agency to fund their designated projects, is responsible for making the initial cost higher than many collectors are willing to pay. Many of the modern issues are bought as gifts to be passed on to others.

Some themes celebrated on modern commemoratives have also been criticized by collectors as being inappropriate. Take, for instance, the 1991 half dollar commemorating the 38th anniversary of the Korean War. Critics point out that this is a contrived anniversary to celebrate and that it was chosen merely as a vehicle to raise funds for a proposed memorial. Another dollar coin made in 1991 was widely criticized for commemorating the United Service Organizations (USO), and other coins made for the 50th anniversary of World War II were, through some unknown logic, produced in 1993, either before, or after, any anniversary. For these and other reasons there has been a general resistance to collecting some of these coins as a complete series.

It is sometimes difficult to locate sales outlets where modern commemorative coins are sold by the authorizing agency, but during the time of issue, they are always available by direct order from the United States Mint. The Mint also maintains a mailing list that is used to advise customers of new issues and through which commemoratives may be purchased. Contact the United States Mint, Customer Service Center, 1-800-USA-MINT (872-6468), or visit their website at www.usmint.gov.

Packaging for the 1986 Statue of Liberty half dollar.

Historically, the entire series of commemorative coins has frequently undergone a roller-coaster cycle of price adjustments. Those cycles have usually been of relatively short duration, lasting from months to a few years. When prices go down, they usually recover in time, and often exceed previous levels.

Following is a list of some of the more popular and colorful commemorative coins that have been issued since the programs began in 1892. There are many other different types—far too many to list here. For a complete listing, see the *Guide Book of United States Coins.*

Values shown are prices generally paid by coin dealers when these items in basic Uncirculated condition are wanted.

Classic Commemorative Coins, 1892–1954

1892 and 1893 World's Columbian Exposition 50¢. This was the first U.S. commemorative coin ever issued. Its popular theme and ready availability keep it in constant collector demand. A few were placed in circulation after the event. $18.

1893 Isabella 25¢. Always popular, this U.S. coin is one of the few showing a woman, and is the only quarter dollar in the entire series. $275.

1918 Illinois Centennial 50¢. Abraham Lincoln is shown here in a lifelike portrait on the popular Illinois centennial coin that honors him. $125.

1900 Lafayette dollar. The only silver dollar coin in the original series of commemorative coins honors a great hero of the Revolutionary War. $750.

1915-S Panama-Pacific International Exposition 50¢. A set of silver and gold commemorative coins was made to mark the 1915 exposition held in San Francisco. These included a gold dollar, a quarter eagle, and two $50 coins (today worth $50,000 each) as well as the half dollar (worth $500).

1925 California Diamond Jubilee 50¢. The beautiful design on this piece shows a forty-niner on one side and a bear, the state emblem, on the other. $125.

1928 Hawaiian Sesquicentennial 50¢.
One of the scarcest and most popular commemoratives. $1,500.

1927 Vermont Sesquicentennial 50¢. This coin was issued on the 150th anniversary of the Battle of Bennington and the independence of Vermont. $200.

1951–1954 Carver/Washington 50¢. An early commemoration of two prominent black Americans. $10.

Modern Commemorative Coins, 1982 to Date

Values are prices paid by coin dealers for coins in original Mint packaging.

1982 George Washington 250th Anniversary of Birth 50¢. The first and still one of the most popular of the new series of commemorative coins. $9.

1986 Statue of Liberty Centennial $1. Money raised from sales of these coins went to refurbish the statue. $12.

1988 Seoul Olympiad Gold $5. This piece is considered to be one of the most attractive of the modern issues. $500.

1992 Christopher Columbus Quincentenary 50¢.
The landing of Columbus was again remembered in this issue. $6.

1995 Centennial of Olympic Games 50¢. Numerous designs were used on 50¢, $1, and $5 coins for the XXVI Olympiad held in Atlanta in 1996. $10.

1998 Black Revolutionary War Patriots $1. Honoring Crispus Attucks, and others who fought in the War of Independence. $30.

2000 Library of Congress Bicentennial gold-and-platinum $10. This most unusual coin combines two metals into one attractive design. $1,000.

2002 West Point Bicentennial $1. Honoring the bicentennial of the founding of the United States Military Academy at West Point. $20.

2014 National Baseball Hall of Fame 50¢. The obverse of this unusual coin is concave to simulate a baseball glove and the reverse is convex to simulate a baseball. $25.

Collecting Proof and Mint Sets

A Proof is a special specimen striking of coinage for presentation, souvenir, exhibition, or numismatic purposes. Pre-1968 Proof coins were made only at the Philadelphia Mint except in a few rare instances in which presentation pieces were struck at branch mints. Current Proofs are made at the San Francisco and West Point Mint facilities.

The term *Proof* refers to the method of manufacture, not the condition of a coin. Regular-production coins in Mint State have a flashing, frosty luster, soft details, and minor imperfections. A Proof coin can usually be distinguished by its sharpness of detail, high-wire edge, and extremely brilliant, mirror-like surface. All Proofs are originally sold by the Mint at a premium; none are ever placed in circulation at the time of issue. Very few Proofs were issued prior to 1856.

A Frosted Proof half dollar of 1898, with brightly reflective fields and frosted design devices (e.g., the head of Miss Liberty).

A Matte Proof 1914 Buffalo nickel (shown enlarged).

A modern Brilliant Proof half dollar, with consistently mirror-like surfaces (fields as well as design elements).

Frosted Proofs were issued prior to 1936, and then again starting in the late 1970s. These have a brilliant mirror-like field with contrasting dull or frosted design.

Matte Proofs have a granular "sandblasted" surface instead of the mirror finish. Matte Proof cents, nickels, and gold coins were issued from 1908 to 1916; a few 1921 and 1922 silver dollars were also struck in this manner.

Brilliant Proofs have been issued from 1936 to the present. These have a uniformly brilliant mirror-like surface and sharp, high-relief details.

The Mint occasionally makes other variations (such as Reverse Proofs, which have brilliant details on a frosted background) as special collector items.

Prooflike coins are occasionally seen. These are specimens from the first few impressions of regular coinage dies from any mint. They are not true Proofs, but may have most of the characteristics of a Proof coin and generally command a premium. Collectors should be wary of coins that have been buffed to look like Proofs. High magnification will reveal polishing lines and lack of detail on those coins.

A 2024-S Silver Proof Set, with the half dollar, dime, and five quarter dollars in 99.9% fine silver. The Mint calls the transparent holder a "lens."

Proof coins are made from selected dies that have been inspected for perfection and are highly polished and cleaned. They are again wiped clean or polished after every 15 to 25 impressions and are replaced frequently to avoid imperfections from worn dies. Coinage blanks are polished and cleaned to assure high quality in striking. Older Proofs were hand-fed into the coinage press one at a time, each blank receiving two or more blows from the dies to bring up sharp, high-relief details. The coinage operation today is much more efficient because of special equipment but is still done at slow speed with extra pressure. Finished

Proofs are individually inspected and are handled by gloves or tongs. They also receive a final inspection by packers before being sonically vacuum-sealed in special plastic cases.

After a lapse of 20 years, Proof coins were struck at the Philadelphia Mint from 1936 to 1942 inclusive. In 1942, when the composition of the five-cent piece was changed from copper-nickel to a silver alloy, there were two types of this denomination available to collectors. The striking of Proof coins was temporarily suspended from 1943 to 1949, and again from 1965 to 1967; during the latter period special Mint sets were made. Proof sets were resumed in 1968 and continued thereafter.

Prior to 1950 Proof coins were sold individually by the Mint. All issues since that time have been sold as sets in special packages. Proof coins made from 1936 through 1972 include the cent, nickel, dime, quarter, and half dollar. From 1973 through 1981 the dollar coin was also included. Regular Proof sets issued from 1982 to 1998 contain the cent through half dollar; thereafter, some sets include the State quarters and the dollar coins. Special sets containing commemorative coins or other issues are also sold at a premium.

Collecting annual sets of Proof coins is a popular way to acquire choice examples of each year's coinage. Proof sets are also widely used as gifts and presents to friends and beginning collectors. When storing them, be sure that they remain safely in their original packaging and away from excessive heat and humidity. Proof sets are available for purchase directly from the Mint only during the year of issue. Sales information about Proof sets and Mint sets may be obtained from the United States Mint at www.USMint.gov or 1-800-USA-MINT (872-6468).

Uncirculated Mint Sets

Official United States Mint Sets are specially packaged sets of new coins that are made up by the government for sale to collectors. They contain Uncirculated specimens of one year's circulating coins for every denomination issued from each mint. Unlike the Proof sets, these are for the most part normal coins intended for general circulation, and were not always minted with any special consideration for quality. Sets issued from 2005 through 2010 have a special satin finish that is somewhat different than on normal circulation issues. In recent years, Mint Set coins have been made using specially prepared planchets (cleaned by a process informally known as *spalecking*, which tumbles them in a vat of cleaning slurry) and struck with slightly greater pressure than normal circulating coins.

Coins struck only as Proofs are not included in the Mint sets.

Uncirculated sets sold by the Treasury from 1947 through 1958 contained two examples of each regular-issue coin. These were packaged in cardboard holders that did not protect the coins from tarnish. Nicely preserved early sets generally command a substantial premium above their normal value. No official Mint sets were produced in 1950, 1982, or 1983.

Planchets, destined to be struck into coins for 2015 Uncirculated Mint sets, being cleaned in a Spaleck machine at the Denver Mint.

Since 1959, when packaging was changed to single sets, they have been sealed in a protective plastic envelope. In 1965, 1966, and 1967, Special Mint Sets of higher than normal quality were made as a substitute for Proof sets, which were not made during that period. The 1966 and 1967 sets were packaged in hard plastic holders. Privately assembled Mint sets and those produced for sale at the Philadelphia or Denver mints or for special occasions are valued according to the individual pieces they contain. Only the official government-sealed full sets are generally collected by those who save Uncirculated Mint sets, and those original sets are considered slightly more valuable than the individual coins, which are often broken out for use in date collections of each denomination.

Both Proof sets and Uncirculated Mint sets have a limited following by collectors. They seem to be purchased more often by the public and given as gifts to celebrate some special date or occasion. For this reason, the values of these sets have remained relatively low for many years. Prior to 2006 the government sold one to two million Uncirculated Mint sets each year, and that seem to be more than the coin-collecting market could absorb, so prices have remained low. In recent years sales have rarely exceeded a half million sets. They should not be ignored, however, as they may be relatively hard to find in the future when they could be the only source for choice collectible coins.

BULLION GOLD, PLATINUM, AND SILVER COINS

United States bullion coins are unlike regular issues because they are not made for circulation and are not sold to the public at face value. They are intended solely for sale to investors, speculators, and collectors, and are sold by the government at a substantial premium above the denomination assigned to them. They are made in response to a demand for gold and silver in a convenient form that can be saved by those who see this as a hedge against inflation, and a safe haven for stored wealth. U.S. bullion coins have been made since 1986 to compete with similar issues of other nations.

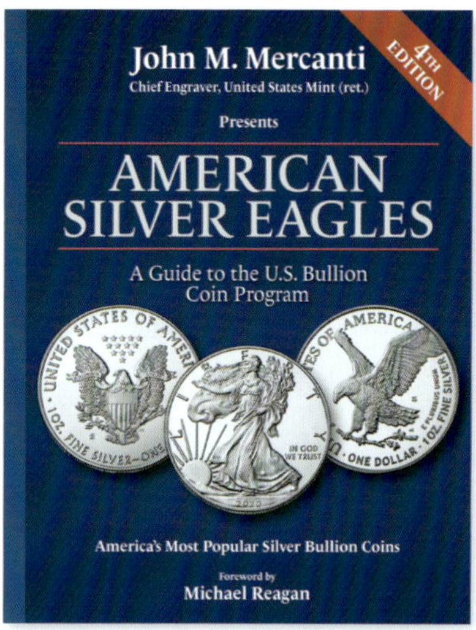

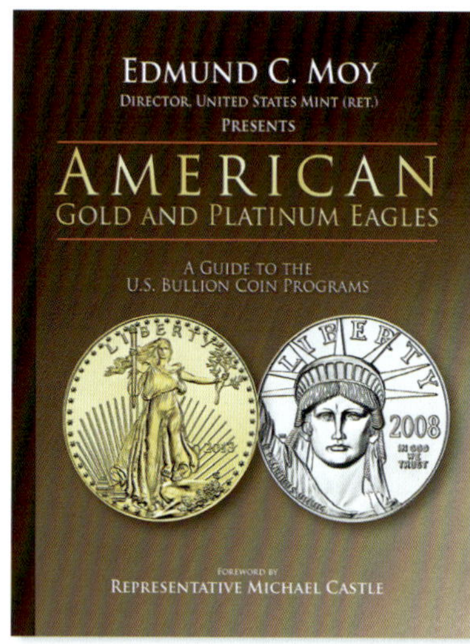

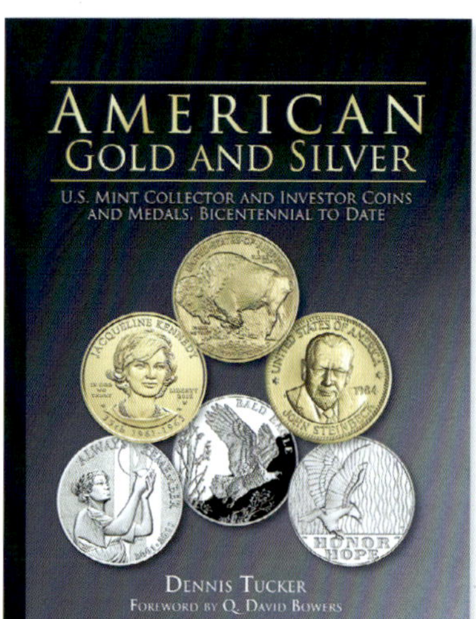

The United States' bullion programs are explored in detail by Edmund Moy, John Mercanti, Miles Standish, and Dennis Tucker in these standard references. Moy, Mercanti, and Standish cover the American Eagle coins in silver, gold, and platinum. Tucker covers "everything else," including the American Buffalo 24-karat gold coins, First Spouse gold coins, America the Beautiful five-ounce silver coins, and others.

Silver and gold bullion bars are made in many forms and sizes. They are used mostly for investment purposes, although some called art bars, are collected for their attractive designs. Perhaps the most coveted collectible bars are those made by United States mints in the past century as a convenient way of storing or transporting precious metal.

The American Silver Eagle is a one-ounce bullion coin with a face value of one dollar. The obverse has Adolph Weinman's Liberty Walking design, which was first used on the half dollar coins made from 1916 through 1947. The reverse design is a rendition by John Mercanti of the U.S. heraldic eagle. These coins are legal tender for the stated face value, but are only sold at a price commensurate with the fluctuating spot price of silver. Each coin contains exactly one ounce of pure silver.

An American Silver Eagle.

Former Whitman publisher Dennis Tucker examines stacks of American Silver Eagle planchets in the West Point Mint. Production Manager Jennifer Butkus and Deputy Superintendent Tom DiNardi are in the background.

Freshly struck American Silver Eagles at the West Point Mint, May 2014.

The American Gold Eagle bullion coins are made in four denominations that contain one ounce ($50), one-half ounce ($25), one-quarter ounce ($10), or one-tenth ounce ($5) of pure gold. The obverse features a modified rendition of the Augustus Saint-Gaudens design that was originally used on the U.S. $20 gold pieces from 1907 until 1933. The reverse displays a family of eagles motif by sculptor Miley Busiek.

Bullion-strike American Gold Eagles are not sold directly to the general public, but to a group of authorized buyers. These buyers obtain the bullion coins from the Mint based on the current spot price of the metal plus a small premium. The coins are then sold to secondary distributors for sale to other dealers and the public. Proof and Burnished (called Uncirculated by the Mint) versions of the gold Eagles are available during the year of issue directly from the Mint for sale to the public.

An American Gold Eagle.

The American Platinum Eagle coins are also made in four denominations and sizes, but they are different from the gold coins. The one-ounce platinum coin has a $100 denomination, one-half ounce is $50, one-quarter ounce is $25, and the one-tenth ounce denomination is $10.

An American Platinum Eagle.

Several other bullion coins are closely related to traditional numismatic items and include five-ounce silver pieces with designs similar to the America the Beautiful quarters; several denominations of gold coins mimicking the Buffalo nickel design; a $20 gold piece with the Saint-Gaudens design; a series of $10 gold coins honoring all of the nation's First Ladies; and high-relief gold coins with modern representations of Miss Liberty.

Bullion coins cannot be redeemed at a bank like other U.S. currency, but must be bought and sold through dealers. Most professional coin dealers handle bullion transactions at a small margin of profit that is based on supply and demand.

An American Buffalo 24-karat gold coin in Proof format.

The 2009 Ultra High Relief $20 gold coin in its Mint packaging.

A First Spouse gold coin. Each coin in the series weighs one-half ounce.

The 2015 and 2017 American Liberty High Relief gold coins.

ANTONIO WAYNE DUCI EXERCITUS
GATTEAUX.
COMITIA AMERICANA

Chapter 10

Oddities, Counterfeits, and Other Coins

When exploring the wonderful world of numismatics, you are bound to run into items that do not seem to fit into any of the normal categories for United States or even foreign coins. These can be exciting things to investigate because there is no telling what they may turn out to be. First, you must determine if they are actually coins, or if they might be tokens or medals. Remember that true coins always contain the name of the issuing country, the date, and (usually) a denomination, while tokens, chits, and privately made coins do not. Medals may look like commemorative coins, but they, too, can be identified by their lack of the three basic elements of an official coin.

Sometimes a questionable piece meets all the criteria for a coin but still does not look quite right. Perhaps it is not listed in any of the standard catalogs, or it has a mintmark or date that should not exist. These are all clues that something is amiss. The chance of finding a new coin that has escaped the attention of all collectors in the past is almost nil. There should be an explanation for every coin that you locate. If you cannot classify a problem coin after exhausting your resources, then it is time for you to consult with a more experienced collector or dealer.

Coins are not always what they seem. This silver 50 centavos coin (shown enlarged) says UNITED STATES OF AMERICA on it, but it was made for use in the Philippine Islands at a time when they were under American sovereignty. Also pictured: Philippines senator (and later president) Manuel Quezon.

Among its thousands of reference books, the library of the American Numismatic Association has information on just about every kind of coin, medal, or token ever made. Members may borrow books, and sometimes a knotty question can be quickly clarified over the telephone or by email (719-482-9821, or library@money.org) or through the use of a specialized reference. More often than not, the answer to a problem coin may be that it is not a coin at all, but rather a medal or something that just looks like a coin. In the worst-case scenario, it may be counterfeit. Such things do exist and show up more often than anyone would like. To protect yourself you should learn how to spot one.

The American Numismatic Association's lending library provides research facilities to its members, including thousands of reference books, catalogs, and Internet access.

A Closer Look at Counterfeits

Have you ever seen a counterfeit coin? Probably not. They are unusual in circulation, and quite rare even in numismatic circles. If you ever got stuck with one you would remember it forever. Not only might there be legal problems with owning one, but you could also be out whatever money the bogus item cost you. Fortunately for collectors there are ways to detect counterfeit coins, and no self-respecting dealer would ever knowingly sell a bad coin to a customer. Even better, if a mistake is ever made, it's up to the seller to refund the buyer's money. Everyone takes great pride in keeping the coin market as free from fakes as possible. Unfortunately, they still creep in, mostly from foreign channels, and cannot be ignored.

There are many kinds of false coins. The ones we hear most about are the street counterfeits that are made to fool the public. Today, with prices being what they are, counterfeiters are making mostly paper money, usually in high denominations. That is the easy way to go because of imaging and computer technology, but in the past there were many low-denomination and gold counterfeit coins in circulation. Those kinds of fakes would not fool any seasoned dealer or collector because they are usually too amateurish to deceive anyone who takes a close look at them.

If you receive a counterfeit coin or bill in change, you should turn it in to the Secret Service (www.SecretService.gov). You can contact them through your police department or perhaps a local bank. Unfortunately, the person with a counterfeit coin in his or her possession has to take the loss. Never try to pass such a piece on to anyone else. The penalties for passing counterfeits are severe. Chances are that you will never encounter one, but if you do, and if you cannot return it to where you received it, then it is your civic duty to turn it in and take your loss. This is especially true of paper money. Saving a single fake coin for your collection is not considered an offense. In over 50 years of carefully looking for such things, I have only received one fake coin in change: a lead dime. The odds of seeing a circulating counterfeit, especially a coin, are slim.

The kinds of fakes that are troublesome are the numismatic copies made to deceive collectors. These are made to pass even the most careful inspection. Sometimes even the experts cannot immediately tell if such coins are real or not. Over the past 20 years the art of making false coins has reached new heights of technical excellence. Many of these are made in China and exported to this country, where they often appear for sale on the Internet. Fortunately for all of us, the art of detecting them has advanced rapidly and the professional grading and authentication services reject them as soon as they appear. Whether by luck, skill, or providence, counterfeit detection has managed to keep ahead of the fakers, and there are no dire threats to the integrity of numismatic collecting.

A deceptive counterfeit Morgan dollar.

In 2017 the nonprofit Industry Council for Tangible Assets (www.ictaonline.org) formed an anti-counterfeiting task force directed by hobby advocate and former *Coin World* editor-in-chief Beth Deisher. It focuses on law enforcement, networking, education, research, packaging security, transport and storage security, laws and regulations, and related topics.

Keeping ahead of the scoundrels who make copies of rare coins is a job that is taken seriously by all dedicated dealers. It is probably safe to say that most professionals could not be easily fooled by a bad coin. They are experienced experts who carefully screen every purchase to be sure that each coin is genuine. When you buy a coin from a reputable source, you can be pretty sure that it will be genuine.

Sometime around 1954 a clever counterfeiter made reasonably good copies of nickels dated 1939, 1944, 1946, 1947, and 1953. Posing as a canteen vendor operator, he deposited many of them in banks, and perhaps never would have been caught except for some sharp-eyed coin collectors who observed that the 1944 coins were made of the wrong metal and did not have the proper large-size mintmark over the building on the reverse. Thanks to their vigilance, the counterfeiter was caught and many of the coins confiscated before they ever reached circulation.

A difficult task that all authenticators face is determining the metal content of a coin or medal. This must be done using nondestructive methods, because by their very nature the items involved could be rare and valuable. It would be easy to test gold using a special acid, but that is not an option. A simple nondestructive method for establishing a coin's metal content is by studying its color. Most metals have a distinctive color and an experienced authenticator can tell quite accurately if a piece is made of gold, silver, copper, or platinum.

However, determining alloys, such as brass or bronze, by color alone can be extremely difficult, and cannot be relied upon for accuracy. It is also impossible to judge the fineness of gold or silver on the basis of color. Fortunately there are other nondestructive ways to determine those qualities, and sometimes whether or not a coin is genuine. A coin's magnetic properties can also provide clues to its metal content. For example, iron, steel, and pure nickel are easily detected with a magnet. Want to test a 1943 cent, which should be steel but appears to be copper, to see if it is really copper or just plated? Try a magnet. You will get a quick and accurate answer. A common steel cent will jump to the magnet, while a very rare and valuable copper 1943 cent will not be moved.

The more precise indicator of metal content is the specific-gravity test. Metals have varying densities that can be detected by weight per given volume. A specific-gravity test compares a metal's density to the density of an equal volume of water. The resulting value is referenced to a standard chart, which indicates specific gravity for particular metals or alloys. For instance, a cubic inch of pure silver weighs 10.55 times that of an equal volume of pure water. Some metals or alloys have a specific gravity that is very similar or even identical to that of others, such as copper (8.92) and nickel (8.90), but there the color difference can usually be relied upon to make the distinction.

Surface X-ray analysis is another way to determine the metal content of a coin, but the equipment is expensive and impractical. For most coins the use of a good quality 10+ magnifying glass will reveal all that is necessary to make a determination. If the suspected piece does not match a known genuine example, the chances are that it is bad and should be avoided. When buying expensive coins, it will pay to learn the basics of authentication on your own, but not everyone has the time or inclination. The next best thing is to buy coins only from reputable dealers—especially coins that have been certified and encapsulated—to avoid all possible mistakes.

Professional authentication of rare coins for a fee is available through the same agencies that perform grading services. All coins that are graded and encapsulated are automatically authenticated.

Alterations

Coins are occasionally altered by adding, removing, or changing a design feature (such as a mintmark or date digit); or by polishing, sandblasting, acid etching, toning, or plating the surface of a genuine piece. Changes of this sort are usually made to deceive collectors. Among U.S. gold coins, the 1927-D double eagle and 1911-D quarter eagle are commonly found with an added mintmark. On $2.50 and $5 gold coins dated 1839 to 1856, New Orleans "O" mintmarks have often been altered to "C" by hand engraving to imitate the mark of the rarer Charlotte, North Carolina, mint.

Over a century ago $5 gold pieces were imitated by gold-plating 1883 Liberty Head five-cent coins without the word CENTS on the reverse. Other coins that were fraudulently created by alteration include the 1799 large cent, and the 1909-S V.D.B., 1914-D, 1922 "Plain," and 1943 "copper" cents. The 1913 Liberty Head nickel has been extensively replicated by altering 1910 and 1912 nickels. Scarce, high-grade Denver and San Francisco Mint Buffalo nickels of the 1920s are often altered by adding a fake mintmark. False 1916-D dimes and 1932-D quarters have been made by altering genuine coins of other dates or adding a mintmark. Careful inspection usually reveals these deceptions, but caution is advised when purchasing any of these coins.

The Mint admitted that it made a mistake by not including any indication of the denomination on the first issue of five-cent coins made with a new design in 1883. The oversight was corrected later that same year, but not before some of the pieces were gold-plated or crudely colored and passed off as the very similar-looking $5 gold coins that were also in circulation at that time.

Detection

The best way to detect counterfeit coins is to compare suspected pieces with others of the same issue. Carefully check size, color, luster, weight, edge devices, and design details. Replicas generally have weaker details than their genuine counterparts when studied under magnification. Modern-struck counterfeits made to deceive collectors are sometimes an exception to this rule. Many Chinese counterfeit coins are extremely well made, and sometimes even presented in counterfeit certified slabs, holders, or albums. Any questionable coins should be referred to an expert or authorized certification service for verification. Any coin offered for sale by an unknown person or agency on the Internet should be subject to doubt.

An authentic 1858-S half dollar (left), and a crude Chinese counterfeit.

Casts

These are usually poorly made with "mushy" letters and details, and sometimes have an incorrect weight. Base metal is often used in place of gold or silver, so the false coins are lightweight and often incorrect in color and luster. Deceptive cast pieces have been made using proper metal content and modern dental techniques, but these, too, usually vary in quality and color. Detection of false coins sometimes involves comparative examination of the suspected areas of a coin (usually mintmarks and date digits) at magnification ranges from 10+ to 60+. Coins of exceptional rarity or value should never be purchased without a written guarantee of authenticity.

Forgeries

Many of the copies struck from false dies are of the rarer colonial and United States pieces, or of rare ancient gold and silver coins. Modern technology is now capable of reproducing very deceptive copies, and even some relatively common coins have entered the market from overseas sources. Most can be detected by anyone familiar with the original coins, because the weight of the forgeries is almost always incorrect. The lettering and design are usually slightly different than the genuine.

Electrotypes

The front and back of electrotype copies are made separately and then bonded together. They can often be recognized by the marks on their edges that show where the two sides were joined together. They are also usually of the wrong weight. As a rule electrotypes are not made to deceive collectors, but are often made as copies of very rare or unusual coins to serve for display purposes (in museums, for example) where originals cannot be obtained.

An electrotype from the Hermitage Museum in Saint Petersburg, Russia.

Restrikes

Restrikes are pieces made in a mint from the original dies but at a later period than the date on the coin. Among American coins there are restrikes of the dollars of 1801 to 1804 and the half cents of 1831, 1836, and 1840 to 1849. Restrikes do not command anywhere near the price of the originals. In modern times dies are destroyed at the end of each year. Restrikes are really not counterfeits, and are classified as a separate category. They are sometimes referred to as *novodels*.

Misstruck Coins and Error Pieces

With the production of millions of coins each year, it is natural that a few abnormal pieces escape inspection and are inadvertently released for circulation. Sometimes such coins are found in original bags or rolls of new coins. These are not considered regular issues because they were not made intentionally. They are all eagerly sought by collectors for the information they shed on minting techniques, and as a variation from normal date and mint series collecting. All mint error coins are interesting, scarce, and valuable because of their unique nature and often bizarre appearance.

Nearly every misstruck or error coin is different in some way, and prices generally vary from coin to coin. Despite their diversity, they may all be classified in general groups related to the kind of error or manufacturing malfunction involved. Collectors value these pieces according to the scarcity of each kind of error for each type of coin. Non-collectors usually view them as curios, and often believe that they must be worth a great deal of money because they look so strange. In reality, the value assigned to various types of errors by collectors and dealers reflects both supply and demand, and is based on recurring transactions between willing buyers and sellers.

The annually issued *Guide Book of United States Coins* gives retail pricing for many of the most popular types of misstrikes and error coins.

In 2002 the Mint initiated stricter inspection and quality controls in an effort to reduce the number of error coins entering circulation. Because of that, misstruck coins made since then are relatively scarce and often more valuable than similar errors of older years.

Minting mistakes sometimes happen even to rare-date coins, and it is always difficult to price such items. Often the price of those coins is considered to be less than for a perfect coin, or the same value as a common date with the same type of error.

Coins with minting imperfections must not be confused with ordinary coins that have been mutilated or damaged after leaving the mint. Examples of such pieces include coins that have been scratched, hammered, engraved, impressed, acid etched, holed, or plated by individuals to simulate something other than a normal coin. Those pieces generally have no numismatic value, and can only be considered as altered coins not suitable for a collection.

Among the most common minting errors are small clips, or missing pieces of metal caused during preparation of the blank planchet. Minor coins with these errors are generally valued at $1.50 to $5.00 each. The next most common oddity is a coin that has been struck off-center, and has only part of the design showing. Those coins are valued at about $3.00 to $20.00 each, depending on the date and denomination and how far off-center the design is.

An off-center Flying Eagle cent.

A clipped-planchet Liberty Head nickel.

Various off-center modern coins.

Blanks, or planchets, sometimes escape being fed into the coinage press and end up in rolls or bags along with finished coins. Values placed on blanks vary from $1.50 for cent size to as much as $300 for a silver-dollar piece.

Coins that have gone through the minting press twice and received two impressions from the dies are even scarcer and are more valuable, with some early types bringing as much as $500.

Overdate coins and *doubled dies* are other types of oddities that are of interest to many collectors. An overdate coin is one where the numbers of the date have been altered *in the die* and changed from one date to

Post-Mint Damage vs. Misstrikes and Mint Errors

Coins that are holed, scratched, or otherwise damaged after leaving the mint are generally considered uncollectible. They end up in dealers' junk boxes, sold as "culls" with little numismatic value.

This Eisenhower dollar offers an example of post-Mint damage (sometimes seen abbreviated as "PMD"). Somebody abraded its surface on purpose or by accident. Either way, this is not considered an error coin, and the damage destroys any numismatic value the coin had.

Numismatic historian Bob Evans discovered this 1855-S gold double eagle among the treasures of the SS *Central America*, a steamer that was shipwrecked in 1857. While conserving the coin Evans noticed that someone had scratched a pipe into Miss Liberty's mouth! Most hobbyists would consider this a damaged coin and would seek a more pristine example for their collection, but Evans notes the "charming" aspect that "contributes marvelously to the coin's history."

This 1807 dime (shown enlarged) would be worth hundreds of dollars if it hadn't been bent and damaged in circulation. These kinds of imperfections should not be confused with production errors that happen during minting.

Notches on this Buffalo nickel suggest it may have been used as a necklace pendant.

A double-struck State quarter.

another. This was a common practice in the early years of the Mint when dies were so costly that it was necessary to continue using them for production as long as possible. Many of the early large cents, like the 1807 Over 1806 variety, show traces of an older date that was changed to a new year.

The intentional practice of changing dates on dies was stopped at the turn of the twentieth century, when new equipment and techniques made it practical to replace old dies with new. All overdate coins of the twentieth century seem to have been made by error rather than by design. All of them are scarce, avidly collected, and valuable. Some examples are the 1918-D nickel with 8 over 7, the 1942 dime with 2 over 1, and the 1918-S quarter with 8 over 7. Don't expect to find any of these in your pocket change. They are all gone from circulation and are now valued at prices ranging from $200 to $2,000, depending on condition.

Traces of both dates can be seen on this 1807, 7 Over 6, cent.

The date on this 1942 dime was applied on top of the 1941 date in error, when dies were being made at the end of the year during wartime pressures. Unlike the early overdated pieces that were made to conserve metal, all twentieth-century overdate coins were probably made by accident.

Doubled-die coins are pieces made from dies that have been impressed two times with the master design slightly different positions. The result of this mishap is a die that shows a doubled image. All coins made from such a die also show the same doubled outline to all features such as the date, lettering, and sometimes even the main design. The degree and severity of doubling has much to do with the value of doubled-die coins. A coin like the famous

1955 doubled-die cent, where the date and obverse letters are noticeably shifted, is extremely popular and wholesale-valued around $800 for a Very Fine specimen.

The die that made this 1955 cent was impressed twice by the master hub, with one image slightly out of register. Every coin made from this die has a doubled image and is of great value to collectors who enjoy owning such oddities.

Other Interesting Areas to Collect

Collectors who want to extend their attention to other areas of numismatics can find a world of exciting items to explore. Take, for instance, the money that was used by the settlers of this country before the establishment of the United States Mint. The early coins of colonial America are all scarce today. Occasionally a specimen will turn up in an old family accumulation and perhaps start a collector on a quest for additional pieces. The early settlers used a great many foreign coins before they were able to make any money for themselves. In time, several of the states made their own coins each with a different state design. Each of these is an important part of American history and our national heritage.

A Massachusetts half cent from the 1780s. (shown enlarged)

Some collectors specialize in this series and collect even the most minor die varieties of the state coins in order to be able to trace the history of each piece. Numerous books have been written on this subject, and a collection of this nature might be considered the most sophisticated of all American collecting. The time and money involved in forming a specialized collection of colonial American coins are beyond the means of most collectors, but a type set of coins representing each period of colonial development, or from some of the individual states, is not an impossibility and presents an exciting challenge.

Massachusetts was the first British American colony to issue coins. Their silver pieces were dated 1652, some say to make the king believe that it was a very small one-year issue, while the coinage actually continued off and on for more than 30 years. Making these coins in defiance of British sovereignty was, in effect, the first declaration of independence for this country. (shown enlarged)

Another highly specialized field of collecting is that of foreign and ancient coins. It is always a pleasure to show interesting coins to friends, and a few ancient coins in a collection will add greatly to the story of history and art that can be told by such a collection. Common Roman coins can still be purchased for under $20 each. Larger and more attractive ancient Greek coins are also available and well within the means of many collectors, but because of their superior style and attractiveness, they are more eagerly sought and generally costlier than Roman coins.

Small Roman bronze coins like these of Emperor Crispus (AD 317–326), and Constantine II (AD 337–340), are often available to collectors in Fine condition for prices under $20.

Minor Greek bronze coins that saw use in daily transactions throughout the ancient world are also readily available in worn condition, although quite scarce in higher grade. They are available at modest prices because of a lack of interest by most collectors. Curiously enough, the large silver coins saw little circulation and were mainly hoarded as a reserve of wealth. It was the bronze coins that were the circulating money of their time, and they deserve more consideration by collectors today. With diligent searching a collector can form quite an impressive collection of interesting Greek and Roman coins. The cost of such a collection would ultimately be no more than that of a carefully formed set of United States coins. The knowledge and pleasure gained from forming such a collection might far outweigh that of a comparable United States collection.

Foreign coins represent another very popular facet of numismatics. In this area a collector has a choice of forming many different types of collections. Some prefer to collect one coin or each date from as many foreign countries as possible. Others like to accumulate a type collection of each different issue from one or every country. Still others specialize in collecting coins of one denomination or size from each country, and occasionally a collector attempts to collect all foreign coins by date and mint. Normally a collector of foreign coins simply tries to accumulate as many different pieces as possible. As such a collection grows it is often possible to form topical groups of coins depicting birds, animals, ships, famous people, and so forth.

This attractive silver thaler from Austria (showing Empress Maria Theresa) was first minted in 1780 and because of its popularity as a trade coin it continued to be made up to the present with the same date and design. Uncirculated specimens can still be purchased for little over silver melt value.

Coins of Canada are the most popular foreign coins for American collectors, followed by the coins of England and Mexico. The popularity of these foreign coins is largely due to their availability and the fact that they are easily attributed. Many European coins are available, particularly those which were brought back to this country in large quantities by servicemen during the two world wars. Coins of other countries are equally interesting, but some with inscriptions in Arabic, Chinese, or Japanese are undecipherable to the average American collector, and are not so eagerly collected. A well-rounded collection will eventually contain at least a few from all of the different categories of numismatic items.

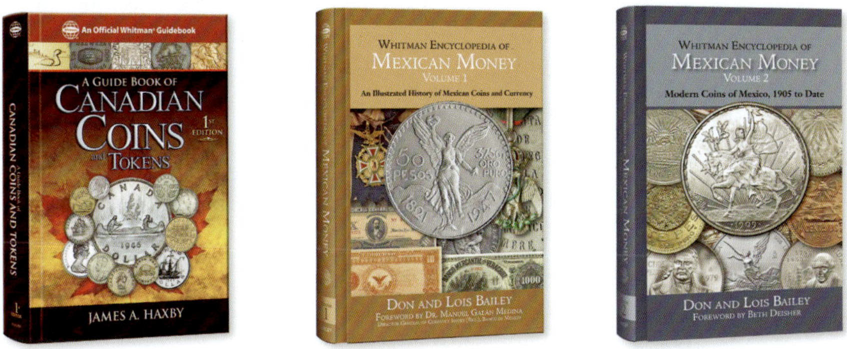

Canadian and Mexican coins are among the more popular non-U.S. collectibles.

PATTERN COINS

In addition to the traditional designs that have been used on United States coins, there have been many experimental pieces that never made it into circulation. Whenever a new design or change is considered for our coins the Mint necessarily first produces trial pieces to evaluate the design or coinability of the proposal. These experimental pieces are called pattern coins. They are never placed in circulation and rarely seen by anyone outside of government circles, but in the past specimens were given to interested parties and even sold to collectors. Despite the cost and general unavailability of these pieces, they are eagerly sought by numismatists.

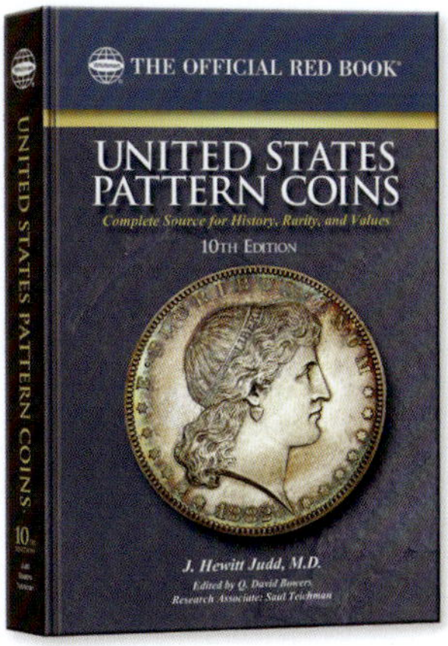

Dr. J. Hewitt Judd wrote a guide to U.S. pattern coins. It illustrates hundreds of beautiful and unusual designs.

Pattern coins are the caviar of United States coins. All are rare and valuable examples of designs that were never accepted for production. Some of the designs are arguably more artistic than those that have been used for circulation, and a study of pattern coins reveals much about the history of styles and artistry of this country.

"What might have been"—various U.S. pattern designs that never made their way to circulating coinage.

TOKENS

During the Civil War there was a shortage of small change, and many merchants were forced to coin their own tokens to accommodate customers. Those Civil War tokens are generally divided into two categories: political tokens, which depicted national heroes or patriotic slogans, and merchants' cards, which carry an advertisement of the firm that issued them. Most Civil War tokens are dated from 1861 to 1864, are about the size of our current cents, and were made of copper or brass.

Civil War tokens were used extensively during the Civil War coin shortage. (shown enlarged)

A variety of other privately issued tokens have also been made during past years. A particularly large group of them occurred during the coin shortage of 1834 to 1841. These are generally referred to as Hard Times tokens. They bear both political and business-related themes. Most are slightly smaller than the old large copper cents. Examples of both the Civil War tokens and the Hard Times tokens are readily available. Prices paid by coin dealers vary according to the popularity and rarity of each piece, but are generally in the range of $6 to $12 for Very Fine specimens.

Hard Times tokens, shown enlarged.

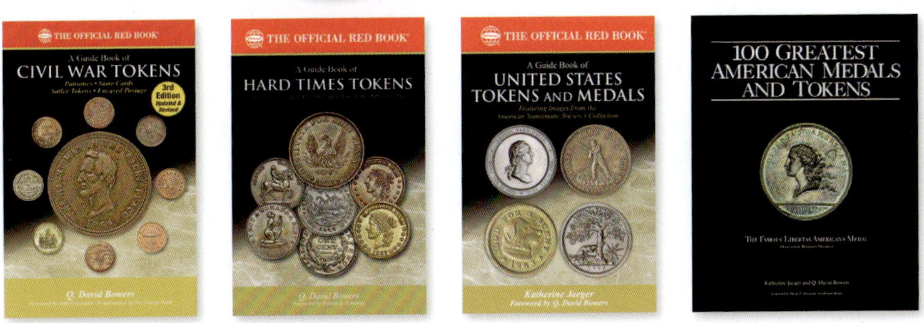

Many entertaining and informative books have been written about American tokens and medals.

Wooden nickels, elongated coins, and other novelties also fall into the category of privately issued tokens and form an interesting part of some collections. These are souvenir tokens made to commemorate special events, and while they rarely have any lofty numismatic value, they are colorful and interesting. Other private tokens that are even more avidly collected are the gaming chips and "coins" used in gambling casinos throughout the country. Tokens, medals, and game counters also form a part of numismatics, and while some collectors specialize in these fields, they are generally considered an offshoot of the basic hobby.

1882
LIBERTY
PLURIBUS

Appendix

Gallery of Actual Coin Sizes

In the early decades of the United States Mint, the diameters of American coins were changed from time to time. The sizes of United States coins have been standardized since the 1830s (or 1840s for silver dollars and some gold coins). Coin types today have uniform diameters for each denomination.

Comparing your coins to the illustrations in this gallery is one way to check their authenticity.

Half Cents and Large Cents

Half cents from 1793 through the 1830s varied (from type to type) from 22 mm to 23.5 mm. Starting with the Braided Hair type in 1840, half cents measured 23 mm in diameter until the end of the denomination in 1857.

From 1793 into the early 1830s, the Mint occasionally altered the diameter of copper large cents, with the coins measuring 26 mm in the early years and increasing to 29 mm. Among certain types, the diameter could vary slightly (by a millimeter or so) even from coin to coin. Starting with the modified Matron Head type in 1835, large cents were standardized at 27.5 mm.

Braided Hair half cent, 23 mm.

Braided Hair large cent, 27.5 mm.

Indian Head cent, 19 mm.

Small Cents

Since the Flying Eagle cent debuted in 1856, all types of this denomination have uniformly measured 19 mm in diameter.

Two-cent piece, 23 mm.

Two-Cent Pieces

All two-cent pieces measure 23 mm in diameter.

Silver three-cent piece, 14 mm.

Three-Cent Pieces

All *silver* three-cent pieces (trimes) measure 14 mm in diameter. All *nickel* three-cent pieces measure 17.9 mm in diameter.

Nickel three-cent piece, 17.9 mm.

Shield nickel, 20.5 mm.

Nickel Five-Cent Pieces

The Shield nickel, introduced in 1866, measured 20.5 mm in diameter. Starting with the Liberty Head nickel in 1883, all types of this denomination have consistently measured 21.2 mm.

Buffalo nickel, 21.2 mm.

Half Dimes

The earliest half dimes were approximately 16.5 mm in diameter. From 1796 into the 1830s the coins measured about 16.5 mm, later reduced (from 1829 to 1837) to about 15.5 mm. Starting with the Liberty Seated type in 1837, half dimes were standardized at 15.5 mm until the end of the denomination in 1873.

Liberty Seated half dime, 15.5 mm.

Twenty-Cent Pieces

All twenty-cent pieces measure 22 mm in diameter.

Twenty-cent piece, 22 mm.

Dimes, Quarter Dollars, and Half Dollars

Early dimes measured between 18 and 19 mm in diameter. The diameter was made a uniform 18.5 mm from 1828 to 1837. Starting with the Liberty Seated type in 1837, dimes were standardized at 17.9 mm, and this has been the denomination's size since.

The earliest quarters were approximately 27.5 mm wide. In 1831 the diameter was reduced to 24.3 mm, which has remained the standard to date.

Half dollars measured approximately 32.5 mm in diameter until the Capped Bust, Reeded Edge, type of 1836 to 1839, which was 30 mm. Starting with the Liberty Seated type in 1839, the coins' size has been a uniform 30.6 mm.

Mercury dime, 17.9 mm.

Liberty Seated quarter, 24.3 mm.

Barber half dollar, 30.6 mm.

Morgan dollar, 38.1 mm.

Silver Dollars

The Flowing Hair and Draped Bust silver dollars (1794 to 1804) measured 39 or 40 mm in diameter. Starting with the Liberty Seated type in 1840, and continuing through the Peace dollar series (ending in 1935), silver dollars measured 38.1 mm. This was also the diameter of the Eisenhower dollar.

Liberty Head gold dollar, 13 mm.

Indian Princess Head gold dollar, 15 mm.

Gold Dollars

The Liberty Head gold dollars (1849 to 1854) measured 13 mm in diameter. The Indian Princess Head types (1854 to 1889) measured 15 mm.

Liberty Head quarter eagle, 18 mm.

Three-dollar gold piece, 20.5 mm.

Quarter Eagles, Three-Dollar Gold Coins, Half Eagles, and Eagles

The quarter eagle started with a diameter of about 20 mm, later was reduced, and finally was standardized at 18 mm with the Liberty Head series starting in 1840.

All three-dollar gold pieces measured 20.5 mm.

Early half eagles measured 25 mm. This size was reduced in 1829 and again in 1834, and finally standardized at 21.6 mm from 1840 to 1929.

Gold eagles were approximately 33 mm in diameter in the 1790s and early 1800s. With the debut of the Liberty Head type in 1838, their size was made uniform at 27 mm.

Liberty Head half eagle, 21.6 mm.

Liberty Head eagle, 27 mm.

Double Eagles

The double eagle denomination entered circulation in 1850. All coins of this denomination measure 34 mm.

Saint-Gaudens double eagle, 34 mm.

Commemorative Coins

Commemoratives, both classic and modern, are the same size as their circulation-strike denominations (half dollars, silver dollars, etc.).

GLOSSARY OF NUMISMATIC TERMS

Over the years coin collectors have developed a special jargon to describe their coins. The following list includes terms that are used frequently by coin collectors or that have a special meaning other than their ordinary dictionary definitions. You will find them useful when you want to discuss or describe your coins.

alloy—A combination of two or more metals.

altered date—A false date on a coin; a date altered after the coin was made to make it appear to be one of a rarer or more valuable issue.

bag mark—A surface mark, usually a small nick, acquired by a coin through contact with others in a mint bag.

barter—The act of exchanging goods or services without the use of coins or money.

bilingual—Referring to the inscription on a coin that is in two languages.

billon—Base silver, usually a low-grade mixture of silver and copper.

A billon French mousquetaire, 1710.

bit—A cut piece from a Spanish milled dollar or piece of eight. A bit from the Spanish dollar was worth 12-1/2 cents. Therefore the expression "two bits" refers to a quarter dollar.

blank—The blank piece of metal on which a coin design will be stamped.

Blue Book—R.S. Yeoman's *Handbook of United States Coins*, edited and updated annually to report current dealer buying prices for U.S. coins.

body bag—The return package for a coin that has been refused by a third-party grading service because it cannot be graded or authenticated.

bourse—The sales room for dealers at a coin show.

bracteat—A very thin medieval European coin with the design impressed on one side, and showing through to the other side.

brockage—A misstruck coin, generally one showing the normal design on one side and a mirror image of the same design on the other side.

A 1943 steel cent brockage.

broken bank note—Paper money privately issued during the nineteenth century. Many firms or individuals issuing such currency went "broke," hence the term.

bronze—An alloy of copper, zinc, and tin.

bullion—Gold or silver in the form of bars, ingots, or plate. This term is also frequently used to designate modern non-circulating precious-metal coins that are generally valued for their bullion content rather than their stated denomination.

business strike—An Uncirculated coin intended for eventual use in commerce, as opposed to a Proof coin. More properly referred to as a *circulation strike*.

cameo—Mirror-like fields and frosty devices. See also *reverse cameo*.

cartwheel—A large coin, generally one the size of a U.S. silver dollar or larger.

cash—An old Oriental copper coin with a square hole for stringing.

cast coins—Coins that are made by pouring molten metal into a mold instead of in the usual manner of striking with dies.

cent—One one-hundredth of the standard monetary unit. Also called a *centavo* in Mexico and some Central and South American countries, a *centesimo* in Italy, a *centime* in France and Switzerland, and a *centimo* in Spain and Venezuela.

certified coin—A coin that has been graded, authenticated, and encapsulated in plastic by an independent grading service.

cherrypicker—A collector who finds scarce and unusual coins by carefully searching through old accumulations or dealer's stocks.

chopmark—A merchant's test mark (usually Chinese) punched into a coin to verify its weight.

A chopmark on a U.S. trade dollar.

Civil War tokens—Unofficial pieces made to the approximate size of current U.S. cents and pressed into circulation during the Civil War because of a scarcity of small change.

clad coinage—United States circulating coins made since 1965 that have an inner core made of base metal and outer layers of copper-nickel or silver bonded to each side. The term may also be used to indicate the cladding or plating of any coin with a central core covered with various other metals.

clash marks—Impressions of the reverse design on the obverse of a coin (or the obverse on the reverse). This is caused by damage to the dies when they impact each other with great force without an intervening planchet.

cob money—Crude irregular silver coins of Spain, Mexico, Central America, and South America.

collar—The outer ring, or die chamber, that holds a blank in place in the coinage press while the coin is impressed with the obverse and reverse dies.

commemorative—A coin or medal issued to mark a special event or to honor an outstanding person, place, or thing.

computer grading—The (now obsolete) process of grading a coin by use of a computer analysis of surface conditions and marks.

contact marks—Minor abrasions on an Uncirculated coin, made by contact with other coins in a bag or roll.

counterfeit—An illegal, privately made replica of a coin or piece of paper money.

countermark—A stamp or mark impressed on a coin to verify its use by another government, or to indicate revaluation.

crack-out—A coin that has been removed from a grading-service holder.

crown—A dollar-size silver coin; specifically one from Great Britain.

denarius—A standard ancient Roman silver coin about the size of a United States dime.

designer—The artist who creates a coin's design. An *engraver* is the person who cuts a design into a coinage die.

A Mexican 8 reales counter-stamped for use in the Philippines.

die—A piece of metal engraved or impressed with a design, and used for stamping coins.

die crack—A fine raised line on a coin, caused by a broken die.

die defect—An imperfection on a coin, caused by a damaged die.

die variety—Any minor alteration in the basic design of a coin.

dipped, dipping—Refers to chemical cleaning of a coin with dilute acid.

disme—One-tenth of a dollar. An early spelling of the word "dime," and pronounced the same way.

dog—A coin in extremely worn or worthless condition.

double eagle—The United States $20 gold coin.

doubled-die—A die that has been given two misaligned impressions from a hub; also, a coin made from such a die.

doubloon—Popular name for a Spanish gold coin originally valued at $16.

drachma—The standard Greek monetary unit. A small silver coin approximately equal to the Roman *denarius*.

ducat—A famous gold coin used by several European countries. Originally an Italian coin of the twelfth century.

A 1756 gold ducat of Poland (Saxony).

eagle—A United States $10 gold coin; also refers to U.S. silver, gold, and platinum bullion pieces made from 1986 to the present.

edge—The outer periphery of a coin that often contains a series of reeds, lettering, or some other decoration.

electrotype—A reproduction (of a coin or medal) made by the electrodeposition process. Electrotypes are frequently used in museum displays.

electrum—A naturally occurring mixture of gold and silver. Some of the world's first coins were made of this alloy.

encapsulated coins—Coins that have been authenticated and graded, and sealed in plastic by a professional service.

engraver—The person who cuts the design into a coinage die. This term is also currently used to designate a person who produces a coinage die through modeling by any other medium or technique.

error—A mis-made coin not intended for circulation.

exergue—That portion of a coin beneath the main design, and separated by a line.

face value—The stated denomination or value of a legal-tender coin.

field—The background portion of a coin's surface not used for a design or inscription.

filler—A coin in worn condition, but rare enough to be included in a collection. Derived from such a coin "filling a hole" until a better example is acquired.

fillet head—A portrait showing the hair tied with a band, generally on the forehead.

fineness—The purity of gold, silver, or any other precious metal, expressed in terms of one thousand parts.

First Strike—An unofficial term once used to indicate a coin struck shortly after a new die is put into use. Such coins often have prooflike surfaces and resemble Proofs in certain (but not all) characteristics. Polished, previously used dies sometimes also have these characteristics. The term has also been applied by marketers to any of the coins made within the early months of release of a new issue.

flan—A blank piece of metal in the size and shape of a coin. Also called a *planchet*.

flip—A soft plastic 2" x 2" coin holder with pockets for two coins.

Fractional Currency—Paper money in denominations less than one dollar, issued for regular circulation by the United States during and after the Civil War. Specific issue dates range from 1862 to 1875.

gem—A coin of exceptionally high quality.

half eagle—The United States $5 gold coin.

Hard Times tokens—Pieces of a political or advertising nature, privately made and used as money during Andrew Jackson's presidency (1834–1841). Most are approximately the size and value of the then-current U.S. large cent.

hub—A positive-image punch used to impress the coin's design into a die for coinage.

incuse—The design of a coin which has been impressed below the coin's surface. A design raised above the coin's surface is in *relief*.

inscription—The legend or lettering on a coin.

intrinsic value—The bullion, or melt, value of the actual precious metal in a numismatic item.

investment grade—Generally a coin in grade MS-65 or better.

jeton—A small medal, counter, or token.

juice—Additional cost or profit made in a coin transaction.

junk silver—Common-date silver coins (originally taken from circulation) worth only bullion value.

"France Prepares to Aid America" jeton, silver, 1777.

key coin—The scarcest or most valuable coin in a series.

laureate—Description of a head crowned with a laurel wreath.

legal tender—Money that is officially issued and recognized for redemption by an authorized agency or government.

legend—The principal inscription on a coin.

lettered edge—The narrow edge of a coin bearing an inscription, found on some foreign coins, early United States issues, "golden" dollars made after 2009, and certain modern bullion coins.

Lettered edge on the 2017 High Relief American Liberty gold coin.

luster—The shiny "frost" on the surface of an Uncirculated or Mint State coin, medal, or token.

Maundy money—Small English silver coins specifically struck for distribution by the reigning monarch on Holy Thursday.

medal—A commemorative display piece made to honor a person, place, or event. Medals are not coins.

micro—Very small or microscopic (markings on a coin).

milled edge—The raised rim around the outer surface of a coin. Not to be confused with the reeded or serrated narrow edge of a coin.

mint error—Any mis-made or defective coin produced by a mint.

mint luster—The shiny "frost" on the surface of an Uncirculated or Mint State coin.

mintmark—A symbol, usually a small letter, indicating which mint struck the coin.

Mint set—A set of Uncirculated coins packaged and sold by the Mint. Each set contains one each of the coins made for circulation at each of the mints.

money of necessity—Emergency coins struck during battle; also called *siege pieces*.

moneyer—In old England, an authorized mint master or coiner.

motto—An inspirational word or phrase used on a coin.

mule—A coin struck from two dies not originally intended to be used together.

net grade—An expression used to indicate that the grade opinion is based upon a consideration of the averages of positive and negative aspects of a coin, rather than strict adherence to the technical qualities or grading standards for the grade.

notgeld—Emergency money, including coins and paper. Usually that issued in Germany, Austria, or France during the post–World War I inflationary period.

Gold-plated bronze 10,000-mark notgeld from Westphalia, Germany, 1923.

numerical grade—The grade of a coin as expressed in terms of numbers from 1 through 70.

numismatics—The study of coins, tokens, money, medals, and orders and decorations.

obsidional coins—Emergency coins struck during battle, also called *siege pieces*.

obverse—The front or face side of a coin, generally the side with the date and principal design.

overdate—A date made by superimposing one or more numbers on a previously dated die.

over-graded—A coin in poorer condition than stated.

overstrike—An impression made with new dies on a previously struck coin.

patina—The green or brown surface film found on ancient copper and bronze coins, caused by oxidation over a long period of time.

pattern—An experimental or trial coin, generally of a new design, denomination, or metal.

pedigree—The record of previous owners of a rare coin.

piece of eight—Spanish or Spanish-American silver-dollar–sized coins used extensively in trade throughout the world during the seventeenth and eighteenth centuries. The forerunner of the American silver dollar.

A Mexican piece of eight, 1733.

planchet—The blank piece of metal on which a coin design is stamped.

PQ—Premium quality. A "gem" coin.

Proofs—Coins struck for collectors using specially polished dies and planchets.

Proof set—A packaged set of each of the Proof coins made during that year and sold at a premium by collectors.

PVC—Polyvinyl chloride plastic. Not recommended for numismatic storage, because of potentially damaging chemical interaction.

quarter eagle—The United States $2.50 gold coin.

raw—A coin that has not been encapsulated in plastic by any grading service.

reeded edge—The edge of a coin with grooved lines that run vertically around its perimeter. As seen on modern United States silver and clad coins.

Red Book—R.S. Yeoman's *A Guide Book of United States Coins*, edited and updated annually to report current retail market conditions.

relief—Any part of a coin's design that is raised above the coin's field is said to be in relief. The opposite of relief is *incuse*.

restrike—A coin struck from genuine dies at a date later than the original issue.

reverse—The (back or tails) side of a coin carrying the design of lesser importance. Opposite of the *obverse* side.

reverse cameo—On some modern Proof coins, the contrast between a brilliant mirror-like portrait or devices, and frosted fields in the background.

rim—The raised outer portion of a coin that protects the design from wear.

round—A round one-ounce silver medal or bullion piece.

series—A set of one coin of each year issued from each mint of a specific design and denomination. As an example, Lincoln cents from 1909 to 1958.

scrip—Privately made paper money or chits, not issued as regular government currency.

semi-numismatic—A common-date coin whose value is based mostly on the value of the bullion it contains.

shinplaster—Slang term for early United States paper money and fractional currency.

siege pieces—Emergency coins struck during battle, also called *obsidional coins* or *money of necessity*.

slab—A hard plastic case containing a coin that has been graded by a professional service.

spot price—The daily quoted market value of precious metals in bullion form.

stickered—A reference to a certified coin that has an additional label attached to indicate that a second independent service has rendered its opinion as to the quality of the piece.

Landau (Germany) siege money, 1713.

token—A privately issued piece that has an exchange value for goods or services, but is not an official government coin.

trade dollar—A silver dollar issued especially for trade with a foreign country. In the United States, trade dollars were first issued in 1873 to stimulate trade with the Orient. Many other countries have also issued trade dollars.

truncation—The sharply cut-off bottom edge of a bust or portrait.

type—A coin's basic distinguishing design.

type set—A collection consisting of one of each coin of a particular design, series, or period.

Uncirculated—The condition of a coin that has never been used or worn in any way and has retained its original new surface and luster. Also called *Mint State*.

unique—An item of which only one specimen is known to exist.

variety—A special feature of a coin's design that sets it apart from the normal issue of that type.

watermark—A symbol or image that is made part of a piece of paper, especially that used on paper money as a counterfeit deterrent. Watermarks can generally only be seen when the paper is held before a light source.

wheaties—Lincoln cents with the Wheat Ears reverse, issued from 1909 to 1958.

whizzing—Artificial luster made by brushing a coin to make it look like a higher-grade piece.

year set—A set of coins for any given year, consisting of one of each denomination from that year.

BIBLIOGRAPHY

Listed here is a selection of general books on United States numismatics and other references that collectors find useful to consult.

EARLY AMERICAN COINS AND TOKENS

Bowers, Q. David. *Whitman Encyclopedia of Colonial and Early American Coins*, Atlanta, GA, 2009.

Crosby, S.S. *The Early Coins of America*, Boston, 1875 (several reprints).

Noe, Sydney P. *The New England and Willow Tree Coinage of Massachusetts*, New York, 1943; *The Oak Tree Coinage of Massachusetts*, New York, 1947; and *The Pine Tree Coinage of Massachusetts*, New York, 1952 (all reprinted 1973).

GENERAL UNITED STATES REFERENCES

Bowers, Q. David. *A Guide Book of the United States Mint*, Pelham, AL, 2016.

Breen, Walter. *Walter Breen's Encyclopedia of U.S. and Colonial Coins*, New York, 1988.

Bressett, Kenneth. *A Guide Book of United States Currency*, Pelham, AL, 2017.

Bressett, Kenneth. *Welcome to Coin Collecting*, New York, 1998.

Bressett, Kenneth, and Kosoff, A. *Official A.N.A. Grading Standards for United States Coins*. Whitman Publishing, various editions.

Fivaz, Bill, and Stanton, J.T. *The Cherrypickers' Guide to Rare Die Varieties*. Whitman Publishing, various editions.

Lange, David W. *History of the United States Mint and Its Coinage*, Atlanta, GA, 2005.

Yeoman, R.S. *A Guide Book of United States Coins*. Edited by Kenneth Bressett. Issued annually by Whitman Publishing.

Yeoman, R.S. *The Handbook of United States Coins*. Edited by Kenneth Bressett. Issued annually by Whitman Publishing.

UNITED STATES COINS BY DENOMINATION

HALF CENTS AND LARGE CENTS

Bowers, Q. David. *A Guide Book of Half Cents and Large Cents*, Atlanta, GA, 2015.

Breen, Walter. *Walter Breen's Encyclopedia of United States Half Cents 1793–1857*, South Gate, CA, 1983.

Cohen, Roger S., Jr. *American Half Cents—The "Little Half Sisters"* (2nd edition), 1982.

Grellman, J.R. *Attribution Guide for United States Large Cents 1840–1857* (3rd edition), Bloomington, MN, 2002.

Noyes, William C. *United States Large Cents 1793–1814*, Bloomington, MN, 1991.

Noyes, William C. *United States Large Cents 1816–1839*, Bloomington, MN, 1991.

Sheldon, William H. *Penny Whimsy (1793–1814)*, New York, 1958 (reprinted 1965, 1976).

Wright, John D. *The Cent Book 1816–1839*, Bloomington, MN, 1992.

SMALL CENTS

Bowers, Q. David. *A Guide Book of Lincoln Cents* (2nd edition), Pelham, AL, 2017.

Lange, David W. *The Complete Guide to Lincoln Cents*, Wolfeboro, NH, 1996.

Snow, Richard. *A Guide Book of Flying Eagle and Indian Cents* (3rd edition), Atlanta, GA, 2016.

Wexler, John, and Flynn, Kevin. *The Authoritative Reference on Lincoln Cents*, Rancocas, NJ, 1996.

TWO-CENT PIECES

Flynn, Kevin. *Getting Your Two Cents Worth*, Rancocas, NJ, 1994.

Half Dimes and Nickel Five-Cent Pieces

Bowers, Q. David. *A Guide Book of Buffalo and Jefferson Nickels* (2nd edition), Pelham, AL, 2017.

Bowers, Q. David. *A Guide Book of Shield and Liberty Head Nickels*, Atlanta, GA, 2006.

Blythe, Al. *The Complete Guide to Liberty Seated Half Dimes*, Virginia Beach, VA, 1992.

Bowers, Q. David. *A Guide Book of Liberty Seated Silver Coins*, Atlanta, GA, 2016.

Dimes and Twenty-Cent Pieces

Bowers, Q. David. *A Guide Book of Barber Silver Coins*, Atlanta, GA, 2015.

Bowers, Q. David. *A Guide Book of Liberty Seated Silver Coins*, Atlanta, GA, 2016.

Bowers, Q. David. *A Guide Book of Mercury Dimes, Standing Liberty Quarters, and Liberty Walking Half Dollars*, Atlanta, GA, 2015.

Brunner, Lane, and Frost, John M. *Double Dime: The United States Twenty-Cent Piece*, 2014.

Greer, Brian, *The Complete Guide to Liberty Seated Dimes*, Virginia Beach, VA, 1992.

Lange, David W. *The Complete Guide to Mercury Dimes*, Virginia Beach, VA, 2005.

Quarter Dollars

Bowers, Q. David. *A Guide Book of Barber Silver Coins*, Atlanta, GA, 2015.

Bowers, Q. David. *A Guide Book of Liberty Seated Silver Coins*, Atlanta, GA, 2016.

Bowers, Q. David. *A Guide Book of Mercury Dimes, Standing Liberty Quarters, and Liberty Walking Half Dollars*, Atlanta, GA, 2015.

Briggs, Larry. *The Comprehensive Encyclopedia of United States Seated Quarters*, Lima, Ohio, 1991.

Cline, J.H. *Standing Liberty Quarters* (3rd ed.), 1996.

Half Dollars

Bowers, Q. David. *A Guide Book of Barber Silver Coins*, Atlanta, GA, 2015.

Bowers, Q. David. *A Guide Book of Liberty Seated Silver Coins*, Atlanta, GA, 2016.

Bowers, Q. David. *A Guide Book of Mercury Dimes, Standing Liberty Quarters, and Liberty Walking Half Dollars*, Atlanta, GA, 2015.

Overton, Al C. *Early Half Dollar Die Varieties 1794–1839*, Colorado Springs, 1967; third edition, 1990, edited by Donald Parsley.

Tomaska, Rick. *A Guide Book of Franklin and Kennedy Half Dollars* (3rd ed.), Pelham, AL, 2017.

Wiley, Randy, and Bugert, Bill. *The Complete Guide to Liberty Seated Half Dollars*, Virginia Beach, VA, 1993.

Silver and Related Dollars

Bolender, M.H. *The United States Early Silver Dollars from 1794 to 1803* (3rd edition), Iola, WI, 1982 (reprinted 1987).

Bowers, Q. David. *A Guide Book of Liberty Seated Silver Coins*, Atlanta, GA, 2016.

Bowers, Q. David. *A Guide Book of Modern United States Dollar Coins*, Atlanta, GA, 2016.

Bowers, Q. David. *A Guide Book of Morgan Silver Dollars* (5th ed.), Atlanta, GA, 2016.

Bowers, Q. David. *Silver Dollars and Trade Dollars of the United States: A Complete Encyclopedia*, Wolfeboro, NH, 1993.

Newman, Eric P., and Bressett, Kenneth E. *The Fantastic 1804 Dollar*, Racine, WI, 1962; Tribute Edition, Atlanta, GA, 2012.

Van Allen, Leroy C., and Mallis, A. George. *Comprehensive Catalogue and Encyclopedia of U.S. Morgan and Peace Silver Dollars*, New York, 1992.

Gold Coins

Bowers, Q. David. *United States Gold Coins. An Illustrated History*, Wolfeboro, NH, 1982.

Bowers, Q. David. *A Guide Book of Double Eagle Gold Coins*, Atlanta, GA, 2004.

Bowers, Q. David. *A Guide Book of Gold Dollars* (2nd ed.), Atlanta, GA, 2011.

Bowers, Q. David. *A Guide Book of Gold Eagles*, Pelham, AL, 2017.

Fivaz, Bill. *United States Gold Counterfeit Detection Guide*, Atlanta, GA, 2005.

Garrett, Jeff, and Guth, Ron. *Encyclopedia of U.S. Gold Coins, 1795–1933* (2nd edition), Atlanta, GA, 2008.

Commemorative Coins, Tokens, Medals, Bullion, and Other Specialized Subjects

Bowers, Q. David. *A Guide Book of Civil War Tokens* (2nd ed.), Atlanta, GA, 2015.

Bowers, Q. David. *A Guide Book of Hard Times Tokens*, Atlanta, GA, 2015.

Bowers, Q. David. *A Guide Book of United States Commemorative Coins*, Atlanta, GA, 2004.

Swiatek, Anthony and Breen, Walter. *The Encyclopedia of United States Silver and Gold Commemorative Coins 1892–1954*, New York, 1981.

Adams, Edgar H. *Private Gold Coinage of California 1849–1855*, Brooklyn, NY, 1913.

Breen, Walter and Gillio, Ronald. *California Pioneer Fractional Gold*, Santa Barbara, CA, 1983.

Jaeger, Katherine, and Bowers, Q. David. *100 Greatest American Medals and Tokens*, Atlanta, GA, 2008.

Jaeger, Katherine. *A Guide Book of United States Tokens and Medals*, Atlanta, GA, 2008.

Judd, J. Hewitt. *United States Pattern Coins* (10th ed.), Atlanta, GA 2008.

Kagin, Donald H. *Private Gold Coins and Patterns of the United States*, New York, 1981.

Lange, David W. *A Guide Book of Modern United States Proof Coin Sets* (2nd ed.), Atlanta, GA, 2010.

Margolis, Arnold. *The Error Coin Encyclopedia* (2nd ed.), 1993.

Mercanti, John M., with Standish, Miles. *American Silver Eagles: A Guide to the U.S. Bullion Coin Program* (3rd ed.), Atlanta, GA, 2016.

Moy, Edmund. *American Gold and Platinum Eagles: A Guide to the U.S. Bullion Coin Programs*, Atlanta, GA, 2013.

Rulau, Russell. *Standard Catalog of United States Tokens 1700–1900*, Iola, WI, 1997.

Pollock, Andrew W. *United States Patterns and Related Issues*, Wolfeboro, NH, 1994.

Tucker, Dennis. *American Gold and Silver: U.S. Mint Collector and Investor Coins and Medals, Bicentennial to Date*, Atlanta, GA, 2016.

World Coins and Paper Money

Bruce, Colin R., and Shafer, Neil. *Standard Catalog of World Paper Money*, various editions, Iola, WI.

Klawans, Zander H., edited by Bressett, Kenneth. *Handbook of Ancient Greek and Roman Coins*, Atlanta, GA, 2003.

Krause, Chester, and Mishler, Clifford. *Standard Catalog of World Coins*, various editions. Titles cover coins of 1601–1700, 1800–1900, and 1900 to date. Iola, WI.

Lobel, Richard. *Coincraft's 1998 Standard Catalogue of English and UK Coins 1066 to Date*, London, 1998.

Sales, Wayne. *Ancient Coin Collecting* (volumes I, II, III, and IV), Iola, WI.

Sear, David R. *Roman Coins and Their Values*, London, 1988.

Sear, David R. *Greek Coins and Their Values* (volumes I and II), London, 1979.

Carson, R.A.G., *Coins of the World*, New York, 1962.

Shafer, Neil. *United States Territorial Coinage for the Philippine Islands*, Racine, WI, 1961.

Whitman Publishing. *Mega Red (Guide Book of United States Coins, Deluxe Edition)*, various editions, chapters on Hawaiian coinage, Puerto Rican coinage, and Philippine coinage struck under U.S. sovereignty.

About the Author

Kenneth Bressett has actively promoted the study and hobby of numismatics for more than 60 years. His published works on the subject cover a wide range of topics and extend from short articles to standard reference books on such diverse areas as ancient coins, paper money, English coins, and United States coins.

Throughout his career he has worked as an author, editor, and publisher of books and products for coin collectors. He has also taught the subject to hundreds of students through courses at Colorado College and other places. From 1983 to 1988 he served the American Numismatic Association as director of Coin Authentication and Educational Programs. Subsequently he served on the ANA board of governors, and as vice president and president.

Bressett was appointed to the U.S. Assay Commission in 1966 by President Lyndon Johnson, and in 1996 was made a member of the Citizens Commemorative Coin Advisory Committee. He has received numerous awards in recognition of his service and dedication to numismatics, including election to the National Numismatic Hall of Fame, the American Numismatic Society's Distinguished Service Award, the American Numismatic Association Medal of Merit, and the ANA Ferran Zerbe Memorial award.

Credits and Acknowledgments

Many photographs of coins, tokens, and other collectibles and historical items are from the author's collection. Others are from the **Whitman** image archives. Some are courtesy of the **United States Mint** and the **Library of Congress**. **Stack's Bowers Galleries** contributed some images of coins, paper money, and other numismatic items.

Special appreciation to **Owen Linzmayer** for reviewing sections of the fourth edition.

Pg. 2: The photograph of a collector studying a coin is courtesy of the **American Numismatic Association**. *Pg. 10:* The portrait of Thomas Jefferson (copy of a painting by Gilbert Stuart, circa 1805) is courtesy of **Everett Historical**.* *Pg. 13:* The coin-board photograph is courtesy of **Rangeclock**. *Pg. 15:* The photograph of bags of old coins is courtesy of **Littleton Coin Company**. *Pg. 16:* The photograph of Indian Head cents is by **John S. Sfondilias**.* *Pg. 19:* The photograph of a grandfather and grandson studying coins is by **VITA PIX**.* *Pg. 20:* The image of silver dimes in a cloth bag is by **Steve Heap**.* *Pg. 24:* **Prixel Creative** supplied the photograph of silver coins.* *Pg. 25:* The image of old coins in a cash drawer is by **trekandshoot.*** *Pg. 29:* The engraving of a goat is from the *Natural History of Animals* (1880), courtesy of **Morphart Creation.*** *Pg. 39:* The photograph of a German hound medal is from the collection of **Dennis Tucker**. *Pg. 40:* The photograph is by **Sergey Ryzhov.*** *Pg. 43:* The oil painting of George Washington is courtesy of **Everett Art.*** *Pg. 44:* The photograph of Eunice Kennedy Shriver is by **Bob Crandall.*** *Pg. 47:* The engraving of Benjamin Franklin (by J. Thomson, as published in *The Gallery of Portraits With Memoirs*, 1833) is courtesy of **Georgios Kollidas.*** *Pg. 49:* The image is derived from the work of **Rawpixel.com.*** *Pg. 50:* The photograph of the Metropolitan Coin Club of Atlanta is courtesy of **David Crenshaw**; the photograph of collectors admiring a coin is by **fakezzz***. *Pg. 51:* The view of ANA headquarters is courtesy of the **American Numismatic Association**, as is the photograph of the ANA library on pg. 55. *Pg. 58:* The photograph of coin exhibits at the ANA is courtesy of **F. David Calhoun**. *Pg. 68:* The photograph of "junk silver" is by **Badr Alzamil.*** *Pg. 69:* The photograph of the Bluegrass Coin Club is courtesy of **Jeff Garrett**. *Pg. 70:* The mailbox photograph is by **Gaetan-L.*** *Pg. 72:* The covers of **Numismatic News**, **Coin World**, **The Numismatist**, and **COINage** are courtesy of their respective publishers. *Pg. 73:* The photograph of a bank teller is by **Syda Productions.*** *Pg. 76:* The two photographs are by **yingko.*** *Pg. 78:* The photograph is by **Sergey Ryzhov.*** *Pg. 80:* The photograph of a padded surface is by **Beth Deisher**. *Pg. 81:* The photograph of a gloved hand is by **Beth Deisher**, as is the photograph on page 82. *Pg. 84:* The photograph of a Whitman Classic® album is by **Brent Cook**. *Pg. 87:* The photograph of gold coins is by **Netfalls Remy Musser.*** *Pg. 90:* The photographs of PVC damage are courtesy of **James Bucki**. *Pg. 95:* The photograph of coin tubes is by **W. Scott McGill.*** *Pg. 96:* The photographs of PVC damage are courtesy of **Cody Charlton**. *Pg. 97:* The photographs of the Eisenhower dollar are courtesy of **Bill Fivaz**; the photographs of the Lincoln cent are by **Syd Martin**; and the photographs of the Indian Head cent are by **Jonathan Roche**. *Pg. 98:* The photograph is by **allstars.*** *Pg. 101:* Photographs are by **Dennis Tucker**, published with permission of the **United States Mint**. *Pg. 103:* The photograph of a damaged war nickel is courtesy of **Bill Fivaz**. *Pg. 111:* The background image is by **Tischenko Irina.*** *Pg. 112:* The coin-auction photograph is courtesy of **Q. David Bowers**. *Pg. 116:* The photograph of coin rolls is by **R. Mackay Photography, LLC.*** *Pg. 119:* The photographs of holed coins are by **Kevin Day-Thorburn**. *Pg. 120:* The photograph is by **trekandshoot.*** *Pg. 124:* The photograph of old coins is by **Siaivo.*** *Pg. 126:* The photograph of coin collectors is by **Tupungato.*** *Pg. 130:* The photograph of a collector sharing his collection is by **Alan Roche**. *Pg 132:* The photograph of a handshake is by **pikcha.*** *Pg. 140:* The photograph of the American Numismatic Association exhibit is by **Douglas Mudd** of the ANA. *Pg. 144:* The photograph is by **Netfalls Remy Musser.*** *Pg. 216:* The unveiling-ceremony photograph is courtesy of the **United States Mint**. *Pg. 218:* The 1885 Barnum poster is courtesy of **Everett Historical.*** *Pg. 219:* The portrait of Mark Twain is courtesy of **Everett Historical.*** *Pg. 236:* The American Numismatic Association library photograph is courtesy of the **ANA**. *Pg. 244:* The photograph of a box of damaged coins is by **David Luftig**; the Eisenhower dollar is by **Isaiah Hageman**; the 1807 dime is by **Mike Angelo**; the Buffalo nickel is by **Tom Koolick**; and the Smoking Liberty double eagle is by **Bob Evans**. *Pg. 243:* The photographs of off-center coins are courtesy of **Phil Iversen**. *Pg. 248:* The photographs of the Maria Theresa thaler are courtesy of **APMEX**. *Pg. 252:* The photograph is by **Cryber.*** *Pg. 256:* The photograph is by **Voronin76.***

* via Shutterstock

INDEX

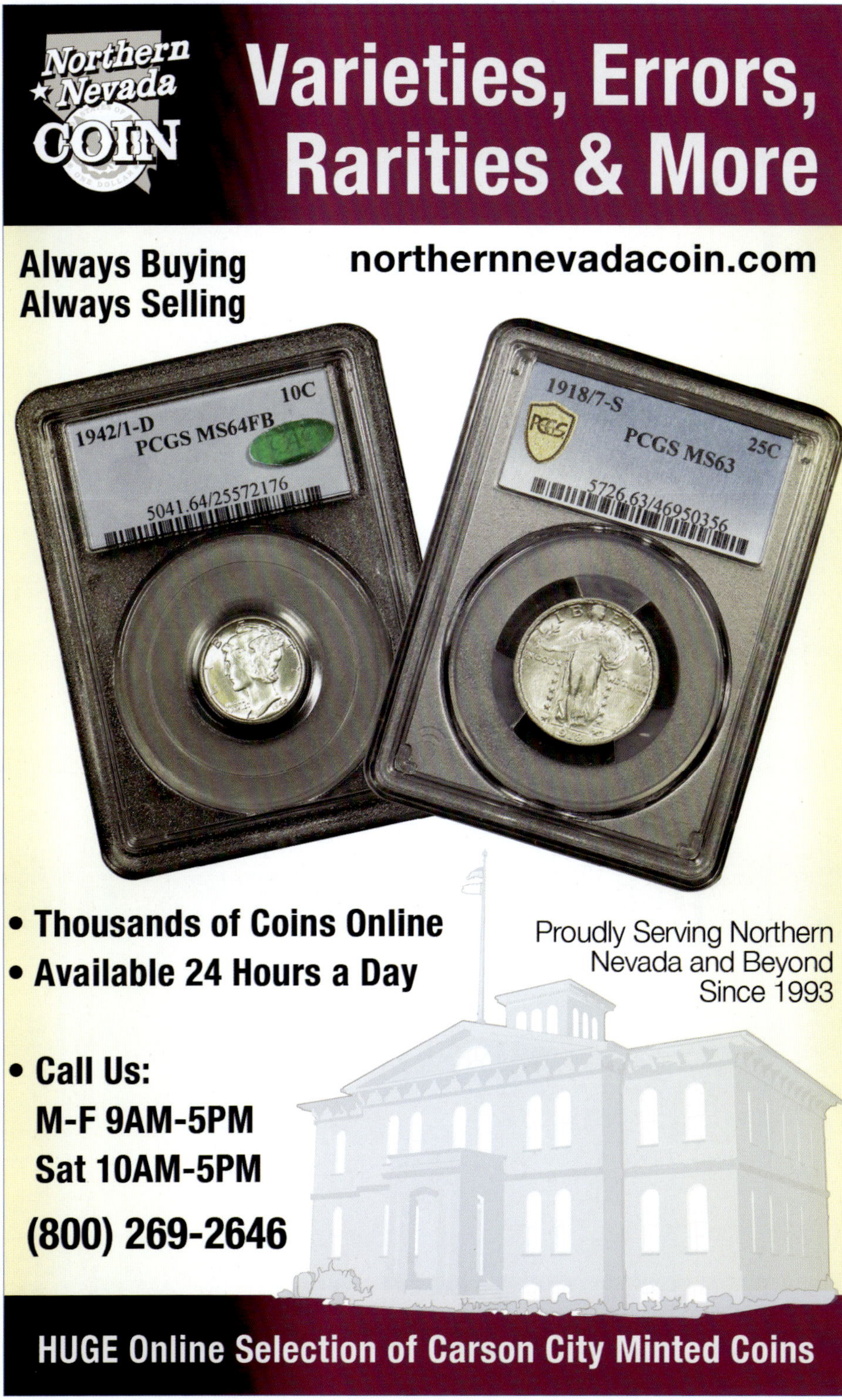
Northern
Nevada
COIN
Varieties, Errors,
Rarities & More
Always Buying
Always Selling
northernnevadacoin.com
1942/1-D
10C
PCGS MS64FB
5041.64/25572176
1918/7-S
25C
PCGS MS63
5726.63/46950356
• Thousands of Coins Online
• Available 24 Hours a Day
Proudly Serving Northern
Nevada and Beyond
Since 1993
• Call Us:
M-F 9AM-5PM
Sat 10AM-5PM
(800) 269-2646
HUGE Online Selection of Carson City Minted Coins